# THE
# INTER-MUTUAL STATE

# A LABOR CATECHISM

OF

# POLITICAL ECONOMY.

*A Study for the People.*

COMPRISING THE PRINCIPAL ARGUMENTS FOR AND AGAINST THE PROMINENT DECLARATIONS OF THE INDUSTRIAL PARTY, REQUIRING THAT THE STATE ASSUME CONTROL OF INDUSTRIES.

By OSBORNE WARD.

"Nature often apportions talent, genius and capacity to those whom society repudiates."—GODIN.

TWENTY-FIRST THOUSAND.

PRESS OF THE AUTHOR; No. 214 NINTH St., S.W.,

WASHINGTON, D.C.,

1877-1892.

# PREFACE.

SINCE the first issue of this work in 1877, there have been many editions published and sold or given away. It is well known among the now rapidly increasing friends of government ownership of mines, telegraphs, railroads and factories, that this book, being the pioneer, was met by a powerfully organized resistance, which worked and dealt blows in the dark. On an old, hard-running press, in a cellar, editions, numerous but small, were struck off; and the meagre returns from their sale went to buy more paper and pay rent, while the author earned his bread by teaching.

Many reviews and editorials appeared from time to time in the newspapers, and numberless criticisms, letters, meetings and discussions, as well as club-organizations in the towns and cities followed. Then came Mr. George's less pronounced but more popular "Progress and Poverty;" afterwards Mr. Gronlund's "Co-operative Commonwealth" and still later, the socialistic books and essays of Dr. Ely, and the phenomenally happy "Looking Backward," of Mr. Bellamy; all of which have not only tacitly endorsed but evidently built upon, the carefully studied arguments delineated in these pioneer chapters, written in 1870–1875.

The good effects which have cheered the author more than compensate all the sad ones acting personally upon himself. Splendid results of radical agitation of those days came in form of a law, the effect of which was to establish at the National Capital, a genuine socialistic money-manufactory, the beneficent power of which has already been used to checkmate combinations of persons gambling in money and overproduction.

In some of the large cities the book-piracy, argued against in this volume, was raging at the moment of its first appearance, to such an extent that it conflicted with the compulsory-education law of the public schools. Children too poor to buy books at contract or monopoly prices had either to stay out and defy the law or be placed on the degrading indigent-list and furnished by a humiliating species of charity. High-minded workpeople's sons and daughters would not be thus debased. Once this wrong clearly shown to the people, they reacted against it; and the book-piracy has given place to the pure and permanent socialistic system.

Hundreds of the first, second and third editions were read by the gentlemen of the City Halls of Brooklyn and New York. It was during the construction of the great inter-urban bridge. The author's pleadings that this magnificent monument of skill and labor in a common cause, should be done by the two cities and out of the common purse, were thoroughly considered at the time and most of the suggestions have already been conceded; for the majestic structure is already a common property of that great community and the barbarism of toll-taking will soon be a relic of the past.

The book also reached the Sachems of Tammany, not long afterwards, and might have exerted a strong influence upon New York politics, particularly in so far as the public works are concerned, had it not unfortunately lost powerful aid, by the death of Mr. John Kelly who had a clear, practical perception of the ideas involved in state control of industries; for he promised the author's friends to exert his future influence in applying the principles herein set forth, as a policy of the city of New York whereby much of the prevailing distress and crime might have been ended. But he was met by fierce opposition, defeated and soon afterwards brought down by death.

In the great public libraries of the country, the generous Librarians wherever in charge, have for many years, been in a habit of ordering from its shelf the LABOR CATECHISM in response to the numberless inquiries, by members of Congress, Legislatures and Municipal bodies, when questions of labor pressed for a solution.

The author's personal communings with his much loved friend, Courtlandt Palmer, began soon after the first edition appeared, through a letter addressed by that gentleman, as an inquirer in 1878, on the subject of its contents; and he ever afterwards declared that his views had been greatly influenced or guided by ideas herein set forth. To that brave, exquisite nature, now passed away, the author has dedicated his more recent work on "The Ancient Lowly."

To Mrs. Elizabeth Thompson the book owes its existence. As stated above, the CATECHISM was written four or five years before it appeared. Nobody would undertake its publication and the author was roundly berated by the wealthy manager of a large firm, for presuming to offer him such a manuscript of heretical problems. Finally, Mrs. Elizabeth Thompson took the matter up and furnished the author means for bringing out the first two or three editions. After this, it plodded, under frowning skies, through four more editions. By this time the author had become so impecunious and obscure that his thankless work had to be temporarily suspended.

About 20,000 volumes of the Catechism have thus been scattered along the by-ways of toiling humanity, from Maine to Texas and California, even to Canada, Great Britain and Australia.

And now, since the recent appearance of the "Ancient Lowly," whereby old readers and converts of the Catechism are informed that the author is still among the living, a swarm of letters of kind inquiry, confessing to a re-awakened love of justice, pours in, persuading him to bring out this enlarged and revised edition to meet an ever-growing want.

## *CONTENTS OF THE CHAPTERS.*

# INTRODUCTION.



## CHAPTER I.

## CHAPTER II.



## CHAPTER III.



## CHAPTER IV.

## CHAPTER V.

## CHAPTER VI.



## CHAPTER VII.



## CHAPTER VIII.

## CHAPTER IX.



## CHAPTER X.

## CHAPTER XI.



## CHAPTER XII.

## CHAPTER XIII.

# INTRODUCTION.

The coming subject of discussion and agitation among the people, and especially the Laboring People, is to-day, the same which has been more or less discoursed in private and in public, ever since the dawn of the philosophic age of Greece.

How much do men know? How much are they capable of knowing? These questions were asked by Zeno, by Socrates, by Aristotle, nearly four hundred years before Christ. It was denied by some of the sages of those times that man was capable of positively knowing anything. Aristotle said that the only method man could take, by which to arrive at an unmistakable knowledge of truth, was by beginning with small things; by investigating through comparison, reason and analysis; by beginning with the least and working out to the greatest; leaving nothing neglected, nothing unstudied, nothing which investigation had not wrought some brilliant of truth from, or added some hitherto unknown gem to the diadem of knowledge. The question is the same now but more pointed. How much POLITICAL ECONOMY do we know? Can men take mutual care of themselves? However much, the world has repudiated that old doctrinal question of the great philosophers of Ancient Greece, it is plain to every one who reviews the methods of the world's moral and mechanical development, that progress has ever followed, and is still following the lesson given by them. The mind of man is evidently still in its infancy; and it seems susceptible of growing ripe and rich, only as it attains these separate auxiliary gems by the light of each successive investigation and experiment. The true secret of advancement lies in an instrument. This instrument is mechanical. With it the unpolished mechanic is moving the world. He is at the helm of mechanics. There is not a science that does not develop from mechanics. The figures of Leverier were useless without the accompanying telescope and pen. The glory of the nineteenth century is due to the invention and application of steam, of the telegraph, of the printing press, and of a thousand other forms of mechanics.

Now the application and diffusion of these instruments of science, of human knowledge, is just that which is making the world wise; and the happiness of the human race does, and ever must depend upon the wisdom with which these mechanical instruments, mostly the product of the humble worker, are applied in the production and the distribution of our means of life and development. The merest tyro may, therefore, see that this is *Political Economy* in its widest and most practical sense.

This ancient plan of research and investigation, by both theory and experiment suggested by Aristotle, led to the establishment of great laboratories, museums and libraries at Athens and in Egypt, three hundred years before Christ;

and nearly all the inventions, charts and books in the world had to be collected into small compass, in order to attract the attention of scholars, while the great masses of the people scattered over the world, were not only without their uses, but were ignorant of their existence.

The world's subsequent labors reversed these conditions. Now, all such instruments are *diffused;* scattered over every part of the civilized globe; and the people are using them.

In those days, it was easy for an ignorant adventurer to send his brutal squadrons to Alexandria, and destroy those invaluable specimens of books and invention, of which no duplicates existed. Now, every individual specimen of either book or mechanical appliance possesses hundreds, perhaps even millions of its kind; and thus the destroyer can no longer annihilate them because they are in actual use, throughout all the lanes of life.

The subject of discussion, therefore, although similar to that of more primitive ages, varies in its almost infinite diffusiveness. The ancient asked how an instrument of human knowledge and development could be made. Curiosity and desire of self culture, brought men from the antipodes to see it. The modern, seeing the instrument constantly before him, asks how it shall be applied to use. What is the wisest method of applying all this science, art, invention, so preëminently capable of producing the necessaries of human existence, and of producing them with such marvelous rapidity? What shall be, in future, the control or management over them? Shall the labor-saving instrument be a monopolizable thing? Must our potent sciences, enveloped in wealth, woven with railroads, electric instruments and lines of steamers, busy with factories, farms, literature be forever operated by the same narrow, competitive process that the comparatively ignorant ancients used? Must it still do in our age, when they have multiplied by millions, and have diffused themselves to such a degree that the eye and the ear encounter them at every turn? Among the ancients, the isolated family, the individual, the competitor, were the only source of government recognized, as applied to the manipulation of labor and its products. All things ruling outside the labor societies, were operated from a central principle of competism. Every kind of business had a conservative character. The tendency was constantly to aggregate. At the present day, the constant tendency is to disperse; and humanity becomes diffused, in a direction of levelism.

Is the competitive principle applicable then, to modern humanity? The competitive system was natural to the ancient mind because religion was exclusive, and favorable to individualism. The family was a world by itself. Over it the father held supreme power. He could punish his wife or his child with death. Back of that monarch—the ancient family despot—there was no appeal. From the family arose phratries, tribes, cities, nationalities, modeled from the same ignorant and bigoted usages, and consequently established under the same despotic *régime*. Jealousy, self-love, and many concomitants of absolutism, and competitive rivality were quite natural, even consistent with a public opinion which such a state of things produced. But christianity, it is said, broke the pagan religion down. Why then, does the competitive system still hold unlimited sway? The competitive system of control is natural to individualism and human selfishness; yet the race is drifting, by the light of science and its instruments, into liberalism; and governments are becoming democracies or republics. Why then, should the control of the scientific labor-saving instrumentalities so infinitely more diffused than those of the ancients, continue in the hands of individualists? If governments, which were manipulated by competing individuals in ancient days, have changed from the despotic to the democratic form, why may not the control of the people's industries be also relatively changed from the despotic, or competitive, to the democratical form?

Public opinion must bend to knowledge; to demonstrable truth. It cannot always remain the poltroon of a monopoly-hugging, competitive system, however delusive its inculcations and natural instincts. The control and ownership of production and distribution tend to escape from the hands of the individual, and to be assumed by the people themselves; and this variation of its control, and ownership must keep pace with the variation of the form of government, from the despotic to the democratic.

It is a mistake to suppose, that there ever was a time when the people of Greece and Rome could have enjoyed a votive franchise and elected their own choice of men to control politics. The popular idea is, that they did; but this opinion is derived from the fact that those ancient governments were called *republics*. Research into the truth reveals to us, however, that magistrates—who were religious priests, by a rite of the ancient religion—used to consult the heavens at night, in search of the will of the gods, concerning the eligibility of candidates! The people were too unenlightened and superstitious to see these tricks of priestcraft; and it often happened that an unpropitious star, meteor, or phosphorescent light was interpreted by such priest-soothsayers as unfavorable omens against the favorite of the poor majorities who, on the day of elections, felt themselves obliged through awe and intimidation to speak and decide against themselves.

Political control is rapidly outgrowing despotic control. The mind of man has, since those days, changed from the exclusive ideas that led to concentrativeness, into ideas of fellowship, that lead to business cooperation, joint management, republicanism. By whatsoever the present generation has developed, through the repudiation of religious superstitions, the inroads of mechanics, public schools, postal bureaus, galleries and museums of art and science, general enlightenment, which all come from the errors of the past as well as the successes of the present, and the hopes of the future, by just so much is modern GOVERNMENT better than ancient. And yet notwithstanding all this, there has scarcely been a jot of improvement in the control of business which produces the means of existence and of happiness of the millions, for whom these governments are made! There has been much political and scientific growth, bnt no corresponding economic growth among the proletarian classes.

Out of this mechanical enginery produced by the study and toil of working people, we see much social improvement among the wealthy and medium portions of the community yet nothing but degradation among those whom society tenaciously persists in making no provision for. People still refuse to take control of the manufacture and distribution of their means of life, in a similar manner in which they have been so successful, in the coutrol of political governments.

It is the belief of the author of these pages, that it is as possible for any enlightened people, who possess such facilitating instruments of research, and of Industrial Economy, both in production and distribution, to govern their economical methods of labor, as it is to govern their political methods of law-giving. The people of this country make their own laws collectively. Why should they not make their own bread collectively? They can agree so far as to elect representatives, and send them to Congress and Legislatures, pay them for their work, watch over their actions, study and criticise their motives, approve and accept, or censure and repudiate the laws which they create. Why cannot they, also, elect representative men to take control of their cotton mills, instead of leaving this important branch of supply forever in the hands, and at the caprice of irresponsible individuals, without the least improvement (except in mechanical instruments) upon the methods that prevailed in the days of the CÆSARS? Political government has become democratical. Why is mechanical government still monarchical?

These thoughts lead us to ask whether it is possible for the mechanical, or more properly, the economical affairs of mankind, to be assumed under a democratical or communistic form. But we do not reflect that this same question once was asked of republicanism, or government by the people. There now remains no longer a doubt of the perfect capability of the people to govern themselves. Every experiment proves it. Every new republic acts as a purifier of human intelligence, and the plan is growing more popular every year throughout enlightenment.

But has the plan of a democratic administration of our economical and household affairs ever been submitted to a similar collective test? Certainly; and on a vast scale; and by the government! Nothing can be more intimately connected with our household, our private, and our business matters than the business of the great Post Office. It is a natural part of the people's business which political government adjusts; but it is intimately related to our economical means of producing and enjoying the means of life. It is so vast that it cannot be operated by an individual.

Besides, the people, collectively, are eternal; while as individuals, they are fleeting. Individual, and even joint stock enterprises, however large and prosperous, are fleeting and perishable. They owe their present, and their future to a man or to a certain set of men who, while they live, are the supreme rulers of their industries. Thus the people are supposed to have no right to question arbitrary dispensations; because they are beyond their collective control.

The reverse is the fact in regard to all business enterprises which are the undertakings of a state or government. Although any individual, be he a private, or a ruler, may die, yet the COLLECTIVE individual, the great Body Politic, *never dies.* In the modern form of elective republicanism, this mutual collectivity is not only eternal, endowed with a constantly self purifying tendency, but it is *supreme* in its control. This collective control dispenses the laws. It operates from year to year, all the vast practical business as well as theoretical functions of a great government.

Auxiliary to this government is the Post Office. The Postal Department grew out of, or rather out-grew a joint stock company. While a company carried the mails of the nation, the people were supposed to have nothing to say; they were obliged to submit to paying prices for their letter carrying service, such as in these days, would be considered insufferable. Gradually, however, the people have assumed this business. Instead of the old monarchical form, this business is now conducted under a democratical form;

and experience has made it very dear to the people generally. It will be shown in these chapters that it is yet far from being perfect, but it is made to answer the purpose very well until we are enabled by our own experience, to see light more clearly.

The public schools furnish another important instance of the application of the principle of democracy to the practical uses of great masses of people by the collective, instead of the individual control. This institution is democratical and a reverse of individualism in principle; however imperfect its details may be, owing to ignorance of the people who control it. It is an institution which is rapidly assuming enormous proportions. It is so democratical that it educates the poor man's child with the rich man's money; and this collective power, the people find, is a safeguard to the perpetuity of their democratical form of government; because it develops one of the most important resources of national prosperity and happiness—the intellect. It is impossible to compute the immense importance of this intellectual development, to a nation.

When the people, as a collective unit, have grown, by experience, in appreciation of this importance, they will doubtless convert the public schools into colleges, with preparatory and graduating departments; and make them vie, in every respect, with the noblest colleges of the world. These schools are controlled by the people in common, who have already established laws in some states, rendering it compulsory upon the children to attend. The public school is a vast business undertaking of the people, who by their votes and labors, control it collectively; and through it, the monarchical idea of business control, is being effectually expelled.

Still another important example of the growth of collective over individual control is seen in the system of hospitals and dispensaries. The reason of this steady growth is, that the public are more careful than the household, of the sick.. Experience teaches that a private house, even if it be a home, is a poor place to take one, afflicted with a contagion; and altogether the wrong place for the sick generally. The public are also becoming aware that a great wrong is being practiced upon them by druggists who, in collusion with doctors, exact exorbitant prices for medicines; and especially, for the prescriptions of these physicians. The continuous tendency, therefore, of the public is to supplant this ancient system of the individual, by means of which he exacts large private profits, with public hospitals and dispensaries.

These institutions are maintained mostly by appropriation from Congress, Legislatures or municipal government, over which the people preside. They are consequently, democratical, and the people make the management of them, a legitimate subject of discussion and of political action. Thus people are forced into the supervision, economical as well as medical, of their own sick and suffering. The people, in common, are learning to take charge of themselves. They must, in the logic of such a system, be constrained to do it well. They must make the noble and growing dispensary, a home. The idea that these institutions are eleemosynary in character, and that, to frequent the dispensary for medical service is akin to beggary and therefore degrading, is false and foolish. It does not belong to sober business economies. Nor does it savor of sound judgment. It is an idea based mainly upon vanity. The people make the dispensaries. They own and control them. Is it not respectable then, for them to enjoy that which is their own? These carpings at mistaken respectability, are unbecoming the sound judgment of a great public.

They have almost entirely outgrown this vanity in its application to the public school. Why should they not be equally dignified in patronizing any other common interest?

It is the often expressed doubt of many whether the true theory of democracy will, when submitted to a whole people with all their contrarieties of thought, their conflicting interests, their love of amusement and flattery, and their general ignorance, stand a solid and practical trial. The pessimists in political economy and governmental advancement are dismayed by the popular and increasing clamor that surges and roars on every side, bitter with accusation of malfeasance in office, and convicting by scores the chosen representatives of the people. To all such doubters the world is better prepared to-day than ever before to make an agreeable report in the affirmative. The indications are, that this democracy is successful, so far as its theory has gone into practical trial. The dismay caused by the conviction of a defaulter need not discourage us. The fact that individuals are often caught and convicted, does not prove that under more ancient methods of government no such rogues existed. On the contrary it proves that under the democratical system, the people are anxious to see the corruption of their representatives exposed, and criminals punished. This was not the case under the monarchical system where one man, or one set of men held perpetual control.

The consequence is that the business of ferreting out rogues has become popular and lucrative to many persons who enter upon it. The people are honest.

They want to know the truth; and will reward by their patronage, any one who will furnish them with it. This has created of late years an enormous newspaper business. It has also occasioned the modern incentive to writing books containing the opinions of individuals, concerning true principles of political economy, regarding statistics and examples. The same popular craving after the knowledge of the truth, is what makes oratory successful; and thousands of good public speakers are kept busy, canvassing the relative capacity and honesty of the people's candidates. All these efforts shed light upon the inner qualification of the aspirant, and the office holder. No amount of labor or expense is spared to enlighten the people concerning them.

The fire that illuminates the prairie crackles loudly as it burns, and purifies the ague swamps; but it is the loud crackling that dismays the timid one. He will not open his eyes to see the light. If he would, he would see the miasma disappear, the dark forms of public robbers lurk away for safety. He would seek to have them caught and brought to trial. In old times, and under less favorable systems, these robbers prowled and glutted themselves upon the people's accumulations unmolested. Indeed they were sovereign. There was no light to expose them. They held the masses in subjugation. In modern democracy the reverse is true; and as the light of honest truth is requisite to collective prosperity, the public will pay for it. The great newspaper is consequently assuming the function of the censor, the tribune, and the lictor. Humanity may rejoice rather than be frightened at the result!

Nine in eleven of all the individual enterprises of this country are, by statistical count, known to end in failure.

About one half the joint stock companies fail. But in relief of this, four fifths of all the *government enterprises* succeed. These cardinal facts alone, are sufficient to embolden the advocate of government employment, or the employment mutually, of the people, by the people, for the sake of the EMPLOYMENT and the PRODUCT, rather than for the sake of profits to a controling few.

If nine out of eleven of the individuals who venture time and money upon business enterprises are found to fail, it is time to doubt the capacity of an individual to conduct business at all. It is also time that the people, who must be supplied by some means, should begin to cast about for a method that will be more successful. Why does the individual so frequently and so ingloriously fail? Is it not because he lacks the requisites of means, of judgment, of tact, that are indispensable to success. and if so, do not a large number of individuals, say a nation of people, if they can come to terms of agreement, possess just these various requisites of money, of judgment and of tact, that would ensure success? It is doubly evident that they do; since they also possess the labor, which they always prefer to sell to themselves, rather than to others.

If one half of the joint stock company enterprises of the country, that are undertaken, prove failures, is it not high time that the great masses who most suffer by such failures by reason of the dearth of employment the financial depressions, and the demoralization they create, should launch out upon the study of a method that will add better factors of success? And does not the fact that a larger percentage of enterprises under the direction of companies succeeds, than under the direction of an individual, prove that the *factors* of success in business lie in the *variety of requisites which numbers furnish?*

There is always one danger which the masses have to fear from corporations; — that which has given expression to the maxim, that "corporations have no souls." Yet this selfishness that makes so cruel a saying true, is undoubtedly just, as applied to the welfare of all the members of that corporation.

What a powerful argument, then, does this black maxim furnish, in favor of augmenting the number of the company in control until it includes the majorities of the people! The reason why the corporation has no soul is because the business formula of rules and of discipline governing, and agreed to, by that body, render it possible for the individuals to shirk *moral* responsibility.

Business rules are inelastic and void of conscientiousness. Individuals are not. The individual operates a business for himself, and fails nine times in eleven.

The joint stock company runs a business for itself, and fails five times in ten. No one will deny that each individual engaged in these enterprises is actuated by motives of self interest. But what makes a number succeed so much more frequently than a single person? The answer is easy. It is because, in a number, who understand the principle of agreement, there are more factors of success. There is more capital and a greater variety of talent, which is requisite to the well-being of the business. If there is agreement, there is certainly a number of individuals, each with his peculiar aptitudes of business tact and pecuniary means. This is evidently the reason why the joint stock companies succeed so much more frequently than the individual, who has only his own resources, and is often devoid of experience. The whole argument, then, suggested by these statistics, shows that there can be no danger from this augmentation of the numbers engaged in an enterprise, even though this number include the entire people.

First, because collective ownership and control dissipate, effectively, the danger mentioned regarding the soullessness of corporations. The corporation works only for the interests of the half dozen individuals who form it. It is gruff and heartless to all others.

The people's collective enterprise is equally selfish; but it includes the *entire people* and consequently must consult the welfare of all. Secondly: admitted that it possesses elements of agreement, it certainly possesses all the factors of variety of talent, of adaptiveness, of aptitude, of genius, and, not the least among its indispensable requisites, it has means and labor of its own which it prefers to appropiate to its own business rather than sell to others.

If four fifths of the government enterprises succeed, does it not show that agreement is a possible thing?

It is possible for joint stock companies to enlarge their numbers so as to include not only a dozen or a hundred thousand members and agree so perfectly, as to perform the most difficult functions of business;

both legislative and mechanical. It may be said that co-operation of large numbers instead of the joint stock companies of a few is a new thing in the world; and therefore, a precarious example to judge from.

Not so; for if we are to believe the history of Christ, and his apostles, the co-operative principle was carried into operation successfully; and further, that it assumed so radical a form, that not only labor, and the product of labor were held, distributed, and enjoyed in common, but the co-operative societies of the early christians, were churches, or mutual self-help curies. Let no one fear that co-operation does not possess elements of success. On the contrary, it is as much more successful than joint stock companies as the latter are more successful than the single individuals.

The co-operative societies have accumulated vast sums of money which they appropriate to many of the different industries, with perfect success. They have no longer any difficulty in owning and controling in common their immense flouring mills, steam engine works, printing establishments, and cotton and woollen mills. They make many of their own shoes, bake their own bread, own and operate their chop and sausage works, tan their own leather and are among the best inventors and discoverers of methods for economizing, and adapting labor to their own supply. The ratio of progression in these collectively managed, and mutually reciprocal enterprises, is incredible. They are able to build lines of steamers to America for purposes of mutual travel, and supply. A hundred more years of such growth will force the pen of political economists out of its wonted grooves of argument, from the old standpoint of competism, into a broad and bold defense of common interests; for if the social, or co-operative experiments of different people, are not sufficient to convince the reader of the justice and feasibility of collective ownership and control, in productive and distributive, as well as legislative industries, let him consult statistics, on a still more ponderous scale, and satisfy himself, regarding the ratio of progression in collective control by so prodigious, versatile, and mercurial an element, as the population of the United States.

In four fifths of their business operations, the governments—Municipal, State, and General—of this people, have succeeded. In this cast no mention is made of the form of legislation, the manner of conducting wars, or the method of choosing the representatives of the people; simply the actual business operations under government, or rather, popular control.

The people have been quite successful in nearly every thing of this kind they have attempted, as a body politic. Within a century, they have shown their ability to manipulate, in the capacity of a compound integer, or a collective unit, almost every sort of business affair which hitherto had been conducted exclusively by individuals. Many of these enterprises, are brought about and operated, not only for the sake of the improvement they afford, in their various functions of production and otherwise, but notably for the sake of the permanent, and economical labor, which they offer to the people who own them, and in whose collective interest they are operated.

The public schools are an example of this kind of enterprise. The people possess them, support them by their own wealth and industry, educate their children by means of them, develop the grandest resource of their national wealth by them, which is the public intellect; and at the same time, find employment for a great many of their own numbers, in the capacity of supervisors, teachers and janitors.

The general status of the human intellect has, within a century been greatly elevated, both in America and in parts of Europe by the public school; and it is to-day the most potent agent in existence, of human development, driving our superstition and darkness of every form from the world, and shedding much of the luster that distinguishes ours, from ages that are gone.

Much of the advance which has been made in mechanics, that have given the modern world so extraordinary an impulse, is due to the support of governments. Mechanics are at the bottom of national progress. Through the mechanic arts, mankind have made healthful advances in the direction of true enlightenment. Now, no inconsiderable encouragement is being given to mechanics, by governments. This Steam Fire Engine is one of the most perfect mechanisms in the world. It is, indeed, an institution, more perfect, if possible, than the Public School. Such an exquisite labor-saving apparatus, rolling and fuming down our avenues, mounted by heroes of the fire-brand and water tube, is a stirring, but not uncommon sight. It glistens with the polish of its proud keeper; is powerful in nerve, and restive for employment. A citizens home is in flames! And a dozen of these beauteous monsters followed by hook and ladder chariots are quickly centering in, to the rescue of that home. The wonderful telegraph has noiselessly transmitted order upon order and dictating their route thither, indicated the exact spot, named the foreman, and appointed from headquarters, each workman. The central administration has appointed to each, his work, with a science that effects the greatest result from the least number of men. There are no supernumeraries. Indeed, the curiosity seekers are not wanted. They are out of place. The steam pumps are immediately connected to their hose; the couplings are screwed to the hydrants; the men at the nozzles are aiming at the glaring element that is gnawing down the peaceful cttizen's home; and with incredible celerity and unconcern, and with scarcely a visible motion, the burning property is deluged from attic to basement, and the fire extinguished.

This case of the Steam Fire-extinguishing Department, thus comes up before us as an argument. It is, perhaps, the best of the four or five communistic instrumentalities of which the world can yet boast. The Public School is indeed, something magnificent, but this is more mechanical; although they are both industries, and belong to the Labor Question. Every person in the city has an interest in the fire destroyer. His very safety depends by night and day upon its effectiveness. It is far more reliable, and less individually selfish than the fire insurance system of companies; and is superseding and supplanting them. It watches the poorest of the poor, as well as the opulent. Men, women and children, of all conditions are unselfishly protected by this wonderful agent provided it is properly kept and scientifically operated. Now the fact that these operations of this fire-police are unselfish, that they must benefit every individual of the community in order to benefit a single individual, is what makes it an engine of

Communism. It is a branch of mechanical science, applied to the social welfare, and exemplifies the aphorism "each for all and all for each."

But does it enforce the aphorism "each for all and all for each?" How does it make practical the theory of the labor movement, that political economy demands the greatest possible result of labor from the least possible effort? How does it purify itself from corruption in its administration by the watchfulness of the people from year to year? The answers to these questions are an explanation of the phenomena of communism, as the basis of political economy. They expose the absurdities, and the anarchical, and unscientific tendencies of the dogma of individual sovereignty.

In the steam fire engine this is done. It is a political instrument. It belongs to the people. It is a part of their democratic government. The people are voters. The vote of the poor man is as good as the vote of the rich man; and this is the poor man's only guarantee of perfect equality. Take away this attribute of manhood and he is a slave. The city is the commune, of which every voter is a member in good standing. It is also a common property, of which every member owns an untransferable share;—the share of citizenship. Consequently, the voter is constantly on the alert. It is the poor man's only hope. He organizes, watches, criticises its government, employs the best detectives to investigate and report the acts of his agents, and thus forces them to be scientific and thorough. In fact, experience shows that voters have very well succeeded in ferreting out, exposing, and punishing those servants who have dared to subordinate the great principle of collective interest, to the welfare of the individual selfishly. But there remains another great class of Industries which the true Labor Movement alone can force into the care of Governments. Namely: Agriculture, and Manufacture. When we, as a nation of people, learn to cultivate our own crops, manufacture our own cotton, silk, woollen and other goods ; our own boots and shoes ; apply our knowledge of Mechanics, of every kind, for the supply of human wants, to PRODUCTION, the same as we are applying our knowledge of Mechanics to the Fire Department, the Postal Bureau, and the Arsenals; when people can as a *collective* individual, do that which now, is so unkindly done by the isolated individual, and do it as well as it is done in the example of the Steam Fire Engine, then, and not till then, will the Labor Problem be solved. Political Economy is to-day trembling and creaking upon the hinges of this collective control.

# LABOR CATECHISM
OF
# POLITICAL ECONOMY.

## CHAPTER I

........

### CONVERSATION

BETWEEN A DELEGATION FROM THE UNITED SHOP-KEEPERS, BUTCHERS, DRY GOODS MERCHANTS, FUEL DEALERS AND APOTHECARIES.

CHAIRMAN. WE are a Delegation from a mutual Organization for the protection of our special interests. We are sent to the Industrial Council to obtain direct information, concerning the object of the radical movement.

RESPONSE. Our movement is nothing other than an innocent Co-operation of working men and women for Self Help.

DELEGATE. Do you call secret Trade Unions and other schemes for exciting harangue, co-operation?

RESPONSE. This is not a mere scheme for excitement. It is an earnest response, by an oppressed laboring class, to a new proposition which affords them a ray of hope. It is as much co-operation of the poor to obtain, by self help, the several necessaries of life, such as employment, homes, eatables, fuel, clothing and medicines, as the almost perfectly similar co-operations of England.

DELEGATE. English co-operation consists of social societies. They are peaceful and inoffensive; while your movements are political.

RESPONSE. But remember, we are in America, where no class is recognized. Social co-operation involves the same principles that political co-operation does. It is through this social, political union, that Americans must arrive at self supply. We have vainly tried, and are trying, to establish the social system of co-operation as in Europe; but there being no guaranty to the workingmen by the government, that this co-operation shall endure, or remain solvent, and responsible to its creditors, it falls an easy prey to dishonest members. Besides this, the country is so large, and the laboring class so nomadic, or migratory, that nearly as many rogues join in the hopes of getting a chance to fleece innocents, as genuine, and solid members. The society having once been deceived, becomes fickle and dies of discouragement. Add this to the influences brought to bear by your trading class, who now control these necessaries of life, and exert their strength against co-operation, and you have the principal cause of failure that seems to follow every attempt of American Social Combination for self help. There is one other reason that must not be overlooked. The extreme freedom of our institutions renders every person a sovereign of him or herself. In Europe there is a sort of recognized class. Any effort to set up a co-operative concern on a social basis, however sound the principle may be, is, in America, received with coldness by the workingman, on the ground that it suggests compulsory fraternization. The trade union works in principle quite the reverse; for that species of combination is based upon a sort of *demand* in which the idea of sovereignty is uppermost. As long as co-operation for furnishing the people means of existence is based upon helpless social combination by which the member has no positive guarantee from his own organization, or from Congress or State Legislatures, that his funds are safe from embezzlers and that his enterprise is sure, just so long is it logically true that he will refrain from supporting this otherwise promising means of relief. These objections to co-operation a few years ago would have seemed untrue, and perhaps absurd; but unhappy experience on every hand proves them too correct.

CHAIRMAN. Yet this interference of any political government, for the means of existence of *your* half of the population, is an interference directly subversive of the very business and means of support, of *our* half of the population. It is a direct threat; and an attack upon us who now furnish your supplies.

REMARK. Indirectly it bears its suggestiveness, but it makes war upon nobody. Many working and useful people whom no industry can afford to lose, have died from starvation during the last few years in this country. The competitive scheme for their supply upon which your class depend for support, failed to furnish them means of sustenance. They starved! It is not enough for humanity to weep. Humanity has proved, amidst tears, to have done little but nurture charity, and its concomitants of degrading soup houses and humiliating asylums. All this, under your system which has impoverished us, and aggrandized you.

Supposing now, these suffering toilers on the verge of starvation because without profitable employ, were to combine with one another, with Trade Unions and communities, and under competent exponents and advisers should form themselves into a political power so strong, that at the elections they place in office tried men of their own class pledged to enact laws so as to legally effect the establishment, in the city of New York, Boston or elsewhere, of a Bureau of Labor and provision supply. Would that not be co-operation?

CHAIRMAN. Of whom do you propose this Bureau of supply shall purchase its articles?

ANSWER. Of you; or anybody who will sell supplies of the best quality and at the cheapest rates. But it is not to be supposed that any broker is to realize a fortune. Co-operation and speculation are strangers. The success of the social co-operations of England has always been in proportion to their *absence* from speculation. Nothing can be more hateful to a co-operative enterprise than individual speculations. It is just as feasible, in a political, municipal government like New-York, or Chicago, to attempt to furnish a supply of dry goods, eatables, fuel and medicines to its citizens, as it is, for a social establishment at Rochdale with eight thousand members, to furnish the same to half the population of that city. Years of experience prove that this *science of direct transaction* is a truly promising departure from old usages.

DELEGATE. There appears a vein of artfulness running in your argument. You seem to wish us to infer that European co-operation is not only similar, but almost identical with this crazy, eleemosynary proposition of the workingmen that depends entirely for its success upon the shrewdness of the politicians in power.

ANSWER. There are several answers to make to your remark.

First: You seem not to recognize that the poor, starving founders of that immortal enterprise in the north of England were often waited upon by just such delegations as your honorable body; and that they were jeered at by those who, for many years made Toad Lane the mock of Lancashire and Yorkshire. The attempt to establish a co-operative Society on the social, that is to say non-political basis, was treated by the shopkeepers and their friends with every kind of insult; and for many years there was scarcely a newspaper in the land that did not systematically ply its cant and jibe until the poor experimenters forgot that it was cruel to be tabooed, or calumnious to be belied.

Secondly: You do not recognize that this same calumny on the part of the shop-keepers, whose long-time power was thus threatened by the new system, was, and is yet, resorted to in every part of Europe, or where-ever co-operation has exhibited itself.

Thirdly: You do not recognize that co-operation in many parts of England is absorbing a large percentage of the inhabitants; that it is becoming an *institution;*

and in all probability will soon have to be upheld by the *state instead of the social government.* Mr. John Stuart Mill had the shrewdness to foresee this when he made the expression:

"I cannot deny that which is proved by the success of co-operation in the North of England, nor that the future of our political economy hangs upon co-operation; and you may imagine a time when the co-operative idea will be so common and prevailing a thing that it will be endorsed by the government and so end in superseding the competitive system entirely."

DELEGATE. Then the American workingmen propose to commence by a political Party of their own, that shall create, on the political basis, a branch of government to control the sale of the groceries, the dry goods, fuel and medicines which we now furnish. All this they propose to do, without even the experience of the social co-operators of Europe

ANSWER. The American people are amply prepared for it. The workingmen's affair is simply a question of slavery. Theoretically, our political slavery was swept away by the war of the Revolution; and later, our chattel slavery, afterwards political, was swept away by the war of the Rebellion. These experiences prepared us for an attack upon the still more subtle Wages Slavery which must be swept away by co-operation. In this country this last swoop must be made by political power, like both the preceding forms; because the evil is general and because Americans, by reason of the peculiarity of their institutions, cannot deal with matters affecting the interests of the majorities in a small way. It has been found to be not only dangerous, but disastrous; for reasons heretofore described. The wages slavery of the

Europeans, is identical with the wages slavery of the Americans; but the methods of conducting the war against it, are different. There, this method must be social, that is, non-political; because the people are not universally allowed the *political*, or *votive franchise.*

Those who most need these home provisions which are supplied by the co-operative store, are, of course, the poorest, who are not allowed to vote at the great elections. But in the little co-operative government, which they find must be intensely strict and severe, they are allowed the votive franchise. It is the intense love in mankind, of this ennobling franchise, that stimulates the co-operators. But our people are accustomed, in the liberty of their citizenship, to use this franchise at the great elections; and it is no honor for them to amuse, or trouble themselves with the affairs of smaller government. Hence, if this greater government neglects to provide for the home provision of citizens; if the General, State, and Municipal Government do not assume control and become purveyors for the people, then, these majorities must remain forever at the mercy of your competing purveyorship. Granted that co-operation is the only means by which working people can obtain their supplies without the "round-about," "change hands," competitive system, and it is easily proved that direct, "live and let live" deal is the legitimate function of a republican government.

Delegate. Admitting that your workingmen's project, of cheap family purveyance may possibly be practicable in future ages, yet we cannot see in it anything but the wildest vagaries; and we know by business experiences of our own, that the very first experiment in it will lead to chaos. Your proposition is revolutionary. You propose to create a political power and with that power, to force upon a vast municipality like New York or Philadelphia, so immense a business as the market, dry goods, fuel and medicine supply; without once considering that in doing so, you are turning us who have fed, clothed, warmed and doctored you long and faithfully, out into the world, perhaps penniless, and with our business ruined, in old age when it is too late to learn another. This may look very upright to you but we look at the matter from another point of view. We are disposed, moreover, to look at it from a standpoint of your own good. We warn you that this is a direct revolution.

RESPONSE. So is the successful co-operation of England a direct revolution.

DELEGATE. In taking such a distribution of these goods upon yourselves you create a void and confusion in the methods of transacting business!

ANSWER. Do not your own stores remain? And is any man deprived of the right of buying of you and paying your prices for a hundred years to come, if he wishes to do so?

DELEGATE. You destroy the long studied and practically learned functions of a great business economy, before you have reared up even the *business discipline*, to say nothing of the Officers, by which the new method is to be transacted.

ANSWER. This kind of argument is all very plausible and persuasive and deserves to be thoroughly considered. But the people remember very well when the American colonies were suddenly converted, by a severe political contest, from a dependency to a free common wealth, that although the attempt involved worse revolution than this you lament, they were found to be thoroughly prepared for the change; and neither this people nor the human race at large, have ever regretted it. Your objection finds complete rebuttal again, in the more recent event of the great Pro-Slavery Rebellion. A great many people were plunged into consternation. Emancipation was proclaimed before any preparations were made for a new order of things. The abolition of chattel slavery was proclaimed in a day! And in a few short months it became a fact. Yet the country out-lived it all; and great as the change was, involving the destiny of millions, the confiscation of properties, the overturning of systems, and the creation of a new and instructive page in history, yet the first swell of time has launched us into the exercise of a new political economy; and all goes smoothly again. But if history at home is not sufficient to convince you of a falacy in your objection, you need but look at the little decree which in France, instantaneously revolutionized the system of weights and measures. On the evening of one day the old system was in full vogue. On the morning of the next, it was a punishable offence to use any other than the new. Yet in a week everybody was pleased with the change. In Japan and China, mighty revolutions are going on, from the old, barbarous systems, to the more convenient ones of modern science; and almost without a ripple of political discord. Now all these great and sudden changes which involve the destinies of the human race have been effected by governments and are political because anything decided by political action is supposed to be decided by the consent of the majorities, or, at least, by the decree of those in whom the majorities acquiesce, and have confidence. There is no appeal from this decision. It is final. But if it be a mere petty decision like that of a social co-operative scheme, it is laughed at by one, obstinately upheld by another, tried and found wanting by another, by another proved a success, and betwixt the wranglings of indecision, it is about sure, in this country to fail; while the old, one-sided, and advantage-taking system of furnishing supplies, continues.

CHAIRMAN. Can you give us any details as to your proposed method of substituting your so called political management for the present system of supply?

ANSWER. We are too actively engrossed in the preparatory work of organization and general discussion of the great whole, to be able to attend to details. Your very natural question is asked several years too soon. There are, however, several points upon which we are agreed. All Officers entrusted with the management of this business must be elected. Workingmen have been badly misled by the appointing system; and they are learning to agree upon this one point. They want no more of it.

CHAIRMAN. Will not the system tend to destroy the Trade Unions?

ANSWER. On the contrary. In this political co-operation the trades Union assumes the functions of the *co-operative society*. The Trades Unions, or rather the central council of Trades Unions composed of their delegates, discovers any errors and frauds that may lurk in the system, and is thus enabled to bring in all grievances, and to *demand* their correction. If they be not speedily corrected new Officers must be elected to fill the places of those who prove incompetent. The *honesty* therefore, with which the supply of the *whole people* is conducted, will in this manner, prove the incentive of wise voting. *Wise voting is thus forced by the household needs, discussion and practice, upon every man and woman.*

There is no chance for corruptionists in the system because, if the people find their clothes, their table provisions, their coal and medicines come too high, they begin to clamor about it. They agitate. They hold indignation meetings. They take their grievance before their central councils. They take it to their own hearth and home. The irregularity is first discovered by the housekeeper; who is the first to bring her suspicions of knavery to the attention of her husband. The detective proclivities of every newspaper finds its noblest sanction, its harvest and heaven in it. Political economy in this system becomes alike, the poor man's and the rich man's economy. This is the first budding of the true, honest, earnest, just and humanity-saving political economy.

INQUIRY. On what other points have you determined that may come under the category of Details?

ANSWER. It is safe to conjecture that the outlines of the system may consist as follows :

First: An Elected Mayor, or Municipal Governor.

Second: An Elected Common Council.

Third: The Division of the City or Community, wherever it may be, into a certain number of Districts.

Fourth: A Great Central Provision Depot with Rail-Road communication and Telegraph Lines.

Fifth: A Bureau of Fluctuations.

Sixth: An Official Bulletin containing a price-current for each week, and Principles of the system.

Seventh: A system of telegraphy, by which the cook, the housewife and the sick patient may for one cent, send an order for what they want and receive the package required, — the payment for the package being given at the Telegraph Office, at the quoted price.

Eighth: The Delivery, conducted as follows: — First: There is a central market into which the wholesale buyers send the goods. Second: In this market is a general Telegraph Office. Third: Radiating in different directions from this market, and among the people at convenient points, are hundreds of Sub-Stations, connecting by Telegraph, with the General Office. Fourth: A Telegraph Boy or Girl at every office. Fifth: The Delivery Service, with Head Quarters at the general Telegraph Office. This Delivery of goods may be done by horse or steam wagons. All the telegraph Offices are open eight hours each day, and the expedition of the wagons is at least once a day; or more if the people desire. This expedition of the goods is made regularly and at known intervals, and through known and appointed routes. The manner of enjoying advantages of this system is as follows: Each house is furnished with the Bulletin containing a price list. Any one wishing a market bill has only to consult the price list, and from it make out a list on paper of the articles required; and with this go to the nearest Telegraph station, pass in the order, the address, and the money for the goods. This order is then dispatched to the Central Bureau, with the address; and the provisions or other goods thus ordered are delivered at the house by the first delivery wagon.

These are some of the rough outlines. Any subsequent, practical details might show the further venture of ours in relation to operations of a practical kind and their application, to be unsafe.

DELEGATE. Do you consider that the government postal department acts as an example to be patterned after?

ANSWER. In very many respects. The postal system offers the same *incentive* to the people, to study and to require honesty in its administration. It is, like this supply system, a *service* that comes right home to every man, woman and child. Like the supply *service*, it depends upon the *cheapness* with which it transacts its business. Like the supply service, it enters into legislation and depends upon the political intelligence of the people for its success. Like the supply service it depends upon celerity and certainty in its evolutions. But the postal service has many bad elements. The great principle involved in it is badly contaminated by the contract system. It is political only in the merest nominal form. Contractors use it as an instrument wherewith to degrade political action. As all the officers of the postal service are appointed they combine to secure the continuance in the offices of their superiors who appointed them. These appointed office holders, however honest their intentions when they begin, tend to become, on account of temptations that beset their office, the meanest of tricksters. They allow manhood to be trailed in the dust for the sake of keeping their positions, and thus securing the emoluments of a contract. The theory is this: When a new Administration comes into power a new post master is appointed. This man finds it to his political advantage to secure the appointment of such subordinates as are surest to wield an influence toward his reappointment at the close of his term. The administrative ability, therefore, of his subordinates, is not so much consulted as the power they can exert in maintaining *him*. If the people should elect these subordinates would they not vote for administrative ability? The post master, as it is, naturally choses politicians as his subordinates, who are versed in all the various mysteries and trickery of bribing, ballot-stuffing, and contract jobbery; and who often know or care the least about attending to the people's business. Not so in the elective system where the people themselves do the appointing. The appointing system has proved the bane of our republican institutions. It is full of subtlety and intrigue; it is as insidious as treason itself and must not be permitted to enter into this scheme of economic supply.

There is nothing about the postal system that works badly, except this habit of jobbing its work to private individuals and corporations known as the contract system. The people are finding out, through the abuses and annual deficits which involve them in debt, that this system of contracting their work out to labor brokers, is pernicious in a high degree and must be supplanted by government railroads, telegraphs, and other means which shall do this work for them through the *direct* or *co-operative* process; and without the intermediaries at all. Furthermore, all employés should be hired by the year, or day, and not by the quantity, or piece; because the latter holds the seeds of competism. The principles on which this new political, co-operative home supply is based, are, therefore, directly anti-monopolistic. The Officers are *elected* by the people at fitting periods; and all men and women engaged in the service under them are to be paid by the year. The books are kept by law; open to investigation and censure. An annual report must be officially made, and the various articles of dry goods, groceries, fuels and medicines must be furnished to the people at their *minimum* cost. Like the co-operative stores of England, they must be of the first class only; and the country, far and wide must be searched for the best and the cheapest.

It is here again, that the present competitive system of supply is practicing the grossest outrages upon the people. It is conducted *by* individuals *for* individuals. But the most lamentable phase is, that it is not universal but partial. The grocers themselves need, of course, pay no more for their own provisions than the *cost* prices. All the well-to-do people if they have any eye to economy, can buy their provisions at some advantage, more or less. That is to say, they do not pay the full retail prices; they get them less. It is only the working majorities, the poor, who have no advantages of leisure, or of mutual reciprocity, or of prestige, who must pay these bills of extortionate price. It is they who, for want of combination and wisdom, are forced to enrich this powerful, numerous, well combined and better educated class of intermediary dealers which your Delegation represents. And it is these poor people, made poorer in proportion as you are made richer, who have determined at last, and after long ages of hunger and deprivation, to attempt this plan of co-operation for self supply which you very naturally deplore.

DELEGATE. This scheme may look beautiful on paper, but before you accomplish anything you must expect our opposition; and that of all the class in sympathy with us, which is very numerous and powerful.

RESPONSE. Powerful only through wealth and prejudice. Numerous only in the cities and towns. The proletariat or non-favored class are in the majority everywhere;—even in the great centres of congregated labor, like New York, or Manchester; but they are especially in the majority in the country.

DELEGATE. What! Do you expect to be heard, or to be other than scouted by the Farmers' organizations?

ANSWER. Not until they have studied their own interests more thoroughly. Until recently, there has always been too strong a tendency of all people to regard our movements as something disreputable. Fools look upon us with pity. The fact is, the cause of the slavery of working people is attributable to their own stupid acquiescence in the logic of their chains. The farmers, taken as a class are worse imposed upon if anything, than the mechanics. They are just beginning to see great advantages in combination. But in order to see its full advantages they must lay aside their prejudices against what they imagine to be disreputable, and learn to pity less. In short, there is no permanent and complete relief for them, except in this co-operation with mechanics and laborers of the cities. The two classes combined in this political co-operation can in a few years sweep away all kinds of mercenary opposition by dint of political party tactics.

DELEGATE. Will you enlighten us with further details of your methods?

ANSWER. At the great centers, say of New York, Philadelphia, Boston, Chicago, and other cities, a central Bureau of supplies is created by the commissioners, or purveyors of the city, who are elected. Attached to this central bureau or depot are all the modern arrangements of telegraphy and telephony.

Let us suppose, that a central depot is stationed, say at the old Washington Market; New York City. Then in each of the wards of New York, Brooklyn and the environing towns are little telegraph stations. Teams connect from the great central depot with the people who thus receive their supplies through a government railroad and water communication, *with the farmers themselves* in all parts of the country. This system binds producers and consumers together with no possible chance for monopoly.

A board of purveyors, or commissioners of supply is elected annually whose duty it is to inspect every article, keep down rings, permit none but the best to enter the market, buy directly from the best supply markets, and keep the prices of the provisions of each week advertised ahead; so that house-keepers may have only to consult the Saturday's paper containing the official price-list of articles, for the ensuing week. At all convenient points electrical stations connect with the many centres. Any person wanting a beefsteak, or any refreshment, has only to step out to the telegraph station, deposit the amount as advertised, for the article required and go home. When the hour of expedition arrives, the porter is at the door with the package. The feasibility, beauty and cheapness, of this system are self-apparent. By it, the people rid themselves of poisons that now infect, more or less, nearly everything we consume. By it the old English and French co-operations are introduced *practically;* only in a political way through the genuineness of every article bought. By it, the prices may be abated from five to five hundred per-cent.; and the present freebooters in our market system are forced to relinquish their strong hold where they have so long and mercilessly prowled upon the defenseless people.

Any one doubting the practicability of this system, has only to carefully study the similar evolutions of the Steam Fire Engine Department; the only blur upon the analogy being the fact that the Fire-extinguishing Department is a trifle more in the interest of the capitalists than of the non-property holders; since houses, stores, churches—even streets, and cities themselves—are property of a comparatively few individuals; and their numbers are few in comparison with the masses who tenant them. The co-operation for safety from fires, therefore, acts intensely in the interest of everybody; but especially, in the interest of these comparatively few owners; while that of the Municipal Market is more in the direct interest of the poorest class or those who are now too helpless to avoid the exorbitant market prices that keep them poor. Just in proportion, then, as the easier class are able to avoid these high prices by purchasing in large quantities, watching the market eliminating petty rings, and utilizing their commodious cellars which the poor cannot have, in such a proportion, do these well-to-do dealers seek to perpetuate the system which enriches their own class, or those in sympathy with them, by impoverishing their proletarian neighbors.

The Fire Department is a complete co-operative organization of a class of citizens. It is political. Why? Because it involves too large an area of the social fabric to be merely social. The Fire Department is too immense and too important to be contracted out. No junto of contractors can have the Fire Department. The intimate home interests of too many persons are at stake. So the people themselves take it, and operate it in their own sovereign interests at cost; and the perfect success which has crowned the enterprise shows the wisdom of the people. It is a successful politico-co-operative enterprise of the people. The Post Office is another. The Water Board is another. The School System another. Their purity depends upon the absence of brokers or contractors among them. They are too numerous to mention.

Now in the face of all these exquisite specimens of popular co-operation as applied to specific purposes, how long must the people be wronged by a diseased and chronic system of supply? How long must their food, clothing, fuel and medicines be doled out to them, by profit-making persons operating in the dark, concocting bargains, as purveyors for the defenseless masses who are chained too low by their ignorance and poverty, to be dangerous; and binding yearly the thongs of destitution and infatuate slavery around them? How long must this last in the dazzle of such an enlightened age as this, when the people have no better excuse for their miseries than apathy and ignorance? A little political organization of the truly useful classes; a little imitation of these magnificent examples, whose very splendor mocks them; a little wholesome combination of independent work, in the direction of self-help, would sweep away the shackles from their limbs, the cobwebs from their vision, the lethargy from their nerves and launch them out upon a field of co-operative economy, redundant in manhood and gladness.

Delegate. We are here to assure you that we have no fear of the progress of your utopian system for generations to come. The press bases its success upon the opinion of society. The press rules. The public have no opinion whatever of your affair. It is as unintelligible to the public as it is obscure. The press wants money—a good thing which we possess. While we can, as now, organize a pool and have the means of approaching and dictating to the press through our subventions, you will be wrangling with others, incapable of putting confidence in your own managers and too poor to hire managers from our ranks to carry on your business to a successful financial issue.

Answer. The politico-co-operative plan may be paradoxical, but it is far from being utopian. That it depends upon the influence of the press exerted in its favor, no one can deny. Neither shall we attempt to denv that the press has too often sold its honor to monopolies. who are secretly organizing to enslave and degrade the people. This is the mortal ignis fatuus that degenerates the press while ever degrading the people. But there lingers yet, in man, much that is noble; and fortunately this element of honor, too much employed hitherto, is seeking its exponent in the press. The newspaper makes a doubly sad mistake in perfidiously sacrificing honor; sad in the fact that it degrades and demoralizes its inner conscience; sad in the fact that it falsifies the conditions upon which humanity depends for happiness. The history of the newspaper shows that notwithstanding the temporary advantages, sometimes derived from influence, gifts and political subsidies, by far the most successful newspapers are those that energetically take the part of the common people. In the public school it is the duty of the newspaper to expose every evil great or small, that exists, So in political affairs, it is also its duty to bring all defaulters to an account. The people invariably buy such papers. They are sure to get the largest circulation The subject matter of such journals being motived in purity, the tone of their columns becomes spicy. A proclivity to act the part of the detective, grows in the editors and reporters of its staff. The people love to read the revelations of the detective. They want news; and if anything is going on, nobody has a better right to know it than the public. To sift out truth and lay it bare before the eyes of the whole people, in all its sickly phases, and amid all its ghastly surroundings, is the true function of the newspaper; and those sheets that yield to bribery, though they may seem to thrive for a time, are doubly doomed liars; in that they palm off falsehood rather than truth for the people, calling it news, thus demoralizing public opinion, and they lie to their own consciences, thus demoralizing themselves.

DELEGTE. How can the newspaper come to the rescue of a system which few candid persons can subscribe to? It would be death to any newspaper enterprise to attempt to foist an idea upon the people that cannot be comprehended by the average man.

RESPONSE. The press has an extraordinary idiosyncracy or a peculiar belief in regard to its "average man." It is well enough to truckle to mental middlings, even at the expense of manhood, for the sake of maintaining a well filled purse; but not at the expense of common sense. That is going too far. The elements of success are plainly visible in every phase of Politico-co-operation. All the peeple want is a clear, plain explanation. These people are in the majority over the vendors of the day. They are the larger part of the newspaper-reading public. If the feasibility of this plan with all its arguments, accompanied by diagrams, were plainly and boldly set forth by newspapers, as points of the current news, like any other interesting invention, it would find support in the favorable opinion of the public. It is the custom of the newspaper to devote money and space on every important invention. Should the discovery of a motive power be made that were better than any now in use, no matter how many steam engine manufacturers it might threaten or how many millions of organized and operating capital it might bankrupt, or how many thousands of employees it might deprive of labor, the press would nevertheless, take an active interest in the discovery; and it is equally the duty of the press notwithstanding this possibility of a revolution of things, among the market dealers of a city, to take an equally active interest in any new and good system of distributing provisions among the people Let the people organize in clubs, in the different communities and boldly maintain Politico-Co-operation and the press will publish the news.

CHAIRMAN. Not alone the press, and all the most respectable business concerns upheld by public opinion will be against you but also the entire orthodox Church, which includes a respectable majority of the people.

ANSWER. It is the duty of the Church and all other great organizations to contribute their share in all movements for the benefit of man. The Church most especially, ought to aid in the development of a good method of provisioning the people because it is democratic. The Church claims to be democratic; since it seeks to admit and provide for the welfare of all, without regard to race, color, sex or condition. It is, therefore, just the organization that should be foremost in an effort to relieve poor people and place them under the influence of angels rather than of devils.

DELEGATE. Religion has always proved itself out of place when tampering with the temporal affairs of people. The Church is an organization with an exclusively spiritual object.

ANSWER. True, it so claims to be; but souls have some sympathy and business connection with our bodies, more material. To be religious is to have the soul softened into love for living mankind. How can a man learn to love his neighbor as himself when his means of existence set him in ghastly antagonism with his neighbor? It is not enough for a dozen, or a hundred well-to-do persons to be able to co-operate for their own selfish interests. We want advantages opened for the poorest of the poor. The very poorest are those who most need charity, the boasted virtue of religion; yet the Church in giving them no material aid leaves them in the depths of every misery. Not having means they linger in squalor and rags—a condition too profane to admit of the education of emotions or the desire to enter the carpeted halls or sit upon the cushioned seats of church edifices. They are out of place there. Thousands of people, naturally intelligent enough, die every year for the want of fruits which in our seaboard cities can be had by the whole cargo for about one quarter the money they are sold at, by our market dealers on the day after their arrival. There is wanted a practical religion; one of whose tenets shall be to afford the poor, needy sufferers, the *means* of bringing such aliment within their reach. Souls and consciences are always in a state of rebellion so long as they are girdled in by disease, poverty, ignorance and other seeds of crime. Politico-co-operation as a government economy, would save humanity, giving people, in mass, the means of saving themselves from the ravenous wolf of need. Ignorance and suffering are the initial animus of blasphemy and crime. Let the Christian begin right, and show his charity in practical earnest or the critical majority looking at the havoc of unabated sin, will continue to sneer him down as a hypocrite. Religion is assimilated with purity and development. How can a man live purely without the practical means? Religion means goodness. How can you expect this in the toils of squalor and rags? The mistake is that religion refuses to touch the labor queston In truth, it stands in inexpressible need of the practical appliances which characterize successful business. You cannot soften a desperado's heart until you smoothen the approaches to it. To provide these means of distributing food at cost prices, and of furnishing the people with fresh oranges, lemons, apples and other fruits and delicacies direct from the ships and of purchasing them direct, by the cargo, is to repeat Christ's practical benevolence in providing bread for a multitude. But what killed Him was the fact that He was not in the interest of speculators who now hold the monopoly over His Church. How can people get time to elevate themselves to a disposition to obey the mandates of Christ, a lowly workingman, when in a community like New York, Brooklyn, Jersey City and environs, they are summer after summer slowly rotting with disease? Remove the causes of disease. The River Hudson, called one of the most beautiful in the world wafts on its slow waters, millions of tons of malaria-breeding offal, past this great community every year. Horses, cattle hogs, sheep, dogs, cats, rats and even human beings, in all the sickening putrescence of every conceivable state of decomposition. The sewerage of great cities and populous towns, rotting reekings from a thousand hamlets, putrefying excrement, blood and offal from a hundred abattoirs and fish-shambles are vomited forth from great sewer-mains into the mouth of this beautiful river making its water doubly brackish with their foul disintegration—poison, whose noxious emanations floating on the in-bound breezes are swallowed into the stench-abhorring lungs of the poor. The rich and wiser class can escape to the mountains and the waters where the air is sweet. It is the poor and the thus defiled whom it is religion's duty to purify who are abandoned, for want of wisdom and means of escape to all the ghastly summer epidemics and contagions. Men and women of the mire blaspheme God and hate both God and man when under the torture of disease. The remedy must come in the removal of the carrion ; and this, it seems, is too much like work for the Church in easy opulence.

Yet this application of politico-co-operation would soon open men's eyes to a great and double economy. This very offal so fearfully destructive to humanity when left to putrefy in the stagnating eddies of our rivers, is of great value to farms and gardens; and the chemical process is by no means wanting whereby to convert it into a fertilizer equal to the richest guano. In Paris and other cities of the east large sums are paid to city treasuries, by companies, for the mere privilege of sweeping streets, and the cleanliness of the streets of Paris, is renowned. But there is no justice even in letting the work out to companies; for the cities could do this work direct. The filth of our streets and rivers would be worth millions of dollars annually, to the city treasuries, if it were converted into manures for fertilizing gardens and farms; and it is a shame that such resources of disease should be allowed to remain, without either practical or moral protest from churches or boards of public works. The alimentation of the inhabitants of our cities as well as the work of keeping them healthy should be performed by the people in common.

DELEGATE. Do you propose to start this system in your social co-operations?

ANSWER. Certainly. And any council, or club of

co-operators can start it. A dozen men and women may organize. After selecting a nook in which to safely put their goods say the basement of a residence of one of the members, using the parlor floor as a hall to meet in, and partake weekly of the business and social enjoyments—purchasing and auditing committees are created to begin the work. The goods are sold to members who have trade cards or credentials. Bills of purchase, and accounts of sale must be regularly and thoroughly audited and balanced, and then reported to the council. This becomes the head center. Similar associations may exist around it, too far away for families to come for goods.

The telegraph or telephone system when the organization has become strong enough, does away with every difficulty. All purchases and all sales are supervised and audited by the head committee. Whenever the system has grown too large to be merely social it will naturally take the political form like the fire department, the water board or the public school.

Delegate. But what about that great, much talked-of commodity known in commerce as liquor? If you can manage by co-operation the supply of table stores why can you not in the same way manage the supply of beverages? Would not such a method as you have pictured apply also to their distribution, so as to sap the profits of saloon keepers by giving applicants a chance to order a purer article directly from a government storage depôt or warehouse?

Answer. Yes. All liquors may be manufactured, stored and dispensed by government, and upon the same vast scale. By this means the true interests of the people are subserved in two ways: first, by buying the best distilling and fermenting products through the direct, instead of the prevailing roundabout system which is cheating the farmers. High-wine concerns fleece the overtasked agriculturists cruelly to gratify a greedy impulse little better than that of the highwayman. Not unfrequently they cheat in another way, by working poor cereals into the liquors; and cover the deception by adding another, in form of a seasoning of cheap and dangerous poisons. The people, the great conscientious mass, would not allow this if they could rectify the calamity at the ballot box. Secondly, the true interests of the people are subserved by simplifying both the methods of production and distribution. It is co-operation wherein people deal directly with one another without making use of these middlemen at all. Nothing is simpler, for it follows the well-tried lines of business as exhibited in the post office or a fire extinguishing service in a city. The people will thus be emancipated from the powerfully organized greed-incentive of the go-betweens who for their paltry baubles of profit create statutes to legalize and foster fashions and concoctions that wheedle and entice humanity into the envenomed paths of self-destruction. No. There is no solution for this question of rum except to submit it, on these lines of political economy, to the vote of the people of both sexes, relying upon their slow judgment coupled with experience and their honest and tender solicitude for the victims they love. Give the masses this opportunity unrestricted, and they will adjust the manufacture and distribution of liquors to their new, equitable and scientific belongings.

## CHAPTER II.

........

## THE IRRESPONSIBLE POOR.

---

VISIT WITH THE OUTCASTS, UNFORTUNATES, FELONS, AND TRAMPS.

WANDERER. We are told that there is in store for us, a means by which we, the so-called "irresponsible poor," may obtain plenty of that which we all desire, but which is so hard to obtain, viz: work. A guaranty of it and a decent compensation. We represent a class of people, who are said to *infest* the country rather than live in it. We are looked upon as loathsome enemies and treated as such. The only habitations supplied us by your society or government are poor houses, and prisons. Such is our condition by nature and by circumstance. We do not come to hear repeated against us, the world's worn-out complaints. We are just what we are — the out-laws of society — and ever have been. Nothing can cure our case but work, without degradation. If we must suffer the latter, we prefer to degrade ourselves and enjoy the benefits of it, rather than be degraded by employers. There is a certain enjoyment in our degradation and we prefer to have it rather than be subjugated to others.

OBSERVATION. The poor house must become the rich house. That only can cure your case. The government should furnish us all an asylum. Why should you be furnished with a home at the public expense, and we left out in the cold? What makes the poor house life a humiliation and a shame is the contempt that attaches to its accommodations and surroundings. Many a rich house is less lavishly funded, and actually poorer than the poor house. Society is not managed by the people, but by a few individuals; and they, in addition to being poor managers, have stamped a curse upon all those, whose turn of genius and peculiar aptitudes render them incompetent to manage for themselves.

WANDERER. Instead of providing us many honored work-shops we are provided an occasional unhonored one. But we *do* manage for ourselves. If nature has adapted us for anything it is for this; and we are followed by your society from which we are outcasts, because we have this independence to strike for ourselves. We possess adaptiveness, each of us to his or her peculiar sort of business. The tramp among us has both ability and independence. Turned out of work by no matter what cause, he has too much enterprise to sink into slavering mendicancy. He does not hold out the common beggar's hand. Should a war occur—which is his constant hope—he is the first to enlist and fight; for he longs for occupation. In times of profound peace, he wanders in search of employment; and begs or demands, or gets by his wits, that which he cannot get by pillage; for like the plebeian of old, he belongs to the class for whom society makes no provision and has not even a hearth or sacred fire, to worship at. And further, like the plebeian, his increasing numbers and belligerent spirit are likely to gain the priority some day, over those who now fail to recognize his right to live. What is true of the wandering tramp, is, in many respects, true of the worse degraded and downtrodden class of abandons. Can it be said of them that they would not accept and prefer honorable positions, at which to earn a livelihood? The imputation heaped upon them that they are indolent, is entirely inconsistant with truth. You will observe this, when you consider that the labor they actually undergo is far more tedious and wearing than the labor of earning a living respectably. It is not true if you say that these outcasts have not characteristics within them which are valuable, if the world in which they live were leniently and economically adjusted. Nor is it true that such people are naturally heartless and brutal.

Observation. We are willing to admit that what you say in defense of your people is mostly true. But do you not think, that both on your part and that of the world, there is an unnecessary bitterness? What society is mostly in need of, is the knowledge, and adoption, of a system by which all these good points you extol in the people you represent, may be employed and paid in a manner that shall be profitable to all the parties. There is need of more mutual association and less individualism in the management of these talents. Under the individualist system, this cannot be brought about because the individual cravings for profit, keep rife the spirit of competition; and where people strive to out-do each other, there is antagonism and rivality. The country stands in great need of enormous and splendid work houses, sufficiently numerous to accommodate us all rather than the present few degrading ones. In large work shops, working people do not rank by the merits of their antecedents. In this country the question is seldom asked a mechanic, or laborer, where do you hail from, or what have you done? If you are a good, faithful hand it is sufficient for the purposes of the business. We mean by this that there exists little or no aristocracy in the workshop. In the petty work-houses now operated by government, this question is asked; because misdemeanor, or poverty, is the suspected cause of a person being there. But if the people had a work-shop conducted on an immense scale, where there were a demand for employés in large numbers, no such questions would be asked; because the people's *asylum*, would then be merged into the people's *manufactory*. It would furnish both employment and thus correct misdemeanor. It would be proudly yours and be at your bidding. Besides, it would be perfectly respectable. If all the people had such an asylum to work in, *we* should avail ourselves of the opportunity as frequently as you and class you on an equal footing. Governments must learn to provide them for us. This will cure the social evil.

WANDERER. It is useless to waste time in thinking about such an elysium as you paint, in lieu of the poor-house and penitentiary work-shops. There are too many rich rulers of the nation's industries, who operate production on the profit system to admit of any such co-operation of the people for self employment and supply.

OPINION. Not at all. It is true that competitive labor exceeds the co-operative, at present; but the same was the case in regard to the public schools, a hundred years ago. For many years, people of the easy class thought it was compromising their dignity to send their children to the public school, to be educated free. It looked like putting them on the town. The institution nevertheless, prospered; because it was maintained, as it were, by endowment of this well-to-do class themselves, who actually paid for it through taxes, imposed by government.

It was constantly against their pecuniary interest, to cavil with their pride; and the conviction became doubly strong when they saw that by sending their children to select schools they were compelled to pay twice for their instruction. Sober reflection is now rapidly prevailing against prejudice; and the private or select schools are dying out. The public school opens its door free to all; and it affords them great opportunities, benefiting alike, rich and poor, developing national intellect and leveling social grades which after all, are found to be nothing but an idea.

But the difference is infinately greater between the poor-house, or penitentiary work-shop and the Public School, than between the Select and Public School. A government poor-house or county-house is an object of disgust and humiliation. It infects a neighborhood for miles around it. Society which always has a small percentage of indigent, sickly, demented, and otherwise disqualified persons, huddles them together in the common poor-house; and low and distasteful beings are thus forced into contact. Obscenity and profanity meet and greet. Bad habits grow little better, in contact with disrepute. They learn to recognize misfortune which the world's censure and sneers charge them with. Their health may be cared for, but the stamp of obloquy fastens upon their names. They are in the poor-house and this is their disgrace. What can be expected of such a government Institution but a moral stench, infecting society, miles around it? There is no mixture or variety. Its own dreary sameness stagnates; and its natural elements are far from sweet.

The greater government work-shop, obviates all this difficulty, by affording impartial employment for any member of society, mixing all together;—the ungifted, as helpers of the gifted—and rewarding all; not with contempt to one and honor to another—but each according to actual productive merit. It thus entirely leaves relative social merit out of question and cavil, and recognizes all as citizens. Beggars and tramps would gladly avail themselves of such a work-shop; whereas, they dread the poor-house. The result would save society much of the disgusting and demoralizing work of intrusive beggars and marauding tramps.

Wanderer. Education, and its methods are one thing; means of existence, another. They are two very different things.

Response. Yes, practically they are different; but they are identical in principle. The public school is certainly a hundred years in advance of the public workshop. But the public school is as superior to the penitentiary and poor-house-school, as the public work-shop will be, to the penitentiary and the county work-house. It is as much the duty of society to guarantee you labor, where you may all be independent and happy, as it is to furnish you schools where you may receive instruction.

WANDERER. You have passed laws compelling us who are of a certain age to attend school; knowing very well that we have no means to do so. We have no time to go to school. We must pick rags, search ash barrels, pick up coals, coke and wood, black boots, sell papers, grind organs, court paramours, juggle, prowl, pilfer, and otherwise profit off our own wits, and others' hen-roosts. All the time is occupied in getting a bare living; how can we go to school?

CONFESSION. Your question is the same that discovered the discrepency in this law of compulsory education. You are quite correct. You cannot go to school. You must live by some labor; and if the law that would force you to attend the public school fails to provide you a place to work so that you may live, it makes a stupid mistake. It is an incompatibility which can only be rectified by another Institution that shall provide a supply of labor by government. It is clear that you must be guaranteed a comfortable home and work, of some kind during a certain portion of the day. The law of compulsory education ought to provide labor as a necessity for your class; else it can never go fully into force; and this fact is, of itself, sufficiently strong to cause, sooner or later, the establishment of government employment among the people. Compulsory Education, and Government Work-shops go hand in hand.

WANDERER. It would indeed, be a happy change, from our present miserable condition, to be thus favorably benefited, each with a home; to have respectable work furnished us; to be looked upon by our fellow men no longer with contempt and fear, but in the sweet spirit of equality and friendship. Furnish the outcasts — the tramps, the unfortunates, and all others, for whom society now makes no provision — furnish us all a safe, and steady place to work, where our peculiar constitutional adaptibilities may be practically applied; put us where our neglected minds, abused bodies, and broken hearts shall be trained, trimmed and healed; and let us mingle with the good, and profit by their counsel; in short, give to the neglected and despised, this noble asylum of labor that by an impartial and just government, is guaranteed us, by right of our inherited citizenship, and you will rid the world of many an evil doer and illuminate human society, in places now shadowed by the darkness and sin of despair.

REMARK. It should be understood that the social element must enter largely into the methods of labor. It cannot be denied that co-operation contains something of this social principle. But in a system of government employment where manufactories are provided *for* the people, *by* the people themselves, the longed-for *economical independence* of the working portion of society, is readily realized. Yours is a peculiar class of people who of themselves, think little about bringing such an arangement into the world. It must be done by their aid. They will not do it themselves; but when it is done they will accept and sustain it. A *respectable* position guaranteed a girl — no matter what her habits might previously have been — secures her *respectability* and independence. In it, she can always be respected. She need not expect to get this position in a joint stock company, because her claim of citizenship which is all she possesses, has no force. She cannot expect anything of an individual concern, because the espionage of individualism will pass censorship upon her former life. But her SHARE IN CITIZENSHIP, dignifies her claim to a permanent position in an establishment, in the land of her birth. Here only can she demand labor by right of her inheritance. The story of individual industries is as old as history. They have appallingly failed in your grievous case. They must be supplanted by those of mutual care.

WANDERER. Will you give us an idea of the grounds upon which a government industry should be based?

RESPONSE. Your question is one that requires plain language in its answer. The laws of co-operation apply nearly the same in production and distribution. Governments, however, have had comparatively little experience in pure production, whether of agriculture or manufacture. We will suggest one of pure government manufacture. Among the numerous staple articles that lack a thorough and economical administration in the method of production, is bread. There is a surprising waste of time, money, and labor, in its manufacture. In the city of New York there are a thousand bread bakeries. Each is an individual concern, possessing its own little administration. Each has its owner who oversees, and its work men, its salesmen, and porters. There is no system regarding the territory that each is to supply. Consequently, wagons are kept running across each other's routes, and the ground is gone over many times each day, before the distribution is made; thus incurring much loss of time and waste of labor. A careful computation on this competitive interfering with neighbors' routes reveals enormous losses on the part of the people in the economy of their effort, just in this one article of bread. The flour necessary to supply these bakeries is never shipped, in a methodical manner to them from one canal boat, train or ship. It is first allowed to go through the hands of brokers or commission-men; each one of whom sends it to his particular customers. The smaller and more numerous these bakeries and the more isolated their business administrations the better are the opportunities offered for adulterating the flour and deceiving in weight. The bakers have all the advantage; the people none. Besides this, many bakers can organize themselves into a protective union and in a mutual and secret way frame rules for the regulation of prices and thus *substitute monopoly for competition;* and while people are made to believe they are getting their bread at low prices, they are actually paying enormously for a badly adulterated article.

WANDERER. What plan do you propose for preventing such wrongs?

ANSWER. In the cities of Lyons, Lausanne, Halifax, and Rochdale, in Europe, there are *co-operative bakeries*, which are owned by a large number of persons. These bakeries supply, not only the families of the member but also all the people who desire to buy of them. Now the members or owners, of the co-operative bakery, have no desire to make money. Their only desire is to get pure, wholesome bread, at cost price. They hire their own bakers, and consequently are an administration of themselves. They have found by a long experience that the larger the average number of loaves baked, the cheaper they can be produced. They get them at cost. Nobody speculates on a pecuniary profit. They hire their own workmen, buy their own flour, employ no brokers, and eat unpoisoned bread. Besides this, *they employ themselves*. Now let us return to the New York bread bakeries. Suppose the people here should erect a great bakery sufficiently large to supply the whole city, from one single administration. In other words, suppose there were an immense bread baking establishment in New York, which had capacity for supplying all the people with bread, daily; and that it were the property of the entire people somewhat like the Fire Departments, the Water Works, and the Public Schools. Do you not see, that it would be co-operation of the citizens, for bread the same as at Lyons, Rochdale and Lausanne? The difference is only in the comparative numbers; not in the principle.

Now we know that the Fire and Police Departments furnish a great many situations for people having children; and that these children are thus afforded means of attending our Public Schools. In law, parents are obliged to send their children to the Public School, in some states. Practically, however, many can do no such thing because they are too poor. If they had work, and even a small recompense, the law might be observed. Many vagrant children like our poor little wanderers of both sexes, our unfortunate girls, our uncultivated tramps or those who become such, would, if the law enforced it, attend school and receive instruction; thus ridding city and country of much ignorance and the attendant crimes and vices natural to ignorance. But without the Public Industry the Public School is unable to perform its true function; and the Law is necessarily a dead letter;—a miserable mockery.

Wanderer. Now you have touched the interesting point of our case. It is true that nothing but the compulsion of law which opens up our opportunities and as rigidly enforces their participation, can ever turn us from wickedness. Many believe we are born to do evil; but although some of us, as of yourselves, are born with evil minds, yet our ranks develop many good citizens; and if we had these excellent opportunities we might develop more.

Remark. In theory, this law is right in compelling your education. The city cannot afford, on grounds of political economy, to allow, either your ignorance, vagrancy, or disgrace. We have no moral right to go prowling in quest of things that do not belong to us; or to do that which is uncomely and pernicious. It is not just that people should live upon their wits, studying nothing but methods of advantage-getting. This robbing hen-roosts, and other pillage and this begging, fighting, tramping and decoying persons in the streets, of which you speak, is, intrinsically, pernicious, when reduced to habit; no matter to what extent, your needful condition may excuse the offense. We ought, all, to be allowed some profitable work. The same law that would compel you to attend the Public School must break away from its own absurdities. It is a dead letter because it is incompatible with circumstances. A bakery would employ thousands of people. They would be employed by the Board of Public Works which has a direct communication with the Board of Public Instruction. The law requires that children attend school. The officers of the law would no longer be baffled in enforcing it; because they would have recourse to the Board of Public Works, in securing situations for parents who are now too poor to send their children to school. If the children have no parents, positions must be assigned them direct, during certain hours each day. As it is, there are, unfortunately, no such positions. There is not a single Public Industry to off-set against the Public School — the very point wherein our political economy is lame. But the public bakery would supply some of this deficiency. It furnishes employment for many thousands; and it is a peculiar class of employment that adapts itself to the capabilities of your particular people. The bakeries of this city employ boys during certain hours each day, as porters, girls as clerks, men as bakers. With the exception of the latter, these are occupied only a part of the day. The remainder of the time may be occupied in study and rest. The demands of the law of Compulsory Education would force the needy of your class into these places as naturally as the law of gravitation fills with air and water, the cavities of nature.

WANDERER. Would not the result of such an industry be to displace from their situations large numbers of needy persons who are already employed in the present baking industry of the city?

ANSWER. This is no more a question under consideration than was the establishment of Co-operative Bakeries at Lausanne, Lyons, and the cities of England. They did it because it became necessary; in order to secure pure bread at wholesale price. In this they have succeeded. At Lausanne the Co-operative Bakery has actually reduced the price of bread in nearly all parts of the Canton Vaudois and taught speculators never more to attempt to make wealth out of profits on this most important and staple article of food, for rich and poor.

Every one who knows the true extent of adulteration and short weight from which many people of America, are suffering in bread-stuffs, cannot fail to see that we have great need of a similar system here. If co-operation cannot be applied as at Lausanne, we must make this many-headed wrong a subject of legislative enactment and introduce the Government Bakery, as a Municipal accommodation for the people.

WANDERER. Will not the establishment of all Government Industries be so contrary to the present methods of production and deal that the competitive rulers will rise against us?

RESPONSE. Wrong must sooner or later give way to right. Individualism governed mankind thousands of years before it was attacked by the old philosophers of Greece, who with all their powers were unable to break it down, because they were divided. This old individualism was so exclusive and so absolute that no two estates or houses were permitted, even to join. They must, by both divine and statute law, be separated from each other. All through those ages harsh laws of primogeniture prevailed, that excluded wills and natural entailments and the whole of this class to which we belong. Before the beginning of our era there were at Rome actually two nationalities of people—the Patricians and the common people. The very touch of the latter, defiled the former. There was an aristocracy of which the poor could not partake. Solon of Athens and Servius of Rome, were about the first of the real, Labor Reformers among the Ancients outside the secret Societies. Before the conflicts carried on by these men, the cruel religious laws made outcasts of daughters and younger sons. Homes were made sullen, forbidding fortresses, whose ceaseless fires were aglow, in the honor of some god of the particular patrimony of each house; and each succeeding inheritor of that aristocratic patrimony became, after death, that god. One will observe then, that, bad as is the condition of the human race to-day, we are much less shackled than in those old ages of comparative superstition and ignorance. The father, and the first born son only, were privileged ones. They owned everything by license of religion, law and usage, all of which they themselves controlled. All others were unprovided for, except, by their own shrewdness and what little they got through charity. Comparatively, therefore, there were in those times, many more people of these predatory classes than at the present time. During all those times, communistic organizations of resistence, formed from the aggrieved outcasts of your class were constantly creating turmoils. There has always been competition in society and always will be, until it receives its death blow by the institution of a system of labor, wherein guaranteed employment and just, and honorable compensation for all shall be established by the people themselves. Little progress can be claimed toward setting wrong right, until the masses of the people themselves take their own grievances in hand, and destroy the huge evil of competism. Competitors in power are now comparatively few, and they cannot hold out against a wise and well directed organization of the people.

WANDERER. Do you claim that the employment of the people by the government is better for our own case than the system adopted by the social communities, such as that at Oneida, and those of the shakers and others?

ANSWER. No. It does not claim to reach so far. These communities you mention, are miniatures of a far future state of society in which there shall be agreement among the people, on points of industry, religion, and social habits. They may be called microcosms of a vast system toward which this government employment may possibly lead and eventually ultimate in. People are proving themselves not only capable of furnishing members with constant employment and plenty, but they also engross some other things which the furnishing of labor to the people by the government, may make it possible for people as citizens, to do, by giving them freedom to act. Our labor party will render it possible for the people as citizens, to step farther, by emancipating them from the bondage of want in which you and many others exist. No sensible person would do anything to stifle the formation or growth of these communities. Such societies ought to augment in numbers, until every hill-side and valley has its example. But it is clear that if they ever become thus numerous their votes will be turned toward the propagation of their principles, until they themselves become a political power, and seek the guaranty and endowment of government on a large scale, by means of legislation. But their system of equal compensations covers too much ground. We cannot hope soon to realize it. We are all in the great cauldron of competitive strife where human society seems forever to be bubbling, sweating and suffering.

WANDERER. Mention was made of a system of equal compensations. Has it been adopted by any associations or any governments?

RESPONSE. Certainly. It is in general use in the family. Because one child of a family of many children is so unfortunate as to be born a cripple, or to be deprived of his physical or mental powers, the just and humane father does not think he should be deprived of the means of life. The unfortunate child, on the contrary, is often more beloved and better provided for than the rest, because of his misfortune.

WANDERER. We can easily conceive of such a thing in the private family although it is seldom our own lot to be so treated. But what of the rest?

ANSWER. A community or an association of co-operators, is, to the same extent, conducted upon this family principle of equal compensations. Now the main point upon which outside society fails, is exactly the point where the family communism succeeds. We repeat that it is too far for us to reach at present.

The idea, however, is as follows: We are becoming agreed that air, land and water are the gifts of nature. They cost nothing, except so far as labor is applied. Therefore, they should have no exchangeable value. All value attributable to them, in justice, is that which the hand of man has bestowed upon them in form of Labor. They are gifts of nature and free to all, except where they are wrongfully misallotted. Therefore, if air, land and water are gifts of nature and cost nothing, so also the innocent *genius* that makes A. a better accountant, B. a better blacksmith, C. a better machinist, D. a superior farmer, is a *free gift of nature.* It costs nothing. They were born with that gift. Now E. a stouter man, having a larger family to support and consequently more wants to supply, works by their side. To learn his trade, he has served a longer apprenticeship and has worked more years. But he is outstripped by A. B. C. and D. who are endowed with a gift. By means of that gift of nature they are adroit in workmanship. This gift cost them *nothing.* Its exercise is their pleasure. It is an unboughten aptitude, which is their pride, their praise, their glory, their noblest recompense. Their bodies perhaps, are smaller. They eat less, wear less, require less; but by dint of this *gift of peculiar adaptiveness* which costs them nothing, they easily excel E. who is stouter, eats more, needs more; and who, ungifted, labors harder, with an equally honest heart. The question before the community and the family and that ought to be before the government, is this: if E. works as faithfully and needs more, is it just to pay him less? Or, let us take another case: A. is a scavenger. B. is a physician. A. works among the débris and the offal. He cleans up the garbage. The sinks and the slummy places in centre and banlieue, are, by him de-odorized and renovated. He is a better community physician than all the practitioners of the materia medica. Yet the world starves and spurns him. If he is willing and useful ought he not to have enough? Ought he not to be educated, refined, loved, and socially privileged with the rest? Ought he not to have enough? It is said he has no *capacity;* and therefore no claim. Yes he has. He posesses the valuable gift of faithfulness together with that most beneficent of gifts, humility. He is adapted to usefulness by *humility*, *resignation*, *un-ambition*, *absence of pride*, that would *disqualify* B, or C, for this disagreeable task. How unjust then, it must be for us, to disdain and cheat *this* indispensable doctor, while we bow in honor to the physician who rides in a carriage and exacts a heavy fee for that which is often of less value. Is it not clear from these illustrations so often repeated in society, that the old egotism resting upon assumed relative merit, constantly applied in the competitive system and so uniformly averse to the idea of equal compensations, is the very argument which, backed by immemorial usage, all the individualists and their joint stock companies, and all the monopolists ever have used and are still using, as a means of getting superior material recompense called *pay?*

Is it not this argument which, based upon a no less fickle and shifting foundation than received opinion, leaves the willing and naturally honest but ungifted multitude to freeze and starve? Is it not this one-sided, non-community of recompense that has ever fostered arrogance and forced crime? These selfish instincts tend to throttle knowledge and development. There seems no possible method of adjusting this apparent incongruity caused by the diversity of our aptitudes and capacities, except by a sweeping adoption of this apothegm, namely:— JUSTICE DEMANDS THAT WE WORK ALL FOR EACH, AND EACH FOR

ALL; and that we struggle for the adoption of equal compensations. There is no judging from an average of each workingman's capabilities. Neither is there satisfactory economy in the aged system of competitions. It is complex with disputes, rivalries, intrigues; and profligate in a concomitant waste industry—the great advertising system. No community or co-operative society can afford this expense nor the enormous waste that attends these friction brakes in political economy. Simplicity, not complication in an invention, is what makes it a practical success. How can we judge the exact relative worth of a producer? Who can discriminate, under the intricacies of circumstance, of prejudice, of influence, of variety of relative grades, of advantages, and disadvantages, to which the mass of human genius and muscle is subjected in the present apportionment of work and pay? Can an honest and wise public afford to be harrassed by the competition, the dissatisfaction, the rivality and tendency to intrigue, that fester in an aggrieved and slighted spirit? Is not the principle of equal compensation which guarantees a sufficiency to all, the true leveller of class? Are JUSTICE and EQUALITY compatible with class?

WANDERER. Do you claim that this system of employing the people by the people themselves, will be better than the system adopted by the close associations whose governments have solved the problem of labor and even that of socialism itself?

ANSWER. There is a resemblance. These associations are fore-runners of the vaster government. The idea of government employment in the one, seems almost identical with that of the other. The well directed little community contains nearly the same elements, both in philosophy and practical detail, as the true empire of a wise and great people. Each works for its members, the citizens; and each realizes that which it works for. But the small close association, because it is small, realizes its ultimatum earlier. It is, however, the same perfection which the greater government, pursuing the same course, will inevitably arrive at with far better satisfaction as to personal freedom. The close associations are based not only upon the idea of furnishing members with constant employment and constant plenty but they drink in also, deeper sentiments, which the furnishing of labor to the people by self-government makes it possible for members to do, by affording them freedom economically. The small society, wisely managed, affords labor to every member. This labor is not excessive. The people have time to think. They agree in joint deal from year to year; and consequently become rich. They live, labor and enjoy, on a method of just compensation. With plenty, and some leisure, and the accumulations of experience, they are better prepared to put in practice the more subtle points of socialism than the outside world. They are a little government. They can better attempt the settlement of questions of mental culture, and even of race culture than those in the midst of withering want and prejudice, such as rage in competitive society. In fact they have advantages which do not exist elsewhere. But the fact that the miniature governments are capable of yielding independence and happiness to a few, does not prevent the growth of the same principle in the *great community* through the aid of a greater government, on a greater scale. The small Community is strictly a government. It is a government by the people. So also a Republic is a government by the people. Its members possess property in form of industries, schools buildings, institutions of pleasure, of profit, and a code of ethics, in common. So also the citizens of a republic, own in common the schools, the institutions of legislation, of jurisprudence, the Postal business, and many other things in common. If you ask why they do not own and control all business, the answer will be that they are not yet as uniformly wise as the people of the small community.

WANDERER. You speak of the true Social Problem; and mention the adoption of methods of race culture. We are interested here, because representatives of a class whose miseries are of ante-natal, more frequently than post-natal origin. We are outcasts from good society, because we are often the children of inebriate, or malformed, or vicious parents. We remember the dark alleys where our infancy was passed; not the tapestried parlors of the opulent. Our females hover nightly on the gloomy corners. The dens they wander from are wanting the luxuries that cheer the more favored homes of cultivated people. What does your beautiful theory promise that shall prevent the contaminating touch of these hideous dens of unchecked and vicious concupiscence. Some of us live in promiscuous incest, the result of being forced together. We are crammed into squalid abodes, which are made to abuse the theory of breeding by making our social habits too prolific. Sheer poverty coaxes us into indiscriminate contact with one another overfilling home with mortals who, in turn, procreate their own bad traits from one generation to another. Could society see its way clear to procure us labor and good influences, would it separate us from this too close contact and mix us with the world?

RESPONSE. We hold that what is wrong *must* be corrected. With Kant, we say, that means *must*, at every hazard be furnished for righting wrong. If the Church, if the Schools and Colleges, if the social influences of Society, if the individual, can do nothing but fail and forever suffer disgraceful and inglorious discomfiture in their feeble efforts to correct such dismal wrongs, then must the PEOPLE, as the federated units of nations, brand your wrongs into their Platform of Party and upon their Flags of liberty, and hurl them into Parliaments and Legislatures for correction. If there is not enough strength in human modesty to recoil from, and revolt against such scurrilous and unsightly scenes, then must the people be incited to look at wretchedness from a view of Political Economy and blazon the fact that neither yourselves nor the world at large can afford to tolerate social ulcers which both degrade and infect community with a death-rot. It is no way to correct these evils by proffering charitable pittances. The recipients of such, learn to sneer at gift-givers and regard gift-giving with the contempt it merits; since it inculcates indolence by nurturing churlish expectancy. Squalor, groveling, packing, drunkenness, are reflections of indolence and ignorance. No nation of people can afford to permit the causes of your complaints; much less the effects. No. Let us strike against evil and urge a forthcoming remedy. The remedy lies in Labor. Labor will purchase your admittance into the Public Schools; and society, respecting you, will extend her hand of love and care. There are gems in your ranks which need but to be thus cleansed and their crudeness rasped away, to sparkle among the radiant brilliants of intellect and of man and womanhood.

Neither city, state, or nation can afford to pay the costs entailed upon society by your condition. The natural consequence of want of instruction and development among the non-propertied citizens, is helplessness. It cannot reasonably be expected that it should be otherwise. This state of depravity then, is *calculable* and might have been foreseen and avoided. Society, calmly looking upon these blemishes, and suffering them, while noisomely imbibing infectious torments from them, yet being furnished with means of prevention and cure, such as a pretentious church, a promising government, a world of exact sciences, all under control, and doing nothing from cycle to cycle to prevent such blight, cannot but feel compunctions of guilt mixed with its crowning shame and humiliation.

## CHAPTER III.

.......

## THE HYPOCRISIES OF COMPETITIVE DEAL.

---

### CONVERSATION
### WITH A MERCHANT'S CLERK.

CLERK. WE HEAR VAGUE reports concerning a proposed new system of distributing goods; and it has occured to us to inquire what the advantages are; whether there need be as much perversion of morals of young clerks, or whether young people need to be thrown into so constant temptation as at present. It being a part of the clerk's qualifications to be a shrewd liar, and indeed the strongest requisite to secure him permanency in his situation, we should be very glad to know of any method that would render such habits unnecessary.

REMARK. There is a method which is calculated to obviate this evil of lying, cheating, and stealing; but to introduce it in the place of present systems is a very difficult affair. That involves the formation and career of a vast political Party; and a succession of battles and skirmishes against a great and vitiating system of deal. This method proposed, consists of Community deal, wherein government, in the interests of all the people alike, takes the place of the two prevailing methods of competition and monopoly.

CLERK. What difference is there between competition and monopoly?

ANSWER. There is much difference. So much, that they cannot be compared together. A competitive trade is isolating and rather repels than attracts others engaged in the same traffic. There is a strife among dealers as to which shall sell cheapest, and this strife or competition too often amounts to mutual hatred. Competition is as old as communities and is seen not only in all varieties of trade, but it exists in the spirit of people. It is competism that causes the sad and often deadly animosities that exist between nationalities. It is competism that keeps cities, colleges, manufactories aglow with strife. In a good sense it makes an element of health in the literary attainments of scholars and is indispensable, as a heightener of all kinds of qualifications requisite to society. In a bad sense, it is pernicious in promoting low strifes like fighting, gambling and rivalry in deal. In a word, it appears from the most careful survey of the history of competism, that it is a natural attribute in man; which when applied in a bad sense, produces not only the thievery and falsehood among clerks, of which you complain, but also almost every kind of degrading result, from the carnage of warfare down to the meanest brawl; but when applied in a good sense it promotes a restless activity of the intellect and results in inventions, discoveries and improvements in science which are rapidly fitting the world for a new economy of Distribution that will render prevarication and deceit no longer a qualification for the clerk.

Monopoly, on the other hand, is a ring of merchants or of manufacturers, or of miners or whatsoever trade, combined to *close in upon the people* and shut them *out* from competition. The clerk engaged in selling articles in a competitive store must demoralize himself by lying and using every art of dazzle and dissimulation, in order to flatter purchasers and adroitly sell them a poor article instead of a good one, so as to win and entice a larger number of visitors. The clerk in a monopoly, is equally demoralized; because he must exhaust his genius in inventing every kind of device to make his customers believe it is fair deal, when, in reality it is extortion. In either case, as a general rule it demoralizes the clerk. It makes him the meanest species of thief; because it makes him steal for others instead of himself. It makes him a confidence swindler, by profession. It makes him a liar and an ingrate by cheating his own society, often his own kindred. It makes him a hypocrite; and the class legislation of his powerful masters legalizes his hypocrisy. When we come to consider that this large class of society's victims, not only covers the clerks of retail and of wholesale deal, but that there yet remain on the category all the clerks of manufacturing deal, and of transportation—in fact all the clerks of both the competitive, and the monopolistic systems as well as the reckoners of their immense accountability—when we consider, that in these legalized hells of falsehood and hypocrisy a large percentage of our population—our best and noblest young men and women—are reared up and paid and well applauded in ratio to their success in such deceit; when we see all this, can we wonder that there is a spontaneous inclination not only on the part of clerks, but also on the part of other working people, of scientists, of all lovers of truth, to rise up in power and blot it out of existence?

Clerk. If, in the competitive and monopoly systems, there can be no hope of reform and no cure for this evil which is making compulsory liars of clerks and otherwise vitiating their morals, to what system must they look for reform?

Answer. They must bend their energies toward the gradual establishment of a system of deal which will require the opposite qualifications for a good clerk. The world needs a system of deal that shall make people honest of necessity. People must study the character and applicaton of *Co-operative deal.* We must learn to deal with each other by direct approaches. Monopolists and competitors are the middlemen of deal. Demoralizing clerks of which you speak, is one of the many pernicious results of their system. Society must destroy the evil by dealing directly with its own membership, without aid of a third person. The only object ( other than common interest he feels in society, )which the broker of the world's deal has in view, is gain—exclusive individual profit In co-operative deal, no thought of exclusively individual profit can be entertained. A *co-operative society never cheats itself.* Its clerks must not lie. In the world's deal, society allows itself to be cheated by the insidious intrigues of which you complain, for profit. Profit lies at the bottom of the evil. You must get down to the bottom, drag out his old cankering lust for profit which fattens middlemen and demoralizes you, and substitute it with a purer one that repels exclusively individual profit and deals with yourselves at cost. Let this be done by your government; and you begin to feel the true incentive of citizenshi|. You then begin to see what the use of a government is and feel your first encouragement to honesty.

CLERK. If the sale of dry goods should be assumed by government instead of the individual merchant it would still have to employ clerks. These clerks would have to be superintended, strictly too; for if they were not expected to steal for others, they might, unless guarded, inspire their present employers' love of profit and practice deceit for themselves. Besides, who is going to guarantee the honesty of superintendents? Are not the oft-repeated exposures of fraud and other betrayals of trust, of our government officials, sufficient to warrant the people in doubting their capability to choose upright men as superintendents of the sale of dry goods?

ANSWER. If the government assumes the sale of dry goods it will be for the majority of the people; and the first principle involved in that sale is the obtaining of the best goods at least cost. The notion of profit does not enter here. So that if their first and all-important object is to obtain genuine goods at low cost, their next object and privilege is to find out and *know* what they have cost. *This is the first great home-duty of a people.* Having ascertained and made a record of the cost of goods in general, they will very naturally inquire into the causes, if these goods are not sold them *at cost.* Do you not see that this investigation leads to a profound and respectable study of causes and effects, right in the little matters of the household? Yet these little matters of the household, so very long neglected, are after all, the subject of supreme importance in political economy. Now tell me how such important but difficult matters can ever be adjusted while the sale of goods to the people intimately interested is given over to the caprices of competitive strife or of the more sweeping monopoly, back of which there is no appeal; where the people have nothing to say and no more power or control than the most abject subjects of a monarchy in the East.

CLERK. It indeed seems very clear that people should look at this proposed change in distribution as a matter of no second rate importance; and once shown that they are really capable of constructing an efficient, distributive service under government, the same as that of the Postal service, or the distribution of water in cities, they will certainly take action toward its establishment. But such a proposition involves revolution. It will seriously interfere with this *profit incentive* you speak of, which combines and makes formidable the individual power of our present managers of distribution. This power, though perhaps numerically small, is immense in influence. It borrows its greatest strength from the usage of ages. It is therefore, acquiesced in even by those whose sons and daughters are demoralized by it. It is a recognized system of our civilization; and though its outworkings are so pernicious as to vilify morals and create and perpetuate the two great castes of wealth and poverty, the very parents of its thus demoralized victims are, in a majority of cases, its strenuous supporters. Now supposing it even to be true, that government as an instrument of popular behest, were perfectly competent to distribute the necessaries of life direct, that is, without any brokers of deal, or profit-paid service, through the management of the people's own chosen supervisors; do you suppose the people could be prevailed upon to make such a gigantic attempt?

ANSWER. Certainly. They will attempt anything, when once convinced that it is right. Of all tribunals, that of a great people is the least susceptible. Before them there is no dodging to please friends. They want unequivocal justice. They are a great while making up their minds what justice is and are incapable of determining, except through prolonged discussion and practical proof through scientific application. But they are convinced by successful specimens; and the practicability of doing away with this profit, or fee pay, has been proved by co-operative experiments. Wherever the co-operation has been honestly and patiently tried, it has yielded precisely the results you seek. Even in America, where the fickleness of membership and sovereignty notions of the people render these experiments precarious and short lived, they have developed this unmistakable tendency to do away with the fee offices and institute direct pay offices in their stead. But in Europe, especially in England, where no such objections exist, they have already become powerful, and are making sweeping inroads upon the old system of trade, based upon exclusive profit to individuals.

CLERK. Do you think the change can ever be brought about by simple co-operation, as in England?

ANSWER. No. There are many characteristic differences between European and American institutions. What Europeans can accomplish socially, Americans find most conformable to their habits and institutions, to accomplish by political means. It is doubtless of little matter how it is done if it is done and well done. It is evident that it can only be accomplished in this country by working up the question on the various forces of experiment, necessity, feasibility and argument, until the people are forced to choose sides definitively. Then it will become a political Party and remain at the option of the voters, subject to their scrutiny. It will be shaken up by party newspapers, until the rule of an enlightened and awakened majority shall be thoroughly recognized.

CLERK. But many enthusiasts overlook the fact that even the most successful co-operative efforts —those of the North of England —have from the first, been in an almost constant wrangle with each other; and that many times they have been on the point of dissolution and are not out of danger yet. It is even hinted that there is an effort on foot to secure the aid of government, or to fortify and consolidate them by a species of absorption into the general government.

ANSWER. Your remark is in theory correct; but you misunderstand the schooling effects of wrangling. The world has prehaps never learned so valuable a lesson as these wranglings of the Co-operators have taught. It is through the jargon of distrust and a thousand other mutual contrarieties to which may be added many fierce personal criminations and expulsions that the ever jealous, watchful, but honest co-operators have fought down this lurking spirit of cheating, lying and money-getting you complain of. For many years the treacherous emissaries of the old system of profit paid deal plied their tricks with a view to disrupt the organizations. In hundreds of cases they succeeded as we succeed in this republic. But every failure was a lesson of experience to the indefatigable organizers of England, who have at last turned the tide of the great battle in favor of themselves; so that within a half century the practical application of the idea of straight deal without the fee profit or commissioners' service has been obtained, with certain modifications. In some parts, this new system has absorbed from ten to seventy per cent of the population. Its effect has been to completely route the incentive to lie, cheat, or steal; making the labor of a clerk pure and innocent. The store becomes the common property of the people. The people are thus the owners instead of the individual competitor or the monopolist, whose only object is to sell for more than he gave, and in that way, which naturally inspires and urges him into prevarication and deceit, make a wealth of profit, exclusively to himself. Co-operation works out the reverse of this principle. It cannot make profit out of itself because it can realize no advantages by profit. Its object is to buy cheap and sell cheap. Sell for the sake of furnishing its owners, the people, with articles at cost. Sell for the sake of convenient interchange; not for the sake of accumulating profit. The clerk who handles the goods has no object in being dishonest. It is this that has already signalized co-operation and made it the nursery of honorable deal. Indeed in the heartless desert of competitive deal, and still later, its all-destroying conspiracy in form of monopoly whose sickening blight corrupts the entire moral atmosphere of human interchange, co-operation is the green Oasis; a speck indeed compared with the boundless wastes within, but full of the balmy verdure of innocence and goodness. Upright deal, and honest manliness, with frankness and cheer, take the place of the shy approach and obsequious servility and cheat of the money-getter and his cronies.

Then as to its being absorbed by the government that is

the most wholesome sign of our age. English Co-operation has only to conquer one half of the competitive system and thus obtain a mere majority to secure its permanent adoption by the government. Deal is that moment out of the hands of middlemen. Deal comes under the control of the people; because the people choose and commission the persons who are to supervise it the same as they now do in the Co-operative Store. Every citizen becomes an equally interested party. It is a vast joint stock company whose members are the citizens; all the people. Can a man cheat himself, lie to or deceive himself, extort profits out of himself? The collective interests of millions are the individual interests of one. All our government services to the people are standing proof of the earnest, honest innocence of the co-operative incentive. It is seen in the Postal service with its impartial precision in distributing the mails at cost. It is seen in the Fire Department with its exquisite and marvelous effectiveness in saving from the devouring element, all property without grudge or favor. It is seen in the impartial politeness toward all at the peoples' Parks; the cost of distributing abundance of water in cities; the democratical and impartial instruction of children at the Public Schools. These are specimens of co-operation in which every citizen, without exception feels an equal incentive to watchfulness, and control.

CLERK. You seem to have lost sight of the fact, that the great English co-operative stores exact a profit.

ANSWER. Not at all. There is by collective agreement, a certain fluctuating percentage taken over and above costs from the receipts, for all articles. This percentage is held by the society as a fund. A provision makes it optional with all buyers to withdraw this percentage, but most of the members allow it to accumulate. This is their fund, their exchequer. They use it as an instrument of levelism. With this fund they, in common, build homes, school houses, splendid central and branch store buildings, debating halls, committee and reading rooms, and other decorations that have made co-operation world-renowned.

None of these improvements are made by the arbitrary decision of a man or even a council of men. The people themselves discuss and decide the most important measures and instruct their executive centers to act accordingly. Co-operation is thus for the people and of the people; and on the whole the people have shown themselves slow but wiser than individuals have been, in creating and adjusting the means of existence and happiness. The government when it undertakes a co-operative enterprise imitates the government of co-operation. The people elect a council or legislature who do as they are bidden. Failure to do right creates the same wrangling and crimination we have seen in co-operation; so by this means we slowly make improvements until, as in the fire and postal departments the people are quite satisfied. The money used for such enterprises, is as in the co-operation of England, invariably the money of the people taken in the same manner, only by vote of the people at the elections, out of the public exchequer; and if it is not as wise as the best English co-operations it is because the people are not as active in guarding their interests. It is because they trust too much to individuals and irresponsible counsel and job their interests out to intermediary persons.

It is easy therefore, to see that there is no analogy between the percentage of profit on retail over wholesale prices in the co-operative store which goes back to the mem ber who issued it and the privilege of profit, which accrues to the outside competitive and monopoly deal. The one is, in truth, the reverse of the other. For in the first case every member in the co-operation is a merchant; in the second, only one person, or the individuals of one company are merchants. In the one, there is a sympathy, compulsory on the part of each, for the other, which amounts to pure mutual care. In the other, the feeling is arbitrary and utterly and mutually selfish. With the one, the profits go back principally to the mutual exchequer for the improvement of the members' common possessions; in the other the profits fall into the hand of an individual and furnish him the means with which if he be unkind, to take advantage of those who have enriched him. In the co-operation the capitalized fund becomes an instrument of levelism. In the outside store it becomes the central force of individualism or oligarchy. Co-operation pays the clerk for his labor in delivering goods to their owners. It takes the cost money and a voted percentage; nothing more. The merchant pays his clerk who sells and delivers goods, for every sort of successful wiles, of allurement, of affected platitude, of lying and subtlety so far as is compatible with the inflated and depraved sense of the people; and the simple reason of all this difference lies in the inherent impossibility in either *system* to do differently under the circumstances.

Clerk. You mentioned that the system of profit making, so bad for the morals of clerks, resembles the fee payment for services rendered to certain public officers.

Response. It does. It also resembles the contract system in which the people as thoughtlessly job their productive industries to work-brokers in place of taking them into their own hands. The wealth owner is a member of a class. Legislation is in this country largely in the interest of class. The wealth owner, because his business makes him rich and respected, is proud of his class; while the toiler, because his business degrades him, ignores class. Consequently the wealth owner is stimulated to organize and procure class legislation for himself and becomes the *darling* of the law, while the poor toiler, ashamed of the drudgery and the compulsory deceit that degrade him, though numerically in the majority makes no effort to procure legislation for his class and becomes the *outcast* of the law. The law recognizes fees. The fee is a legalized price for a professional or official service. The law as distinctly recognizes the profit of a merchant, as a fee. The successful merchants are, therefore, as much the darlings of the law as the feed officials of government. But the great government is nevertheless the property of the people who have seen to the extent their blinded eyes will permit, the fallacy of fee offices; and strong efforts are on foot to abolish fee offices, entirely. When this is done, the payment of a service will have to be direct from the people to *their* employés and class legislation receives a blow; because the people, in this case are themselves empowered to fix the salaries of their employés. Profit in all cases, as at present vitiated by desire to make money, means "get all you can." Fees, where they are limited at all, are limited only upon the same principle.

Both are long-time usages, partialized by legislation in the interest of the classes enriched by them. They both belong to the same voluminous category that overflows the cup of the toilers' woes; and the only sure method of removing the evil is by a toilers' National Party, by force of which, to turn legislation in the interest of these unhonored foundations of national prosperity themselves instead of fee officers and profit speculators. THIS CAN ONLY BE DONE BY DIRECT GOVERNMENT EMPLOY—the surrender to the people, subject to their jealous watchfulness on the first incentive to citizenship, of the whole of the mercantile operations of exchange and the carefully guarded adjustment of them by the supervisory control of the people's chosen agents subject always, to their experience and their ever improving legislation from year to year.

CLERK. In what particular do you see the analogy you speak of between the fee-profit and the contract systems?

ANSWER. Properly speaking the contract system belongs more to the productive than to the distributive industries and therefore, not to a discussion on merchants' profits and their demoralizing barters. But there are some departments in which the contract system, with all its hideous and demoralizing falsehood and deception has invaded the world's distributive service. Among these may be mentioned the Post Office.

Athough the Postal Service as conducted by government, has proved infinitely more able and satisfactory than any company the people ever employed to carry the mails, and has, within the remembrance of many who are now living, reduced the postage on a written communication from twenty five cents down to one cent, still we have not yet been able to shake off competism from our mail service.

As a consequence, we find immense annual deficits in our Postal Bureau. The people, it is true, have the credit of conducting the Postal Department of government, and have by gradual legislation from year to year, corrected many abuses, assumed many duties and reduced the postal tariffs until the poorest may derive the instructive benefits of correspondence. But they have not yet been able to develop the work sufficiently to do it *themselves*. They cannot yet see clearly enough to trust themselves, and they must still submit much of it to contractors. Nobody knows better than these the purse-inflating quiddity of public innocence. So the railroad owners continue to press and the lobby, that modern conclavium of republicanism, still emits its effluvia of job-corruption and the demoralizing, poison-pointed foils of falsehood, faithlessness, simulation and finally of biased legislation throttle the people's hopes, inducing them to surrender rights belonging to a majority. Labor, a natural right, is thus jobbed out to outside parties to favor outside interests, while the people themselves, or a large portion of them, are left ignorant and otherwise destitute of every means of associative employment. Great majorities see annual subsidies voted to such purveyors of their business yearly; yet their work is poorly done. Many other similar examples of this very evil of partial, or individualist profit exist, proving that there is an analogy between the mercantile job-letting, wherein the people give their exchange-service to the brokerage party, and the contract system itself. If then, the people as a unity are able to dispense with advantage the business of governing, of law making, of operating government bureaus and great boards of public works, public health, and other matters of business activity, they need not fear to undertake the further task of administering a system of buying and selling, that will require less perversion of good morals among their employés.

CLERK. We have not thoroughly exhausted this

subject in its bearings upon the weight as models of our regal merchants. We see men of great ability like the Girards, the Peabodys, the Stewarts, applying indefatigable toil, amassing fortunes so huge that people seeing themselves outstripped, shrink in fear from them. Their career is so oversweeping that the timid world shudders; while the followers of fashion and those who are of more obsequious turn are infatuated to idolatry; and the moral atmosphere is soured betwixt jealousy, peevishness and servility. By-and-by, the rich man dies leaving to the astonished world, not only the rich lesson of his work, but also a noble legacy in his property. We ask if, on the whole, though he may have been penuriously business-like, he has not set a good example?

Answer. Such men are undoubtedly doing good in a manner of their own. On every hand we see year by year the methods of business administration verging in a direction of frugalities. Great labor-saving instruments, that result from the energy of our workers, make it possible for our inventive tact to swoop business formulas into larger and more comprehensive areas. Genius now-a-days becomes the fulcrum over which brain and hand labor has a leverage. Formerly this was true only of those born to position; and this only happened among those whose material advantages were most in unison with their natural advantages or heritage. Many of them distributed their gift of genius upon a low level; and so made bad use of their advantages. Inherited or arrogated rights of this kind are believed to be dying away. Free-born smartness is taking their place. Consequently, since genius will have sway, we have merchant princes instead of princes; money kings instead of kings; railroad autocrats instead of emperors; commonwealths instead of empires. Phenomena like these designate the difference between the self-made and the endowed fortune. Now the modern bent of free genius is, in the competitive world to take advantage of scientific appurtenances in use and thus enlarge those intellectual opportunities formerly curtailed for want of them. We see this in the great business enterprises of Stewart, Claflin, and Vanderbilt. They teach an invaluable lesson. Even if they extort undue value from their clerks, they have a certain sort of usefulness as ushers at the portals of a more humane and engrossing business method that may yet absorb competitive methods into those of common interest; uprooting the competing system upon which these men build their fortune and renown.

When we look at the immense capabilities of a single individual of genius we ask whether there is not agreement enough among all the geniuses of a whole people, providing their ultimate object be in the end, realized, and their life-ambitions equally satisfied, to join issues, as a Body Politic, and carve for themselves and for the people for whom they manifest so much death-bed solicitation a new career of wealth-making and of wealth-distributing. This is the question of labor. Solve it and you have overcome the source-causes of your complaints.

# CHAPTER IV.

## MERITS OF THE LABOR CONFLICT BEFORE THE UNIVERSITY.

COLLOQUY BETWEEN MEMBERS OF A COLLEGE FACULTY AND AN ADVOCATE OF THE LABOR MOVEMENT.

PROFESSOR. THERE are few colleges in the land whose faculties and advanced students do not feel a desire to encourage, in their literary and rhetorical societies as well as their magazines, a large amount of radical sentiment. In how much do your theories of government employ conflict with religion; or how far do they in your opinion, project heresies against the established principles upon which most of our colleges are conducted?

ADVOCATE. The people say they are enslaved; that the cause of their enslavement is bad management; that their struggle is for economical emancipation; that bad management is the result of ignorance. Certainly then, the College which professes to teach wisdom, should by all means do its duty to the people!

PROFESSOR. It is not the duty of the College to undertake the education of those outside. Those inside are generally well provided for. Nevertheless there appears a desire to discuss the question of integral education which would, as you state, abate the general ignorance that has enslaved the working people and kept them impoverished.

RESPONSE. This discussion is the first and perhaps most necessary thing. It is of all other things most necessary that our high schools begin at once the discussion of new and launching points of political economy. They educate the young man and start him in life; and generally, the theme of thought inculcated during the college life is that which moulds his future career and builds life habits which a life-time cannot eradicate.

PROFESSOR. Most college faculties are conservative. They are at present hesitating upon prudential grounds. Is it prudent we ask, for us to entertain a line of discussion, that leads in opposite directions from rules of society which is established?

OBSERVATION. There is nothing in the principle of Social Employment of the people by the people that conflicts with any college duty. The idea is based upon *Mechanics:* upon the adjustment of things so that the greatest amount of production and distribution shall result, through Mechanical Economies, from the least *possible amount* of time and effort. It seeks economical applications of machines to the uses of the people. It might not yet have been raised even to the dignity of a question had not certain apt individuals, by a superior tact in management and acquisition obtained the control of these inventions, and applied them to their individual uses, thus encroaching upon the people as a mass by accumulating collossal fortunes from an overplus that accrues from this partial or individual management of inventions belonging, as the Problem of Labor hypothecates, to the Commonwealth.

PROFESSOR. Will you give us an example? Your propositions are too vague and blind. Do not fear to state your question boldly.

REMARK. An example of this misallotment is seen in almost every great invention of recent date. Printing by types is old; and consequently has, through successive stages evolved from their control, and is now rapidly coming under control of masses, though it has for ages, groaned under rigorous censorship of class rule. The newspaper must in order to please the people, throw light into dark places. It must, to be a success for its manager, work for the people at almost cost terms. A scheming editor or a junta of them may, even in the comparative enlightenment of our century, manage to withhold from the public the news and the knowledge of the truth; but this is fast vanishing. The best papers find it the most successful plan and most to their own personal advantage, to steer entirely aloof from combinations for purposes of accaparation and build their reputation upon the ingenuous patronage of the people. So far as they do this we find no fault. We even recognize that the printing press will in course of time evolve from the control of monopolies. This fact is of grave importance as it shows a similar evolutionary tendency in all of the inventions, the monopoly of which is now oppressing humanity. The press unfortunately, has only made one forward step in this direction. There is yet much of the old egoism left, as well as a powerful spirit of exclusiveness but the plainest examples of the accaparation of inventions are found in things more modern. The rail road is a modern instrument of progress. It is an invention. Its patent right has run out and left it the property of civilization. Its economical and impartial use by our race as a collective interest would facilitate to an incalculable extent, the well-being of society. Instead of this it is made the *property* of companies who, by successful business tact have found it possible to control transportation; and thus cut off or dole out, at something like imperial pleasure, the very table supplies of whole nations of people. This abuse is looked upon as a revival of old imperialism under a new form. It is regarded with alarm and should be thoroughly considered within the College halls. All we ask of the College student is that he enlarge the domain of discussion; and freely take into his literary clubs all subjects that come under the head of mechanics applied, or science of economics—uses of mechanical instruments, their benefits to masses instead of particular individuals.

Professor. Will you state a single case of proposed remedy for this so-stated usurpation of a great invention by monopoly merely as a clue for the students?

Response. Interesting examples may be studied in many mechanical contrivances called public highways. But are they public highways, strictly speaking, when they are private property? Can this be called an unequivocal expression? We have an excellent instance in the great inter-urban bridge at Brooklyn. For many years this great population of two cities were chafing in ill content under the individualist system of ferriage across the

Strait that divides them. Municipal authority was powerless because under the competitive system the apothegm "what's everybody's business is nobody's business," is true. The ferry business had grown up in the hands of individuals. Boats proving insufficient as a public highway, the bridge became a necessity. It was too enormous an undertaking for an individual or company to complete. Nothing could consummate it but the combined populations of these two great cities. Power of legislation was all they could bring to bear. But this they held as a most sovereign reserve. With this legislation the two cities by the will of the people, built the bridge. Money was drawn from the treasuries of both. If the bridge belongs to the people instead of a company, it follows that they are the power which in future must adjust the tariffs over it; and a magnificent rapid transit industry is thus whipped into the control of the correct owners. Revolution seems absolutely involved in it; for should other industries undergo a similar metamorphosis you would have communism. People are hereafter to own their means of transit from their homes to their business. Great efforts will be made by them to abate the fare. Further legislation will be resorted to. When the fare has fallen to two cents they will agitate further reduction until the best of rapid transit is enjoyed free. Perhaps the most striking case before us is that of the Telegraph monopoly. The natural remedy for its present dangerous and distressing misuse lies in a similar method of public ownership and management instead of an individual.

Professor. How shall the great people with all their varying opinions, their contrarieties and incompatibilities, their incongruous mingling of shrewdness of one with turpitude of another, of aptitude with inexperience, think of taking the duties of so huge a net work as the telegraph, and of managing it with harmony?

ANSWER. You have asked the question every person should ask; every student especially. It is just the question we desire every College Faculty to present to the Literary Clubs. We strongly urge that they examine it thoroughly, and without bias; because they are to go forth, eventually into the world to reconcile these incompatibilities you speak of and fix the people for assuming their legitimate duties. The world of humanity must adopt a severe adjustment of the mechanical science they possess, and adapt both its management and its results to *masses* rather than to individuals. It is for the college of all other schools, to understand and to set forth this enlightened application of invention, purely as a matter of science. It is not a matter of opinion, belief, morality, ethics or even equity any more than the law of gravity or the laws that govern the force of projectiles. Who is so silly as to falsify nature with such inexplicable crudities as morality, ethics, or equity? Either of these terms suggests volumes of doubt and cavil, when the simplest law of nature after being discovered and applied hushes forever all disagreement by the inexorable accuracy of its fiat.

You know when you send a telegram what will be the results of your action. It is severe science. Apply the telegraph so that dispatches may be sent by every citizen at cost, say at one or two cents for thirty words and you immediately effect a revolution. You abolish letter writing. You do entirely away with secret correspondence, which has been the bane of races. You abolish a large part of the Postal Service with its secret and hateful espionage, its costly jobbing of transit contracts and its tedious delays. You improve the money order system to a degree that intercepts all individual and company commissions and in fact, you simplify and improve the entire Post Office business. And yet the Telegraph is an innocent instrument, harmless and unconscious in itself, of the inroads it is destined to make upon old systems. Now this change comes from the innocent adoption by the people, of an invention which works in accord with natural laws; following them with a severe yet harmonious mechanical exactitude and without any more reference to moral rectitude or ideas of justice and equity than the equally harmonious but greater planetary and solar systems, that form the universe. The morals of ethics change with indoctrinated belief. Science is changeless. This should be distinctly understood; since it clears off all objections to the discussion in schools, of the politco-economic adjustment of invention, on the ground of usages and creeds.

PROFESSOR. How shall the Telegraph be made to work these advantages?

ANSWER. That is a business detail. The government which is the agent of the people and in this country entirely subject to their collective voice, has for many years managed the Postal Department with success. If the Department can improve this service by an invention like the Telegraph, there can be no doubt that the government has a perfect right, if the people order it through their representatives in Congress, to buy up every line of telegraph now in possession of companies. If the companies will not sell, it has an equal right to construct new lines and operate them for the masses of people represented in Congress, which is to say, the entire population instead of the few people who now control them. But this subject needs careful consideration by the people; and who could debate it with more care or impartiality than students of the College?

PROFESSOR. But is it right that the Telegraph companies, after having constructed their lines with so much patience and wisdom—run great risks in the adventure, taught the whole world valuable lessons by developing the application of telegraphs, which is next in importance to the invention itself—is it right, after they have set up so much and enjoyed the use of it so little, that a greater power like an Alaric should descend upon, and sieze it away from them? It may look quite possible but is it not unfair?

RESPONSE. Questions of merely adopted morals scarcely enter into a great mechanical equation. With the people it is only a matter of physical result. Shall the interests of forty millions be ignored to gratify a handful of forty? Shall an important means of life and happiness involving great facilities for gaining bread and knowledge, be denied a whole population for the paltry sake of an almost invisible minority? This query about equity, so dwindles before the importance of *much versus little* that the figures take a new inspiration. The question is for the master mechanic to solve. The people are physicists. They do not ask how much moral advantage is going to accrue from a change like this. They only ask concerning the *material* advantages; or the advantages calculable from a general, economic point of view. In short, the application of the unerring mechanical laws is the base of the ethics of a vast people. What percentage of general gain will the management of the telegraph by the government of the people, result in? And to whom will this percentage accrue? If it can be proved that dispatches can be sent at one per cent less money than letters, the question is settled from an economic standpoint. If it can be proved that a dispatch, which now costs one dollar can, by the Post Service of government be sent with equal reliability and quickness, for three cents, then it *must* be adopted by the people as a mathematical co-efficient of their business. If the whole people as owners and managers can be substituted for the present forty owners and managers, and this change of management results in bringing the entire message Service of the nation down to cost prices, the same being performed as the letter service now is, under the legalized head of the Post Office Department, then it becomes no longer an individual or company affair; but a huge co-operation of the people for a cheap and effective message service; and must be considered from the political point of view. It is no longer personal, but public. It is political economy. The change amounts to revolution; yet its measure of argument is taken dynamically, not ethically; for its conclusion is arrived at by figures, without reference to whether it overset personal interests and theories any more than the calculations of Copernicus and Galileo had reference to theories or creeds upon which millions based their law of ethics and thousands their means of life. The bigotry that prevents the politico-economic application of inventions on considerations of moral right is as intolerant as the bigotry that imprisoned Galileo for making a physical discovery of the earth's orbital path. What consideration of right or wrong actuated Professor Morse, while studying out the vehicles of electric transmission? It was as much the elaboration of the physicist as is the dissection of a newly found creature by the naturalist to gain and impart knowledge. Yet it may produce revolution as subversive of existing methods, their details and usages, as its mechanical superiority proves itself in circumventing the older methods. No consideration of right or wrong will actuate the great majority on questions of adopting it as a substitute, when once they are assured of its superiority and feasibility. But if there were a question of justice involved, it would soon be settled by the *law of preponderance, or comparative claims*, which is the lever of the labor argument. The Electric Telegraph, under the leadership of forty business men as owners, yields wealth, standing, happiness to these forty and their families. Success attends them because having almost unlimited rule, they put the price of dispatches enormously high. But still, these dispatches are available with certain business men. Unfortunately, however, these rates are so high as to be out of the reach of our forty million inhabitants. Not one message is actually sent, where there ought to be, and might be a thousand if they could be dispatched at two or three cents apiece; or in other words at cost.

Now compare this increase of happiness made possible to the forty owners which results from the enlargement of their facilities for enjoyment, with the loss of happiness caused by the exclusion of this mechanism from all the forty millions of population of the land. The comparison is as forty and their families, to forty million. Make this comparison and you at once calculate mathematically, the preponderance of argument in favor of the people's owning and managing the telegraph instead of the monopolies. The preponderance is immensely in favor of the people. At an average the family contains six persons.

Multiply these by the forty owners having families and you have only two hundred and forty persons benefited by their ownership in telegraph stock. What an infinitesimal claim is this, compared with the great collectivity, the people, who would own and enjoy it as a common family, if it were the property of government! But lest this comparison from actual ownership seem unfair we will look at it from another standpoint;—that of APPROXIMATE INTERESTS. The comparison from actual ownership and participation is, however, complete. Approximate Interest is based upon both the first and second incentives of citizenship. By the first incentive to citizenship the great monopolerfeels an honest desire to do a service to the people and the country at large. It is his politico-economic incentive felt in common with the rest; buthis scope is curtailed by his *selfish* or second incentive which prompts him to raise the price so high that comparatively few can enjoy it. So again, on the first incentive, the people feel a strong desire to do a general service to the country the same as the monopoly; but their second incentive, though selfish, is mutual and almost infinitely more diffused; since it is participated in more than the monopoly's service, in proportion as the participants or members of the co-operation are more numerous than those of the monopoly. It becomes at once politico-economic and the people who own and manage it feel two distinct impulses which grow dearer to them as the management improves —the general interest of citizenship and the interest in cheap and effective interchange. The one affords them pleasure because it enhances the prosperity of the country. The other yields them ready cash because it creates them great numbers of good situations and reduces the cost of dispatches to a figure that the poorest person can pay, thus leveling grades. If you ask how this can serve as a leveler of grades then, we answer, it is the same as in the Post Office. In former times when the carrying service was in the hands of individuals as the telegraph now is, the cost of sending letters was so great that few could afford to do it. The consequence was that fewer could write at all and those enabled by easier circumstances to mail letters were most encouraged to learn to write. This caused an aristocracy and resulted in warranting the thus favored in assuming superiority over the less favored class. The assumption by the government which in this country is the people, of the administration of the Postal Service has resulted in gradually reducing the cost of letters and papers through legislation to the minimum sum. Now that all can pay a cent for a postal card and letter communications become possible for rich and poor, the old grades are completely leveled. Aristocracy so far as the interchange of letters is concerned, is totally annihilated. Not so in the Magnetic Dispatch Service, although the actual cost of short communications is less than by the old system and so really preferable that it will doubtless one day supplant it. But the Telegraph is in the hands of monopolies. These monopolies can, and do, to the grief of the poorer people charge such high rates for dispatches that few can use their dispatch service. Those who can, feel triumphant pride in it; and obeying human instincts imagine themselves superior, thereby engendering class. Nothing, we assume, but the assumption of its control by the people, can level down this feeling which recognizes human beings from a standpoint of quantities or acquired possession rather than qualities, or actual merit.

PROFESSOR. Now with reference to the introduction of discussion of this kind into the literary societies, what does all our reasoning teach?

ANSWER. It teaches that while moralists are differing over points of justice, equity, and the science of laws governing society, it often happens that a little innocent, inanimate instrument jumps in and settles the question forever. It teaches that ethics based in doubt must succumb to ethics based in positive truth:— the science of applied mechanics as the only demonstrable and unalterable basis of human society, excepting so far as we regard equity as obedience to known natural law. What else shall ever become our unalterable moral guides?

PROFESSOR. You exercise your ingenuity in presenting the Telegraph as an example; but while you make it appear reasonable that the management of this invention may be absorbed by the government and operated more extensively and more democratically than it is at present, under the control of companies, how far are you going to extend your communism? The Telegraph is not the only great invention in illustration. There are Railroads, Steam Ships, Ocean Cables, Ferries, even Coal, Iron and other Mines, which might with equal propriety be absorbed by the government and operated for the common advantage of the great masses instead of the particular interests of a company. What limit do you set? The proposition magnifies itself into a terror!

ANSWER. Only the limits set by reason and experimental proof. The subject is worth the consideration of every student of economies, of philosophy, or of himself. If the schools and colleges of the land will cast aside that almost hypocritical reserve which in point of progress is leaving them behind the work shop and will take up the discussion of these grave subjects, we, of the experimental trades will prove by exact application what their judgment recommends. Until they do this there must remain too much contrariety, apathy and error. We need the varied judgment of all.

PROFESSOR. Do you observe of late years a tendency in this direction?

ANSWER. Yes. Wrong is being attacked. In view of the great progress already attained through the world's labor-saving instruments, we are slowly but certainly beginning to look upon this subject of equity, of morality, of established ethics as a huge and gradually vanishing infatuation, which is giving way to the more palpable proof that lies in mechanics applied. We are safe only when we base any venture upon severe physics that bring forth perfectly calculable results, as those of mechanics applied.

The rupture of the least law of mechanics is invariably attended with punishment; the obedience to mechanic laws, with foretold rewards. This is without regard to questions of moral or religious observances with which we do not interfere nor wish students to do so.

## CHAPTER V.

## SIMILARITY OF OBJECT RESIDING IN TRADE AND POLITICAL UNIONS OF WORKINGMEN.

### DIALOGUE WITH A DEPUTY FROM A PROTECTIVE UNION OF TRADESMEN.

PROTECTIVIST. WE ARE TRADE UNIONISTS; and hearing of your movements agitating the working people and inciting them to political action, have come to express the views of our order upon your unwarrantable plans and methods of conduct.

ADVOCATE OF POLITICAL PARTY. If you are a trade union please inform us what the true object of this protective union is.

PROTECTIVIST. It is to elevate its members and promote union, equality and fraternity. To secure situations of work for our members out of employment. To establish a benefit fund for the sick and for old age and to promote in various other ways, the social welfare of all the individuals who compose the Order. It is a *government* of the members. It is a government on a small scale and prescribes for the actions so far as possible of all its people. A point upon which it is particularly severe is in relation to politics. No political action has hitherto been allowed. Such Unions are purely social institutions.

RESPONSE. It was mentioned that your trade union government is intended to secure employment to its members who are idle. Such is exactly what the unionists of the political Labor persuasion are trying to do. It is your desire to collect a fund for the sick and the aged. We are doing all we can to accomplish this object. It is your wish to promote the social well being of all members. Who are your members, but the people? So you are endorsing the functions belonging to the State, or Government and presume to accomplish its work as well or better than your own great Government which is yours by virtue of your citizenship.

PROTECTIVIST. Our best Trade organizations, such as the Amalgamated Engineers, the Amalgamated Carpenters and Joiners, the Bricklayers, Typographical Unions, &c. carefully take care of their members. In some of our best Unions this fraternal care one for another amounts to a sweet, reciprocal ownership by the society, of its members, body and soul. The society by joint endearment, one for all and all for one, stands ready to bring into play its combined forces, to help a worthy Brother. All rules of our society are strict, plain, and concise; and none but the law-breakers are censured.

REMARK. Protective Unions then, of this kind, are in all respects, governments. It is a government that takes care not only of its working members in good standing, but also of their wives and children. A member in good standing is not a pauper feeding on its benevolence, but a veritable citizen, clothed with the power of legislation, and ready at any time when called upon, to take the duties of office. Are not all important measures submitted to the deliberations of each council or Branch for approval or rejection, before they can be ratified by the Delegate meeting?

PROTECTIVIST. They are, in our best Trade Unions; such as the Amalgamated Societies of Engineers, and of Carpenters and Joiners. All that have stood the test of time and vicissitude have long since adopted this custom.

REMARK. Trade Union government then, is even more cautious and severe in its legislation than the government of the United States or of England, whose citizens often get deceived and imposed upon because they do not exercise this, of all others most valuable right. Your government is quietly practicing not only the votive franchise, but more. Its members (citizens) not satisfied with the ever erring judgment of its representatives, do not confide to them, final powers. They find it dangerous. They find that representatives abuse their power. Representatives form themselves into juntos; and having final powers, procure money and emoluments belonging to their constituents. This misappropriation cannot be possible, if *all the citizens* in their various councils, reserve to themselves the final ratification or rejection of the laws and measures that govern them, thus making the passage of your laws slow, grave, and sure —even clumsy, perhaps, and tiresome —but laws are grave and solemn things and should not be trifled with. Misfortunes of the working class are largely due to this almost criminal neglect and ignorance on the part of citizen members, in not themselves carefully ratifying every measure before it becomes a law. Your Protective Organization, then, is purely a *Referendum government;* and is the wisest and most careful form of political guidance known in the world. The referendum government makes it obligatory upon each member or citizen, to study and be wise for himself and his family; since the destiny of his whole household depends upon his own legislative wisdom. It will never do to entrust final decisions to representatives, who possess the machinery of deceit and fraud, back of which there is no appeal at the command of the constituency. Is not this statement correct as to the details and out-workings of the most successful and long tried Trade Union Government?

PROTECTIVIST. It is.

REMARK. Our next important thing then, necessary to decide, is with regard to the percentage of the general public who have been absorbed by your growing Unions. How numerous are they in Great Britain and America?

PROTECTIVIST. Why do you ask this question?

ANSWER. To get at facts so that we may talk intelligently; as it is for information that you call.

TRADE UNIONIST. It is impossible to ascertain correctly the number of trade Unions and members of Organizations for trade purposes. They are constantly growing up and falling off, according to their vicissitudes. Sometimes they attempt too much and get defeated; when there usually follows a reaction and we almost lose sight of ourselves. Such reaction is again followed by a steady re-growth and on looking it over, we find that in a few years the Unions are more solid than ever; and what is encouraging, more kindly disposed, more numerous and wiser by both experience and study. Another important feature of this growth, is seen in the tendency of the Unions to amalgamate. In Great Britain they are thus encouraging the growth of numbers, funds and power. In America they are also doing well.

Very many of these Trade Unionists are unmarried men and we have many women. So that no more than three or four persons can be represented by each member, as dependent upon, or directly interested in the Union; footing up the entire number of parties directly and indirectly dependent upon such Unions for the means of life at perhaps five or six million men, women and children in the world. But large as this may seem, they are few compared with the populations of the countries in which they live. In the British Isles where there are thirty millions of people, there are less than three million Trade Unionists, and families looking to the Unions for the means of life. The proportion therefore, of the people, absorbed by the organizations is less than one in ten; or less than ten per cent. In the United States where the population is forty millions, the number of these Unionists is only 350,000, which multiplied by three — about the average number of persons in the family they represent, who are also interested in the success of the Union — gives less than four per cent as the proportion of the inhabitants absorbed by these Unions in this country. We give rough figures but the exact number if we had, we might prefer to keep.

Question. Do all these Associations refer their important measures, such as amendments to their Constitution, heavy benefits to crippled members, decision regarding strikes &c, back to the members for approval or rejection, or do they mostly confide in the judgment and honesty of an elected or appointed Congress, Executive Committee or Delegated Body who may, or may not operate solely for the interests of the society?

WORKINGMAN. They are experimenting both ways; with a gradual growth of the former.

QUESTION. Do you intend to augment your Unions?

ANSWER. We are very incessantly and actively engaged in forming new Unions and enlarging the old ones. Growth of these associations is somewhat brisk at present and the prospect is brightening on every hand. The members are attracted by the now clearly demonstrated fact that the larger the proportion of workingmen in combination in any branch of trade, the easier it becomes to carry a point. The Bricklayers, for instance, when they were a unit, found little difficulty in obtaining the Eight Hour system of days work and in getting good wages. Good organization makes men independent. When we are numerous we can drive out of the city, or force into our own ranks, or otherwise rid ourselves of all intruders who attempt to underbid us. In fact, a single vote has been known to break up and completely route the business of firms that refused to treat the Society with respect. In all cases the power of organization raises the workman more nearly upon a level with his employer. It seems hard, and makes employers who have always supposed themselves superior, wince as though it were an intolerable innovation. But we hold that it is just that the old tide be turned in favor of the unhappy many; and what is just is fair. Mere sympathy for those who, since the world began, have shown no sympathy, cannot avail against the cause of justice and of human equality.

QUESTION. About this we will not quarrel. Do you think the successes you speak of will so advance the trade union cause, that anything like a result you refer to in the case of the Bricklayers, could be obtained in every trade as well as in every part of the country where this trade is applied?

ANSWER. The combination of all, if wisely managed is sure to produce any reasonable result we may demand; but the combination of a part, produces fatal antagonisms among us. Employers well understand this and they resort to every means by which to procure ruptures, through misunderstanding and competition between *us*. To do this they find it convenient to circulate among our most ignorant and credulous numbers, disagreeable newspaper reports and circulars. They make an extremely vicious use of the word "communism." They taunt the workmen who otherwise might be disposed to organize themselves into Trade Unions, with communism and disrespect of religion, and crown their great *coup de stratégie* with cooly importation. This is their growing clue. For this they establish bureaus of immigration, on both sides of the American Continent. Europeans and Africans are imported to the Atlantic seaboard, while Asiatics swarm along the Coasts of California. Such facts are keenly observed by the Organization which sees the necessity of forming protective unions among all nationalities at home and abroad. Contractors of human flesh, or labor jobbers begin immediately to cry against the "Internationalists" who would organize labor Societies in all countries for a common fraternity and a common defense, using their vast power of money and tact, in buying up the vehicles of calumny, obloquy and prejudice against the struggling toilers of all nations.

DEMAND. Do you sympathize with these Coolies,

who are in that way prevailed upon to immigrate hither? Is it the duty of your Organization to protect Coolies?

WORKINGMAN. Yes. Asiatic Coolies would not emigrate of their own will, wretched as is their situation at home. People in the Orient have not the repute of being enterprising in this way. But while we find no fault with their growing spirit of enterprise, we dislike, for their own sake, to see them juggled and wheedled off to America under the conditions described by American Consuls abroad. We find that their appearance on these shores is the result of a deep laid scheme of the Contract System. Men and women from Asia are thus made to enrich labor jobbers by underbidding our rates of labor; and in this manner have inaugurated a system which may eventuate in driving us from the labor market entirely. In former years the African chattel traffic drove white labor from a large territory by a similar and not much less revolting method. We are dealing with a grave question; for if one kind of slavery resulted in horrible carnage, why may not another? Our Coolies, though not confessedly so, are slaves. They are induced to come by treacherous means. Conniving men versed in their religious superstitions, are posted in different localities of the eastern world, and working upon the avarice of equally vicious persons of influence and power, manage to decoy poor working people, by time lease-bargains, mortgages on their labor, glowing promises and other irresponsible overtures; and they are transported by means nearly as cruel as the horrid slave ships; made many times to hover about the odious, sickening slave pens and *enchères*, as negroes were sold in days that make us shudder to recall. The cooly Contract system which may result in starving us, is the dismal opening of another slavery. It is therefore, the *system* under which these people are imported, that must be looked upon as inhuman and enslaving. If these people came here of their own accord and through their own enterprise and would overcome their own prejudices and become citizens, it would alter the matter. We have no more reasonable objections to their coming than we have to our respected and honored Germans, or English, or Irish, who are proving themselves industrious citizens and of whom many of us are a part. But if we attempt to organize these people into unions of self-protection, or if we would combine them at home and enlighten them on these principles of self-help which are proving of such immense advantage to ourselves, we are immediately sneered down as "communists" or "internationalists."

QUESTION. Are we not led to infer by your glowing views, that the growth of Trade Unions ought to be extended all over the world?

PROTECTIVIST. Most certainly. And it should be so considered by every human being depending for his living upon his labor. Never till such union is achieved, can class be abolished, and equal man-hood and woman-hood established. Let me give you an example:—There is an arrangement of these human flesh contractors on the Atlantic Seaboard to supply Manufacturers, Builders and Farmers with cheap labor. Advertisements and circulars are scattered over Germany, Holland, Scandinavia and elsewhere, setting forth in brilliant colors the marvelous wealth and resources of the Americas. Now among the many who are induced to emigrate hither, some are members of excellent Trade Unions who are well posted on all these exaggerations. They take out their card of membership there, which serves to install them into full membership here. Many of them find work through their Union as soon as they arrive; and thus avoid the discouraging and impoverishing necessity of working for almost nothing until they pick up enough of the language and usages of the country to demand higher pay. It is this that the importer of humanity makes his profit upon — this first wear;— this interval of time between the poor immigrant's landing and his acquiring enough knowledge of the language and habits of his adopted country, to inspire him with the presumption to demand more respectable wages. The scheme is to constantly keep a large number of employers supplied with hands at almost nothing. Instances are common where laborers and others are, in the darkness of want and credulity, decoyed off to brickyards and other slave pens, and worked with such fiendish brutality by the foreman that in a week, tired nature gives out, and their very groans and agony are systematically mistaken for revolt and made the beginning of a tumult. The scoundrels then drive the poor wretches off without pay on the charge of insurrection — their treacherous, improvised pretext —and another gang is immediately sent on by the impious knaves in league with them, at the Labor Exchange Offices; and the same outrage is re-committed, times without limit. This damning practice is made to elude the law by presenting a shade of legality in this wise:— A verbal arrangement is made by which the poor are made to agree, through the wiles of interpreters, to work a certain length of time. If they quit before that time they forfeit all their wages except the commission, paid per head, to the city agent, and their transportation ticket from this Labor agency to the place of work. This the law arranges for. The money agreed to be paid those who stay the full time is often a fabulous sum to them but just before this time expires the row or tumult in disguise, is sprung upon them, and the fuss is so cunning and surreptitious, and the yards are cleared so quickly by the hireling police, or other parties, that the poor unsophisticated builders of Babel however innocent, and wronged are assumed to be the only instigators of their own forfeiture. Such fearful injustice cannot be practiced upon the Trade Unionist.

QUESTION. Did you not mention before that some of your best Trade Unions are those imported or transplanted from Europe?

PROTECTIVIST. Yes. Quite a number of our most effective labor organizations are purely British, bringing with them, and conforming to, all the rules of the mother societies. The *Social-Demokratische Arbeiter Vereine*, or Social Democratic Workingmen's Unions, are transplanted from Germany. Among the valuable trade unions from England are the United Order of American Bricklayers, the Amalgamated Carpenters and Joiners, the Amalgamated Engineers &c. These powerful organizations of Labor are becoming rich, and with wealth, they carry their points. Now to my argument. If there were perfect organizations which included a majority of the workers of each trade and calling in existence, in the different countries where these people are, and if there were corresponding Unions here so that each person could be helped by the fraternal energy of his own Union, on his arrival, in short, if there were no chances for these ubiquitous Labor Exchange agents, to swindle the immigrant, what an immense amount of suffering would be avoided!

Once acknowledge this and you acknowledge the need of an International Workingmen's Union of Trades. The world's workers, male and female, are in great need of more Organization in their respective homes and more of the science of international deliberation. There ought to be Trade Unions started in China, Japan, India, everywhere; and our own Organizations at home, would not only be doing a humane deed, but would make honor and progress by sending missionaries to all parts of the world, to teach the benefits of combination among working people, against systems that enslave them.

REMARK. After all you have said you only concur with us although we would avoid using harsh words; because these so called Jobbers of Labor's Profits, are in another way but unhappy victims of the competitive system. The evil is inherent in the system, not in the men.

PROTECTIVIST. How do you agree with us? Instead of advocating these practical means of solidarity among the down-trodden working people, and instituting plans of deliverance from the horrible shambles of slavery which exist systematically at home and abroad, interlinking with each other for the propagation of this disunion among us, avarice among them, and the establishment of a still more extended and exclusive reign of monopoly; instead of this, you would, if we comprehend you, get us mixed up in petty politics and divide us by political wrangles!

RESPONSE. On the contrary you have shown that the very finest and richest as well as most powerful unions of tradesmen are those that exercise most wisely, the votive franchise. The very oldest and most thoroughly established of them, such as have stood the rack of trial, you acknowledge to be those which enforce the discussion by all members, of every project of a new law or change of an old one. It is claimed in fact that your organizations which are producing the happiest results are those that have been practicing the referendum. This is the most radical proposition in political science. Yours is an entirely political manœuvre, because you would have it engross the masses, and you work by ballot. It is a subject of discussion and doubt to-day among classes of education and means, whether the people who compose the CITIZENS of any country, monarchical, or republican, are yet wise enough to assume this function. It is strongly insisted that the citizens, under the government of the American Republic, are not yet advanced enough to legislate for themselves by assuming and executing the ratifying power. Men argue that if the people send their Representatives to make the laws which govern them, it is as far as it will do to trust them. They still insist that such laws will be better made and more strictly enforced by the Representatives than by referring them back to the people at large for final adoption or rejection. In other words, the political economists and scholastic thinkers are of opinion that the people are not clear-headed enough yet to be able to criticise and properly sanction the Bills which their own representatives have codified at their Congress and Legislature. Your trade union experiment is a bomb-shell in their ranks, which explodes a great theory. It proves that a class of citizens who cannot be regarded as possessing a full average of experience, —the mechanics and laborers of England and America the education of whom has been greatly neglected,—*are found perfectly competent to not only ratify their own laws, but also to detect and punish all attempts at mal-administration.* It is not only a fact, but it is a cheering chapter of *news;* whose portent might well be advocated among our political economists who find it easier to gain money and popularity by doubting truth than by telling it. In fact, the experiment of the Trade Union is political; and it is a foretaste of a mighty revolution. Can you not see that the very measures you are advocating, such as the building up of Organizations for mutual protection over the world, is an intensely political movement? Any action for the advantage of large numbers of people, if that action depend for its success upon the casting of the vote, is political. Trade Unions are politico-economical; because, their business is to further the economy of Trade Labor, in a way which it shall redound to the best interest of the members and their families. What more can a Parliament or a Legislature do? The state is a compact of the Citizens within a given territory, to be governed by the laws which are the result of mutual deliberations. Such action of any community is political. A trade union is a compact between each other, of many workmen who are in like manner, governed by laws of their own enactment. All laws, alike of the State and of the Union, are for the general welfare of the members or citizens and their families.

PROTECTIVIST. We do not pretend to deny that the trade organization, on the whole, has a political aspect. But we are opposed to having any thing to do with local politics. The moment we begin to meddle with politics we find that the interest in the organization wanes. Workingmen have been repeatedly plundered by the tricks of political rings. They have learned by grim experience to loathe all politics of the times and place no confidence in the harpies of political jugglery.

ANSWER. This is wisdom itself. But it is clear that

you fail to see that you are yourselves building up a Political Party in your Trade Organization. The moment your Organization becomes so perfect that it can carry its own points, as in the cases you have mentioned and you begin to perceive the strength of your command, you will see the wisdom of applying this strength to crush out the selfish corruptionists. In a country like this, where privileges are not denied those who have the manhood to claim them, such a power cannot remain inactive. In fact, the workingmen are already deliberating upon the practicability of political action; and the result has been rather to combine than to disperse them.

PROTECTIVIST. There is too much vagary about political action. We are practical. We want to apply our effort where it will yield something direct for our families. We want principally the guaranty of work, at good prices, so that we shall no longer feel the dread of poverty pinching at our firesides. How is this to be obtained by politics?

ANSWER. We do not propose to curtail the functions of your Unions. Not in the least. On the contrary, they should be made more effective. What we propose is to extend their functions; not to curtail them. If the Trade Union can educate its members by discussion so far as to effectually refer its propositions back to the entire membership for ratification or rejection, it is safe to conclude that it can vote with wisdom for or against any person whom it may nominate for office.

PROTECTIVIST. What course of action can you prescribe that would commend itself to the Unions we represent?

ANSWER. We would advise no particular course; for that would partake of leadership. The great Labor Movement should shun leaders. In the march of great principles there can be no leaders any more than there can be leaders in science. There may be doctors or teachers but they are mere exponents not leaders. In this political point of view, a leader is, in this movement, a mere political mountebank whom you should always shun as one who seeks to jump on the car you have with toil constructed, and drive it to perdition. Most leaders are designing persons whose scheme is to accomplish the two-fold object of glorifying themselves by distroying you. They wheedle your votes, get elected, betray your trust, work all their influence against you, break up your organization by stimulating dissentions and then leave you, disarmed and disgusted, at the profuse emolument they obtain from the common enemy whom their treacherous betrayal of yourselves has served. Beware of such Politicians. We can only mark out an object to be gained by political action. The manner in which this purpose is realized, it is safest to leave to you. We will simply suppose you represent four Societies: the Iron Workers, the Ship Carpenters, the Riggers and the Caulkers; and that you are located, say in and around Boston. Apart from the multitude of industries, great and small in that busy city, there is one which we hear little about but which is the common property of citizens. Immediately in the vicinity is the Charlestown Navy Yard. It contains all the advantages of a first class industry. Ship-yards, Rigging lofts, Machine shops, and every possible requisite of a great and flourishing business. These immense concerns are the property of the people, and should be conducted by the people in their own interests. These works must get out of war-like grooves and be turned to general use. What is the use of a manufactory if it is not to supply the people? Yet in times of peace, these vast works lie idle because there is no more use for the engines of death. How long must the individual enterprise and the spirit of gain be the chief incentive to manufacture. Rightly considered these are co-operative works; to produce what? Death! The people do not want death; they want life. Now is it not clear that if a company build ships for sale and sell them to the public for what they can get, that they are prompted by a reverse spirit from that which prompts the people when they manufacture their own ships? In the one case it is pure individualism incited by speculation. In the other, it is collectivism; and makes and distributes these necessaries according to the people's own wants, without any spirit of speculation whatever. It is pure co-operation which reverses the old order of things, and avoids the methods of intermediary manufacturers and sellers. The immense difference between an industry conducted upon the co-operative system, is shown in the fact that co-operation saves advertising. Advertising is an enormous branch of human labor belonging to competism. It is neither natural to monopoly nor to co-operation; and if it is used in them it is because they are not the offspring of competism exclusively; and what ever of the advertising trade exists in co-operation or monopoly, comes from the competism that lingers in them.

Nothing but a higher knowledge and practice of Political Economy can ever rid the world of these ravenous and all devouring urgents—competition and monopoly — that feed upon the labor of the poor; and nothing but the combined virtues of wisdom and organized force can eliminate this gigantic and unproductive branch of human labor, the advertising system.

From this it will be seen that there are three very distinct methods upon which society conducts its economies of life:—Competition, Monopoly, and Co-operation.

The Navy Yard alluded to, so long as it performs its own work direct, according to the regulations of government, is a *co-operation.* When the government authorities banter with outside parties for bids to execute the work without regard to the advantage of the citizens employed, then it is no longer co-operation, but *competitive* in its nature. But when Congress orders work and appropriates money for it, and a single individual outside conspires with Senators, Representatives and other persons of influence, to get this work entirely away from the government ship-yards, and shops, in order that he may himself do the work, and by reducing wages, lengthening the day's labor and slighting the work performed, make a fortune for himself only, while his neighbors suffer, then our Navy Yard becomes a victim to *monopoly.* The workingmen, therefore, as a natural consequence cannot fail to see the need of combination in favor of the *purely co-operative management of this naturally co-operative industry.*

Trades Unions are learning by experience that a little combination and energy lend more influence than the promises of Senators or Representatives. With wisdom they can nominate and elect representatives of their own; and with such power can secure all this work to co-operation notwithstanding the wishes of outside competitors and monopolists. A workingman always prefers to work for himself. Now no lover of liberty is destitute of feelings of responsibility toward his government. He must, and does, from the nature of his stock in the government which is his citizenship, feel a pleasure in seeing his ships and other means of defense, in time of war, well constructed. In times of peace, what is to hinder their performing the work of the people? A workingman owns his government, and has a right, in common with all others, not only to look to its best interests but also to be employed by it.

If, therefore, the Navy Yards produce better ships than the outside ship-yards and if they pay and treat the workmen better, then it is easy to conclude that they should be allowed to do the necessary work; even if it be the manufacture of mowers or sewing machines. Manufacture is a thing which every cititzen has an interest in. Its natural peace method is co-operation. Workingmen who must bear the brunt of war, want no more of it. Co-operation means peace; competism, war. Here then we have an industry furnished with all the Stocks, Docks, Shops and fixtures, necessary for a business, which, if set in operation, would employ fifteen thousand workmen, on the cooperative principle. The men are better paid, work less time, produce more genuine ships and for as little money as the outside contractor produces them. Not that the workman's labor is less efficient in an outside concern, but because the proprietor generally requires for his individual profit that percentage, which in good co-operation, goes to the workman in form of increased wages and short hours. The proposition is clear. If you possess organized numbers and social management, you restore the co-operation to yourselves. The simple application of that power, involves political action. In times of peace, when you want social prosperity, men are speculating out of you upon contracts paid by appropriations to build engines of war. Turn these works into social factories of *peace;* for workingmen are the true victims of war; and an International Association of them, if it had energy, discipline solidarity, virtue, might prove the only power, to check the war spirit and turn arsenals and armories into people's workshops and bring about the universal peace.

PROTECTIVIST. The Trade Unionists could not consent to do anything until they are more instructed on the argument you adduce. Most of us are accustomed to work in outside establishments and know little or nothing of the principles you advocate. It might be years before we could acquire sufficient clearness to see the permanent advantages of this sort of co-operation. We cannot understand how co-operation can be so fraternal as to do away with war, although we are its victims.

REMARK. It is plain that it requires something more than a knowledge of the rules of your Order to be a true Trade Unionist. The votive franchise is supreme in this country, and if you will not use it when you see an opportunity to set such an enormous industry as this, in motion, manufacturing the necessaries of life and thereby bringing employment and gladness to the homes of 15,000 families, you must expect that competism will organize its political forces against you and crush you down. When manufacture and distribution are conducted in the interests of the people in general, it will speedily bring forth peace, prosperity and plenty for all. But so long as the Trade Unions and other Labor associations persist in the neglect of these great and important matters in which their happiness and liberty are involved and throw away their golden opportunities to destroy the competitive system, so long must labor remain in subjection.

PROTECTIVIST. You speak only of one Navy Yard.

Are not these government or co-operative industries, as you term them, numerous?

ANSWER. They are already numerous enough to have called forth the attention of the Labor Movement. Jobbers who use them are the true cravers for government employ. Do not therefore, allow your Unions to be influenced by their taunts at you, as seekers after "Government Employ." It is often their own emissaries who, with all the wiles of the competitive diplomate, cast obloquy upon you for that which they themselves are surreptitiously surfeiting on; —government employ. The labor broker not only craves contracts from government which furnish him wealth, but he systematically turns the engines of power and persuasion against you, who neither ask nor expect a tithe of that he receives. He seeks, with the lobby, to use influence in casting obloquy upon your innocent effort to live by using these arsenals co-operatively, while he destroys the virtue of that co-operation and undermines the health of its democracy by using, in his monarchical methods of industry, the appropriations that were intended to be paid you in days' work. The workingman has a right to help his government make ships not only for war but for peace; and therefore, has a right to be employed by his government; while the contractor who gets away this employment and enriches himself on the appropriations, does it by irregular means.

There exist already splendid industries, for which the different governments, Municipal, State, and General, order appropriations annually. They belong to you, the people, and were intended for you; and if you would turn your force towards obtaining them you could all have constant employment on your own premises without fear of being discharged. As it is, you neglect to obey one incentive of good citizenship. You are hired to execute the work, at poor wages and long hours, and caused to slight the duty. Thus you are given bad inculcations against the government you are under obligations to protect. Still you refuse to take political action.

PROTECTIVIST. Will you mention some of these industries for which governments are making appropriations?

REMARK. They are too numerous to mention. There are eight Navy Yards in the United States. One at Brooklyn has accommodations for 18,000 or 20,000 workmen when in full activity. The greatest part of the enormous manufacturing and distributing business of the Post Office is let out on contract. The printing of Postal Cards, Stamps, Envelopes, Official Papers &c. should all be paid for by days' work. Instead of this, the contract is given to others; and you are required to make them, not for government at all; but for parties indirectly, who, in your ignorance of resistance make slaves of the workers. The government pays a contractor about the same amount it would cost to make ships, in the regular way on the ennobling live and let-live system it once adopted;—that of good pay and eight hours. The contractor profits not so much on the government as on you; which is in proportion as he can obtain more of you, in *urging your labor, reducing your wages and lengthening your hours.*

Every city has its enormous public industries, such as street cleaning. Sewer making &c. The necessary business under the management of the different Boards of Education, Public works, and the Departments of Docks, Parks and other public improvements is very great. Still with some few exceptions such as the schools, this vast business is done by contract, or by an irregularity. The building of Edifices for the General Government is accomplished, to a large extent, by petted contractors. In fact, when Trade Unions see the true magnitude of their loss and humiliation, caused by their own prejudice against political action, they will certainly arouse with the farmers, and force the application of more regular methods of work.

PROTECTIVIST. What plan would you advise for a Social Union wishing to keep its members employed in any of these government works?

ANSWER. A plan that will demonstrate to the politician who now hires you and gives positions to those in the collusion in payment for their services at the poles, that they are no longer required. The workmen themselves should be so thoroughly organized that they can make the execution of this work a study. Individuals who now control public works make it a study. Being very few in numbers and having absolute control they often make a bad study of it. This is the way the public work is now done. Of course they study to make money for themselves; and it often happens that it is not the contractor who proves the lowest bidder, but the contractor who offers the politician the highest commission for the work, who gets it! It becomes, therefore, necessary that the laboring citizens who are to perform this work, should make a thorough study of what they are paid for; both for their own and the general good, for no other method can ever eliminate these irregularities from the public works. The honest masses of workmen can be relied upon. *The general public must take charge of the work which belongs to the general public.* The working masses who execute this work, are the general public. They do the work and ought to have charge of it for their own and the general good. If the work is contracted out to an individual, interest in the management of it dies; because interest ceases when control is gone. The public interest is arrested and stifled and irregularity is certain, in proportion as public control is diminished numerically; that is, in proportion as public control is irregularly taken from the people and surrendered to individuals.

PROTECTIVIST. Would you have us use our combination as a *school of deliberation* wherein the subject of study shall be our own means of support?

ANSWER. Exactly so.

PROTECTIVIST. What guarantee then, have the great public, that we shall not be as selfish and dishonest as any of those who have plundered the public treasuries and deprived the workmen of their pay?

RESPONSE. Your question, you will see, answers itself if you will allow yourselves to reflect and study. Every important subject of political economy must be studied through practical lessons. Supposing your organization of laborers is composed of the residents of a Ward in one of our great cities. One main object of the organization, like that of any Trade Union, is to procure work for its members and look to the general welfare of their families. Upon this object exclusively, they are combined. Upon this object they deliberate and vote. Upon this object they are so anxious of success that they dare not trust to their own judgment on matters of general importance; but find it most sure to refer all important projects and decrees back to the members of the different Unions in the country for ratification or rejection.

Are there any opportunities for dishonesty in this? On the contrary so free from secrecy is it, that if all the laborers of the Ward are in the Union they are all required to join in the deliberations. Nothing can be done which the people do not know of and have not inteligently deliberated beforehand.

PROTECTIVIST. But in what light have we deliberated upon it? Have we considered any proposition with reference to the good of the city or of people outside the Union?

RESPONSE. It is upon this that we are coming slowly to an understanding which will set us right, with reference to the motive of your visit. *The judgment of masses is surer and more to be trusted than the judgment of individuals, when they can agree in council.* This is an axiom your Unions have proved. The votive franchise of the Federal Government of America has also proved it by a hundred years of experience. The Referendum Government of the best and solidest Trade Unions particularly proves it. In the business of contracting a job of street cleaning, of the Ward in question, there are not more than ten persons. These ten persons can generally control the entire street-cleaning Department of the city. But even allowing that there are ten to this Ward, they are few enough to conspire against the public at large. Now, how many laborers would be most apt to constitute a Trade Union in that Ward?

PROTECTIVIST. From twenty to five hundred or more according to the population and the necessity or incentive to organization.

RESPONSE. Well, for fairness, we will put it at one hundred and fifty members. There are in this Ward, then fifteen times as many persons interested as citizens in the healthiness, cleanliness and decent appearance of its streets, as there are street commissioners and jobbers who now have control. Is it as likely that one hundred and fifty citizens of these streets, subject to diseases from their foul effluvia of filth, would cast their vote against a renovation of them, as that ten who having wealth, live in splendor, in better places and are not subject to their malaria, would do it? Is this trade unionist a mere animal without any appreciation of health, or decency and utterly devoid of capability to judge in matters of his home comforts? The question needs no answer. He has proved himself an able judge wherever he has found combination possible. Rest assured that such union of laborers would keep their own streets in good order, as the result of unanimous vote of their council. They have two honest, virtuous incentives, distinct from each other, but necessary to good citizenship;—first, to earn a living by their labor, and secondly, to do good work for the health, the convenience and the prosperity of community.

Protectivist. We can admit that they would do it, and that they ought to do it. Unionists are close reckoners on points of health and home interests.

Remark. Well, when they attend strictly to all such points of home interest, we have political action. It begins by an organized protest against all remissness and collusion of political labor-jobbers, who secretly conspire to keep us out of employment and make the innocent people pay contractors for what is left undone. We have poor street cleaning and idle workmen as a result.

Protectivist. Granting all this (and it is political action), how could the trade union administration be made to supersede the present administration of the street commissioners?

ANSWER. It is not pretended they would. Perhaps it may never become a duty of the labor unions to commence political action by tearing down established forms of government. In some cases such extreme measures may become necessary, on the peace basis; but what is at this moment wanted, is a better guardianship, by the community themselves, over the practical things of home life. Wrong in public circles will always exist, unless the masses of the neighbors most deeply interested take not only the labor itself, but also the supervision of the labor into direct control; and become detectives, censors and judges of every public action of their representatives. To do this, requires study and its means—organization and discussion, on these politico-economic incentives.

PROTECTIVIST. Can this line of action be applied with advantage by all the unions?

ANSWER. Just the same. If the ship carpenters or the machinists and blacksmiths do not apply themselves urgently to the task of employing their own members at the navy yards, where there are large government establishments waiting to employ them, the necessary work of government will be leased, or jobbed out to contractors and done on the old wage-slavery system. So long as the contract system thrives, the achievement of eight hours as a day's work, will be impossible; because this system dominates upon the discomfiture of the workingmen, caused by the *profit* to the individualist which accrues from the true producer's toil. It must become clear to the student that the cure for this lies in *direct* employment by the workman's own government in which he has a common interest —the workman's own Government that needs the work and is able to pay for it, *directly* into the workman's hand. It is this same boon of increased wages and short hours which a workman has a right to demand, that makes the contractor rich, by being exacted from the poor, in sweat drenched driblets of slave labor product.

PROTECTIVIST. Is it possible to apply this theory to the advantage of all Trade Unions?

ANSWER. It is as applicable to one branch of supply of human wants, as to another. You own your government. It will do for you anything you bid. But you must cast off prejudices and learn to study, deliberate and vote for yourselves and your wives and children. The great world's contract jobbers are on the alert. They are tasting with a jealous relish, the sweet meats of government employment; and in order to perpetuate their monopoly over it and enrich themselves by its appropriations, which they instigate by bribed legislation, they deceive and decoy you from your duty to yourselves and to humanity, by frowns of assumed superiority and reproaches of heresy.

PROTECTIVIST. There is a desire to work on our religious prejudices.

RESPONSE. Yes, but it is only a subterfuge. Ours is a question of severe political economy. Religion has little to do with it. What we want is more practical business in this question, to demonstrate it by solid physics. It can be solved only by a better adjustment of purely physical relations. The people must be made to understand that this labor movement is intrinsically free both of questions of morality and of religion. Political economy is its province. To attribute to it the province of ethics or religion is to give to it functions that are entirely foreign and will only retard its action. It rests solely upon the application of the means, mechanical and otherwise of *producing the most in quantity, of life's necessaries, with the least labor; and the equitable distribution of the same, on the same principle.* If the horticulturist neglect his plants they become rigid; the earth bakes around their stalks and they choke with weeds or die of drought; but if he waters and weeds them with care and supplies them with such fertilizers as furnish the proper chemical constituents of their growth, there is no further question as to their success. They will produce flowers and fruits in almost mathematical proportion to the labor and science, but particularly the science bestowed upon them. The horticulturist thrives and is happy with his green plants, flowers and fruits. What has this to do with any question of morality or religion? There is a strong question of economy involved, as far as the gardener's happiness and material interests are concerned; but nature never stops to consider whether these plants were reared in the midst of blasphemies or of songs of praise. Nature never stops to consider consequences only in the *physical* or scientific mechanical point of view. Wisdom dictates that the result should be fully known before the cause that produces that result is applied. The solution of the labor problem involves the stern study of causes and effects. Nature deals in no hap-hazards or speculations. Her laws are as rigid and uncompromising as they are immutable; and she punishes every physical error because it is an error, and without regard to the innocence of the tears that fall.

The fact is, the laws of nature are not the laws of ethics, but rather of mechanics; since it is only through instruments that our productive labors can be accomplished.

Nature's work is severe and exact in all its details. If we invent a labor-saving machine capable, with one man's direction, of performing the work of one hundred men and these hundred persons who formerly earned their living doing this work by hand, are wise enough to manage the labor-saving instrument *themselves*, they will get a living for ninety-nine times less trouble than before, minus the wear and tear of machine. But if we allow a monopolist to usurp to himself the usufruct of this labor-saving machine, he will, with its labor, turn out upon the streets to starve, ninety-nine of the hundred workmen, keeping one to operate it; and after paying the one his wages, defraying the expenses of wear and tear, rent &c., he remains master of all the profits which were formerly paid the ninety-nine men now idle, in form of wages or means of life. The machine, therefore, actually becomes a curse to the ninety-nine men, by intercepting their means of life; and all the prayers and tears of ninety-nine starving families will avail nothing. Whereas had the one hundred men a proper knowledge of material economies, they would co-operate with each other in the management of the labor-saving machine, and use it for the common benefit of all. This being clear, it becomes equally clear that any community or state, composed of persons who have established a government for the general good which allows one person to monopolize its instruments of production, and thus distress its members, is itself the victim of the grossest ignorance of the law of demand and supply. Nature punishes this state with inevitable results of its own ignorance which are poverty and crime on the one hand and individual fortunes on the other.

## CHAPTER VI

..........

### AN ENGROSSING QUESTION OF GOVERNMENT COAL-MINES, PUBLIC HIGHWAYS, AND OTHER MEANS OF DISTRIBUTING CHEAP FUEL AMONG THE PEOPLE.

---

DISCUSSION WITH A MEMBER OF THE PRESS ON THE DUTIES OF THE NEWSPAPER.

EDITOR. THE SCHEME OF WORKINGMEN to subordinate the Individual to the State by making government assume an economic guardianship over masses abrogating the competitive system entirely, is an innovation upon society to which Editors can scarcely lend their sanction. It can only be realized by slow absorption at best, and the independent newspaper is certainly the last thing one could think of confiscating.

REMARK. People want an honest and able paper; but can such a thing exist under the competitive system? Could a Commonwealth operate a newspaper better than an individual? These are our questions. In a competitive state of society, if we look at it logically, so long as people allow others, not committed to their welfare to do their work, they can scarcely expect it will be done in their interests. So long as the Editor is the individual proprietor, his paper *must* work for *one* man; not for many, only so far as by pleasing many it advances the interests of one. This is an axiom with exceptions; but it involves a principle that bears its fruits of poverty and wealth. It is well known that the most flagrant corruptions are those which have been upheld by newspapers, subsidized in their interests by money. In other words, Editorial Administrations when tempted by money, have been known to take contracts of suppressing evidence against parties who entertain a scheme to get money without paying an honest equivolent for it. Buzzards of the law making process perch in our Congress Lobbies. In the contract, and for a given sum, newspapers can, unbeknown to the public, sell their honor, and become mere, mercenary auxiliaries of any scheme. Sometimes it is within their power to so far lose dignity as to guffle and rave at all honest resistance, improvising, or suppressing arguments. Individuals are apt to decoy public opinion, (while we possess no Social Press in the interests of the majorities,)or succeed by browbeating and intimidating all honest endeavors of justice to secure fair play. We believe that the only true theory for just and democratic Government is on the basis of Party;—Party strife; Party differences; friction of principles against each other as set forth by Party. Both Parties are common property of humanity. A proposition is launched by the people. It meets with favor from a certain class, say the Workingmen; who upon that principle, or Platform of principles involving new and progressive issues, organize a Party. Another class embracing the older, competitive methods of State hold to old or non-progressive principles, and becomes a Party in antagonism to that of the workingmen. Justice would say:—"Discuss these arguments; weigh them; prove them; apply them; and I will award my verdict according to the result." How can each Party get at discussion without having an Organ in its interest? This principle of Party issues has been successfully tried by the American Republic; and its natural result has been to advance civilization, by hastening the adoption of methods of political economy. Having arrived where they are, the industrious class of people begin to look at each other for mutual assistance in gaining a better livelihood by their labor; and as the State is the strongest, oldest, richest and most natural Organization, they naturally look hopefully to its Government, as the solidest medium for carrying out their aims. No idea is entertained of accomplishing much of this, immediately; but if a Government Press cannot be had, which is completely in their favor, they can, and do, organize a Social Party among themselves and through that organization, build up a Social Press. An arrangement of this sort will answer the purpose, until the Government Press can be created by their power.

Government ought to own and operate a Newspaper in their interest. It is demanded as an Organ of their own. Working people want it to advocate their cause boldly and openly. We expect the Party of the capitalists, or the Party that has so long held us in bondage, will continue its own organization and its own papers. We are willing to match arguments, statistics, wit, tact, genius, and relative claims, against theirs. But we are not willing to allow their papers or those engaged in their interests, to suppress our arguments with impunity as they have been doing in our helplessness, without having a chance to show our share of fact, and force of virtue in our own behalf. We have been treated with intolerance, silenced, kept uneducated, uninformed and but half employed, until driven by the degrading results into the study of social industries, social government, social papers, as sheer necessities, We think we have adopted the only means by which ultimately to establish an organ, able and powerful enough to buffet successfully with the great public press.

EDITOR. You can never in our day effect the establishment of a government paper. Therefore we have but little fear that a labor party will injure the business of the great science of journalism. We may rest quite at ease. Journalism may rest passive also with regard to the workingmen's party. It appears doubtful whether it succeeds in obtaining government aid in co-operation, upon its utopian idea; because the workingmen have not reared political economists and statesmen to take the positions of those they would displace.

REMARK. Does not this show the need among laboring people, of an honest and powerful journal that endorses and advocates labor principles from their depths? Workingmen want an energetic and able organ. They have discovered principles for the ground-work of a democracy which might break up class. It is clear that the industries of a great people are being peddled out second-hand to individuals. Working people want equality, even if it assume a form of the communism of More's Utopia.

EDITOR. By what line of argument do you arrive at the conclusion that collective management can ever be made to succeed in the place of individual management?

ANSWER. Many specimens of labor associations are of themselves vital arguments. Many of the best and most efficient and powerful mutual aid and friendly organizations, are those having the means of supplying their members practically, and to the letter, with everything they promise. Many self-help societies exist which are able to, and *do*, guarantee the promise set forth in their rules; that is, provided for and enforced, in their government. To be a member, therefore, of such a mutual aid society is to enjoy a guaranteed citizenship under a government in which every citizen is allowed to deliberate and vote upon the management of his own business industries on which himself and his family are dependent for support. A society like that of the amalgamated carpenters, or the amalgamated engineers, and many others, is a *bona fide* government, based upon the principles of the Referendum Democracy wherein all new laws, alterations and additions must be submitted to the entire membership, for approval or rejection. These societies are not only doing this, but they are practically, and in this mutual way, taking upon themselves the ownership, so to speak, of each other. They are both the government and the supply-sources of their citizens, that is, members. Success of their government, therefore, like that of any other government, depends upon the education of the voters —their intelligence. As soon as they shall determine to launch out upon an enterprise of their own, this business becomes a co-operation of every individual member of the whole society. This is the natural result of any Referendum Democracy. Citizens themselves assume and execute the right to ratify or veto any law or project before it goes into force. Citizens take to themselves the functions of presidents, dictators and kings.

EDITOR. Can you state an instance, showing how this can be applied?

ANSWER. Supposing the Coal Miners' Association, after passing through all the vicissitudes of that species of warfare their union entails, should at length become so thoroughly combined as to open a Mine of their own. The question immediately arises as to the method of effecting this. The idea of the Miners operating a concern as large as a Mine, involves many difficulties. It requires mining science, strict business management, a high discipline over the work of every department and a submission on the part of all, to the authority of those they have vested in control. Substitution, in fact, of collective for individual control in the business of Mining Coal. In it lies a difference kindred to that which exists between monarchy and democracy; for the individual control of the present system, is a near approach to absolute despotism. Co-operation of the Miners to work for themselves and enjoy, in common with themselves, the product of their labor, is as democratical as communism. Now mere theory is very beautiful and plausible so long as it remains a theory; but when one comes to apply it practically, it generally fails and continues to fail until we become old in experienee; until new officers have learned to take the places of the old and the new enterprise becomes an Institution, assumes forms, habits, systems, by which all its details may act harmoniously in order that the whole scheme may produce the largest dividend. It is not, therefore, to be supposed that these Miners can ever succeed in obtaining a Mine and operating it in their own interests by mere social combination.

Miners have only one way by which this co-operation can be effected;—the ballot. When these Miners become so numerous and so well organized as to wield a strong political power, they can demand of the Legislature or of Congress, that this mining property now used as an instrument of oppression of one and of profit to another, and these Miners' labor, now used to accumulate wealth and aggregate it into focuses of monopoly, carrying with and for it, their vote by proxy, shall be conducted at once in the interest of the people in general, and of the Mining Fraternity in particular. The only way then, by which this change can be effected is by political action. The mining property must belong to the State; and the State must employ the Miners. The Miners will possess a powerful Trade Organization the same as now, and this society must jealously watch and work, giving its votes to none but those who are both qualified and disposed to control these Mines honestly, and in the interests of the Miners who are the people. This is the only means by which the hard working Miner can even expect, ever to enjoy an equal standing, or a generous appreciation of his toil.

EDITOR. Your argument digresses from the subject. What has the Editor to do with the affairs of Miners living hundreds of miles away in the wilderness?

RESPONSE. Everything. From the moment the Miners' Organization assumes power and declares for this principle, it becomes a cogent advocate of a new Political Economy. It begins to look about for a Press commited to its interest. Its action becomes the subject matter of Newspaper talk. The proposition that the State shall assume the control of Mines, involves the great Coal Supply; which is a question of more than ordinary magnitude.

EDITOR. But it is communism; arrant, cantankerous communism.

REMARK. Call it that, or co-operation, or political

economy, or statesmanship. There is no more communism in it than in throwing up a redoubt, by a national army for the defence of citizens. There is not a whit more communism about it than you will find in the Supreme Court of Jurisprudence. When a holocaust like the Chicago fire takes place, the people become panic-stricken, and there being no dicipline, fall upon one another, or become the prey of thieves. It is then that their government steps to the rescue, and order comes out of confusion; the hungry are fed, the injured cared for. This is the work of government. What is wiser? What more effective? Yet it is the very communism that horrifies the editor. When thievish coasters made a piracy of wrecking, our vessels felt a double dread of shipwreck—dread of the accident of shipwreck itself, and dread of pillage by marauders—but now, the people are wiser, better organized, better statesmen, better business managers. They are better communists if you insist upon the term. Statesmanship and communism then become synonymous terms. Why? Because government has stopped all this scoundrelism by establishing light-houses, posts of succor, and vigilance officers, who patrol the shores night and day; and with fog horns, life boats and daring experts, are already regarded by honest people as guardians of their lives and fortunes. Why do you not cry out against this procedure, and stamp it as communism? Yet government mines coming to the rescue of the people are no worse.

EDITOR. Because it bears no adequate comparison with this great proposition to drive out individual companies who now own the mines. Companies have started the coal business at great risk and cost. It would force government, already burdened with duties, to assume the cares, and responsibilities of the whole coal supply. Besides, in most of the cases you have cited, the villainy was aggressive and predatory. The law makes no provisions for thieves and wreckers. One object of the law establishing safety for ships was to rid the country of thieves.

REMARK. It was to destroy the traffic of individualist freebooters and to establish safety for the general community. So far as this branch of the principle is concerned, it is the triumph of con-fraternal, over individual rule.

EDITOR. But how does the principle apply to the Mines?

RESPONSE. Is not the mining of fuel for the people as necessary a business as the coast commerce? Is it not far more so? A large majority of the citizens engaged in this business are the working people. A small minority are those who employ them. They are indeed very few proportionately. Yet this insignificantly small minority are actually allowed to wreck the masses in a traffic that is as rapacious, as cold blooded and far more deadly. They are allowed to set their own prices and force the poor Miners to work under ground amid dangers, the recital of which shocks the ears of the courageous. They are allowed to reduce their condition to a state worse than slavery. When a slave grew old he was maintained by his owner. When wounded or sick, likewise. The true slave, therefore, was spared the responsibility of self support. But when the Miner or his helper is thus disabled he is discharged as worthless and left to die. Sick women, the wives of these poor men, are known to have been driven out of their masters' huts in default of payment of rent and forced to plod homelessly and bare foot with hungry, tattered children, to perish in the snows of winter. Rates of wages have been allowed to be systematically reduced until the men, frantic with approaching wreck, sought relief in strikes which served this minority with an excuse to have them arrested or shot down as rioters. The very brutality of this class law, known as the riot act of Pennsylvania made the men reckless and in their ignorance of wiser expedients, doubtless caused the predatory career of the Molly Maguires and other ruffianism. Then came the wholesale hanging of these men, which was almost immediately followed by the gigantic railroad strike in July 1877. This will be followed by deeper organization, tenderer co-sympathies, and more powerful Amalgamation. Meantime the capitalists who have grown mighty by thus exacting wealth from the over toil of their poor imbruted men, are busy fortifying themselves with class laws. It is thus that the christian spirit of love is being falsified in a christian land. It is a continuous rumble of struggling, incongruous, negative forces that know not each others' welfare because the slaves of self-protection and individualism. Unless the Public Press opens its columns in the advocacy of a remedy, this state of bad management and misunderstanding, must lead to still more fearful rioting if not to all the horrors of a civil war.

Editor. What step is the safest for a paper to take in order to most effectually reconcile both parties?

Answer. An Editor is supposed to understand his own business situation best. We can only say that the Coal Mines and the Rail Roads and Canals leading from them to the people *must become common property*. This is sufficient. It has been resolved upon by all the important Labor Congresses of the world; and rest assured the struggle will go on until the Socialisms of all countries become numerous enough to take this strong hold by treaty or by storm.

EDITOR. For us to take the part of such a radical and revolutionary movement would of course destroy our business speedily.

RESPONSE. By no means. The most widely known Daily of New York is in the habit of showing the feasibility of this plan of the workers. But the laboring classes will not wait for tardy appeals from the capitalist Press. They are now busy creating papers of their own. The great conflict has actually begun and it is too interesting and important to become weary in good works.

EDITOR. If the Miners and Farmers want to have the Coal Mines and Railroads worked by government instead of individuals or operators as at present they evidently will require the help of the Press. They will have to organize themselves into a political power and create centres, or posts, for stumping the country; and by harangue and newspaper labors, show the light and dark spots of their subject. Now if they had the tact and steady determination to really organize this thing, there is something in it; and it is quite possible that newspapers might at length see a clue which they could follow without losing their subscribers. Before this can be done however, the Miners and all those interested in government Mines and Thoroughfares, must do much pioneer work. They must outgrow their habit of wrangling.

REMARK. Here then we have the Editor convinced; but without the energy to venture an idea or a penny in advocacy of a great proposition involving a question not only of fuel for his fire and of reasonable freight tariffs and passenger fares, but of slavery of the human race! What can be expected of these work people while their issues stand friendless? They feel sometimes forlorn and often frenzied, reflecting upon the apathy of those who ought to be their friends. It is this that cultivates a spirit of alternate despondency and malignity which manifests itself periodically in those dreaded spasms that sometimes take the shape of industrial catalepsies and swoons, and sometimes of emotional whirlwinds and tornadoes. Every one of these paroxysmal pangs of the laboring classes, which are growing more numerous year by year, serves as a fulcrum whereby to get new leverage under this communism you abhor, and hoist it into view. Seeing the Editor in an attitude of mercenary indecision and recreant to everything but *self interest* makes them morbid and radical and they rush to extremes;—even to the borders of social cataclysm. This is why they begin to demand a Government Paper. This is why they may soon determine to have the Mines and Railroads themselves. It is one of the keys of the phenomena of labor agitation. The apathy and indicision of the Public Press has perhaps done more than the open action of masters to aggravate and exasperate the men; for they very naturally mistrust a collusion between the masters and the Press.

EDITOR. Journalists are like other folks; and they sometimes stand in need of the joys of conversion before they are themselves fitted to take up their cross and follow. Give us an explanation of the workings of government Coal Mines and Railroads.

RESPONSE. It will probably be a long time before the people are blessed with a thing so unselfish as government Coal Mines and Railroads; but when that boon is realized, the effects will show as follows:— A Government is a co-operative society. It has functions strictly industrial, which can be classed with no other style of industrial functions. Now, a discrepancy prevails among Editors. They are almost universally in favor of any industrial co-operative society and equally averse to a government enterprise; while *fundamentally, these are one and the same thing.* This discrepancy is not seen in the *principle* but in the *numbers* involved. If a score of Miners could buy a Coal Field and work it themselves on a small scale, no one would object; but if *all* the Miners propose to own *all* the Mines, there is a noise about it. Yet it would be better for both Miners and people. The same is true of Canals and Railroads for carrying the coal. A co-operative society is a government as much as Government itself. A great advantage then, certainly would be felt, first by the people at large. We all have an interest in the Post Office and the Public Schools; because they take charge of certain departments of their necessary business and are paid without favoritism from the Commonwealth of the land. Exactly the same interest will be felt if they own and operate the Coal Mines themselves; likewise the Railroads, in common. They would not tolerate a monopoly. They would watch with eager interest, over their own Works. Year after year they would send picked men to the Legislatures and to Congress charged to look after their household interest of fuel and fares. They would gradually grow by this practical urgent of study and become peaceful citizens. Under the present company rule, what has a Congressman to say? Influences are often strongest on the side of wrong. He can sell his vote against the people oftentimes in favor of the Coal and Railroad Companies' lobby Legislation, for which millions are often accumulated in pools. But the interest is so second-hand, so distant, so vague, that the poor people are hoodwinked and bewildered. Could it go so any longer if the government owned these Mines and the avenues leading to and from them? On the contrary; you would see protective organizations among the people which you do not see now. They would study and inquire into the causes of every variation of the price of coal. The housewife would be the one to demand an inquiry. The political club would pass and publish resolutions, and appoint investigating committees. If things still went wrong, the members of Congress from its district would be required to bring the matter before Congress and if the mischief were not speedily rectified, persons more faithful and efficient would find a seat the ensuing sessions. But the healthiest assurance of it all is, that when the business is based upon the Principle of collective instead of individual ownership and control, it will be the *Principle* itself, not its details, that will form the basis of study and organization. At present there exists but one incentive of citizenship. This adds another; *that of being employed by themselves.* Mere details are amendable at will; but a great Principle stands eternal. Not a year rolls round that does not intensify the popular love of this great and successful Principle as exemplified in the Public School system, the Parks, Fire Departments, the Belgian Highways. Yet a public Coal Mine is but another application of the same principle. Under the present system, as has already been seen, neither the Miner nor the consumer of fuel has an accorded right to ask why wages should not be reduced so low as to force men to a stage of starvation, or why the coal should not be raised to ten dollars per ton. The stagnant apathy of the people in such cases of outrage is something sickening. They will not only submit to have the price of coal exorbitantly raised but they will even take the part of their systematic exactors and rail against the poor Miners if they chafe and fret under their hard lot. But this is a mark of popular submission to usage where no great principle is involved. On the whole, it is a good token rather than a bad one. Bring this *Principle* into view, and they will cleave to it with the same dogged tenacity; and the propensity once wheeled and reversed becomes an argument of great power in favor of the reform

In the second place, the advantage would be felt by the Miners themselves. They already possess a Trade Society numbering many thousands. These are all voters. They are, we will suppose, so organized that they submit, almost to a man, to vote for any list of candidates of their own choosing. They are powerful enough to carry an election in certain localities. Add to this the fact that all other Trade Unions and Co-operative Associations in the country are with them in principle, that the Farmers are not without sympathy, and that they have a complete party Organization, and you see no inconsiderable force arrayed and concentrated on the principle. Such forces will work to cheapen coal, to raise the wages of Miners and Laborers, to shorten the day's work and to destroy the profit or speculative incentive. Men claim that the profit incentive and the money wasted in bad management which a Government Mine would avoid by more permanent and scientific appliances, would more than make up for the difference in their wages and shorter time which they need to secure them health and long life. Achieving this difference in wages and time, is raising them from bondage to freedom. So much for the Miners and Railroad employés themselves.

But people at large have an additional interest in the cheapening of coal. The Workingmen do not expect to live by any other system than that of wages; at least for the present. Honorable recompense for a fair day's work is thought by most Workingmen to be productive of about as much liberty and happiness as they can require, so long as they do not cringe under a fear of being dismissed. The Mines being the property of Government and they being voting citizens, each feels himself a stockholder, which intensifies his interest in the work of producing coal for others who are also citizens. There is a feeling always between citizen and citizen, something akin to mutual care. The speculative propensity destroys this. Never till we destroy the speculative incentive or propensity can we enjoy neighbor for neighbor, this feeling of mutual care. Mutual ownership of large works tends inevitably toward it.

EDITOR. Here you strike a subject of acknowledged importance. Journalists who are the closest observers of all forms of social combination, mark that at Labor Congresses, resolutions are always passed which seem, so far as the realization of their import is concerned, utterly absurd. Perhaps there is not one of the many phenomena of this labor imbroglio so obscure as your sweeping proposition regarding State Control over what is now Individual wealth and of subordination of the individual to the State, body and intellect. Workingmen seem bent on forcing out the obvious misnomer which resides in the much mooted term "Commonwealth." But in what manner they ever expect to realize, each his individual competency, by submitting to surrender themselves, or by a complete subversion of individual proprietorship, is a vexed problem. They seem to think that by giving nobody anything they are all going to realize everything; that while all have everything, nobody can have anything!

RESPONSE. We will illustrate this in sweeping prospective views of it. There are forty million inhabitants under the government of the United States. One business of this institution called government, is to watch over and provide laws and regulations for the well being of this government property which is valued at thirty or forty billions of dollars. This entire property, now mostly in the hands of individuals, is supposed to keep us all employed; or at least, to furnish us all some means of support In fact this property is all the people possess by which to get a livelihood. But under the existing arrangement of this means of living, people dependent upon, and eking out a precarious, too often dishonest living from this vast property or Commonwealth, care very little about each other, or each others' happiness. Bickering jealousies and short sighted interests prevent it. But supposing the Coal Mines, in all, worth 100,000,000 were State or Government property; or, what is the same thing, supposing all these Mines were ours in common, instead of being the property of individuals; then each one of the 40,000,000 inhabitants of the nation would actually own, as his, or her share in citizenship or as a vested right, one dollar of value in this Government Property. He would have, not a merely nominal, but a bona fide stock in public property, to that amount. It would not make that citizen rich, to be sure; but it would make him an actual stockholder in that property in common and inseparable with the rest, clothed in the true dignity of guaranteed rights. He can agitate and protest against any infringement of that right. His State becomes a business Co-operation or Society bringing all the mutual interests of neighbors together, which present private ownership in exclusive property fails to do. Now let the government own also the Railroads of the country. They are worth, say $100,000,000 Each citizen then, owns $ 2,50, in Railroads as common property. The Cotton, Woolen, and Flouring Mills are worth as much as the Railroads. So continue adding industry after industry to the government and you continue to augment the value of every citizen's actual, guaranteed claim to this property; the management of which they then have in their own hands collectively; or may have, if they will organize. When all the various properties have been absorbed, each citizen will be worth as many dollars as, 40,000,000, (inhabitants) are contained in the $40,000,000,000, the value of the property of the country; or about 1,000 dollars. This if well managed, will support him for life at six or eight hours of labor per day, which this business is sure to supply. The result will be not only to prompt citizens to augment the value of their property, but also a growing demand for *mutual care* and a steady falling off of the selfish spirit of speculation. These ideas are, during the present century, applying very forcibly to the question of Mines. If the Coal Mines were owned and worked by government, it would behoove all citizens to watch the methods of their management closely. The Miners would sympathize with the citizens and every person must feel it his duty to procure the largest amount of coal with the least labor and cost, and distribute the same most economically, to every household; while the Miners would receive all they claim through the superior economy of govermnent control and the absorption of the speculative spirit of profit.

## CHAPTER VII.

### REASONS WHY RAILROADS, CANALS, RAPID TRANSIT ROUTES AND TELEGRAPH LINES SHOULD BELONG TO THE PUBLIC INSTEAD OF INDIVIDUALS.

Opinions interchanged between members of the Industrial Party and of an association of the Iron and Metal Trades.

---

Brotherhood. There is a subject, too little discussed and too generally suppressed, which touches upon the liberty of the people. As a Brotherhood or fraternal association of the trade or profession of Steam Engineers, a certain society represents not only the family and individual interests of its own members enrolled, but also the interests of many thousands directly and indirectly connected with them. Though it is difficult to unite them all under one administration they nevertheless, interlink their sympathies with the principal organization, because material interests connect, and force them to it. As an instance, the Locomotive Engineers control the destiny of many outside their profession. When a strike is decided upon, it involves the means of life, not only of these experts, but also of all the firemen, conductors, baggage men, brakemen, clerks, porters even the restaurant people and the newspaper boys, those connected with the fuel supply and the way laborers on the route, as well as ticket and telegraph agents, and numbers indirectly connected with this great business along the line of the road.

QUESTION. How does it happen that so small a number as the practical Engineers can command such unlimited, not to say despotic influence over large numbers and varieties of business? And when this question is disposed of, we would like to hear how they defend themselves, if accused, of an outrage upon society, by such an arbitrary action as that of ordering a suspension of the people's important business of transportation and travel.

BROTHERHOOD. Your first interrogative is answered if you recognize that a trade is worth more in practical business, than a knowledge of accounts. To command a complete control of these auxiliaries of the Railroad business, the Engineers have only to organize a small number of these mecanicians themselves. Into this brotherhood they do not admit any whose reputation is bad or who have not received a certificate of qualification through a regular Board of Examination. Such qualification requires the practical knowledge of the machinist trade and considerable knowledge of blacksmithing. Sobriety is required, or the man might wreck his train. Long practice in the art, and close study of the philosophy and construction of the locomotive are required, to make him a perfect master of his dangerous but valuable machine. Good nature is required, or in some unguarded passion he might cause the destruction of the life and property of many innocent people who are often entirely at his mercy. All these requisites of a good Engineer considered, there are few, comparatively, who are competent to pass their examination. Quite different is the estimate regarding a Conductor or almost any other employé of a Railroad. Any trust worthy business man may soon qualify himself for his work. He belongs to a class of accountants; Engineers to a class of practical scientists. It is true their work besmears them and they compare badly in outside appearance with the neatly attired Conductor of the train; but that does not diminish their real faculty. In fact, the Engineers are the true and responsible masters of trains in motion. Consequently a closely organized Brotherhood of all the Engineers of the country can influence the destiny of every individual employed.

Your next interrogative regarding the right of Engineers to suspend an immense public business, requires more elucidation.

LABOR PARTY. Society is like the human body;—formed of great numbers of attributes. It has its vital, its circulating, its repairing, its nervous systems. If you cut off an artery or vein of the strong man even at the extremity of the limbs, you arrest simultaneously the life action at the other extremity. If you destroy a nerve, the death of that delicate organ of vitality may cause also muscle and bone to palsy and die. If you kill the sense of sight the entire organism also gropes in darkness, and intelligence withers because it has lost its means of brilliancy and glory. Any injury to the least as well as the greatest of the innumerable composite parts of this exquisite structure is an outrage to the whole.

So also of society. It is a delicate structure composed of innumerable sympathetic tissues. If you arrest the healthy action of the circulating system, you outrage the whole organism. If you, whose peculiar profession renders you competent to control the interests of greater numbers than yourselves, take advantage of a fortuitous power and order a strike or a suspension of one of the great vital industries of society you instantly cause panic, passion, suffering, to thousands of innocent people a great distance away from the scene. Stop the freight lines and you instantly threaten great numbers of worthy people with starvation in the cities and towns. Yon give advantage to organized speculators on market provisions, who immediately run up the prices of articles which your freight lines convey to market and thus aggravate monoply. Indeed, what else but monopoly in one of its forms is such action of a handful of organized men whose arbitrary, perhaps impassioned decision thus dictates the destiny of ten fold their number?

Brotherhood. Does the Industrial Party condemn the action of this fraternity, in seeking an innocent combination of its members? You speak of society as though it were all harmony; as though its relations were all perfect, and no internal discords existed! But men organize for self protection. A systematic pressure is brought against the fraternity which is a mutual benefit society. Its object is to help the member in times of need by obtaining for him positions, or pecuniary and other friendly assistance. A strike is always a last resort. They have recource to it only when all other means of self-help are cut off and they find themselves face to face before an adversary with bloodshot eyes glaring with greed. This insatiate creature exists in form of a trio of Monopolies;—the owners of all the Railroads, Telegraphs, and Rapid Transit lines, who are inter-combined and bent on reducing wages of all their employés so far as to completely disarm them, while they refuse to reduce fares and freight tariffs in proportion, for the benefit of the people.

LABOR PARTY. Monopoly! Ah; here you touch the true fountain of difficulty. It is one monopoly arrayed against another, with the odds for you in the name of justice. But the difficulty in our comparison just now was that it was intended for society as it *should* be; not for society as it *is;*—disrupted and contorted by competism. In the body there are no elements at war. It is peace. Not a fibre moves that does not thrill in harmony with its neighbor fibres. When this body is in health, all its members co-operate. Nerves, muscles, tendons, veins, arteries and the organs of mind and sense co-work in practical, genial association. No tissue lies idle, but all work. The force and zest of each bears an exact proportion to the task of the whole. The body has its canals, telegraphs railroads, and rapid transit routes for transmitting intelligence, aliment, and exhausted material, to and from all parts, where required. It has engineers, farmers, fuelers, designers, telegraph operators who stand faithfully on duty and never quarrel. Its operatives, humble and pretentious, number millions. No single set of them is in the habit of concocting a strike for higher pay and of suspending work, throwing others out of employment and cutting off the means of support. The body is a sensitive commonwealth which is unaccustomed to brook such spasms. They are death. Every member stands at his post, working, reciprocating composite essentials of a beautiful unity whose glory is mutual love, protection, enjoyment in common, of all the good things of the general whole.

BROTHERHOOD. You overlook a serious decrepancy

in your comparison. We are associated in self defense, from evils of society as it *is;* not in harmony with an imagined society as it *should be.* We find little if any, of the harmonious co-operation you depict in your illustration. Hard experience teaches to our chagrin, that the actual condition of industrial government is the reverse of your glowing example. Instead of common sympathy that thrills life in a living body, there is distracting rivality. Instead of mutual co-operation, or sharing in common, of the labors and products of a railroad, or telegraph, or shipping business, there is one individual or one set of them, to whom is given an unlimited, legalized power to dominate the actual workers, perform no work himself, and arbitrarily, and too often without the least sympathy, dictate to them drudgery and poor compensation. Instead of mutual ownership or life interest in a common whole, the interest is wholly lavished upon this central object of favor, who becomes a despot and all his Engineers, Telegraphers, Captains and other assistants become his slaves. Where mutual co-work and inter-profit resides in the body, nothing but jealousy and distrust resides in the greater worldly body against which this Brotherhood is arrayed in self-defense. Your comparison is poor; for in the place of love, self-support and care, there is little but short-sighted self-interest which engenders a long train of misallotments and their entailments of suffering and petty warfare.

Industrial Party. We understand then, that the cause of your dilemma is the fact that this associated Brotherhood has no common possession of the things to which they contribute their labor. The living body is an industry acting in obedience to the inflexible laws of nature. Nature gives each worker a share of the product of his labor which is amply sufficient for his wants. Nature therefore, or *law* takes the form of government; and all her employes know the law and conform to it. They, from self-interest obey a *principle*; you, crucifying the principle must obey a *master*. Obedience to a natural principle of which he is a part, makes the worker a co-partner in its business. Obedience to a master whom he knows to be prompted only by selfish thoughts for selfish ends, makes the same worker a slave; because in the one case he is himself, *a part and parcel of the principle he obeys.* In the other he is under abject control of *foreign* interests. Nothing then, can remove the difficulty but the *assumption by government of the ownership and management of these thoroughfares* and their operation upon a principle, instead of selfish individual interest. As soon as this is done, your brotherhood will cease to order strikes or otherwise cause a disruption of the business they are entrusted to execute. An instance of the intense, natural interest arising from obedience to a principle, rather than an individual, you will observe in these railroad strikes wherever they threaten to disrupt the business of the Post Office. The brotherhood own this letter-carrying business in common with other citizens; just as one member of the body owns an interest in another; "each for all and all for each." When a strike occurs, this sympathetic feeling shows itself. In the extensive strike of 1877, orders from the leading councils of strikers were issued, forbidding the stoppage of trains carrying the mails. There was a strong feeling on the part of the men in favor of the *mail trains.* This was greatly wondered at by many and was generally observed. It was regarded by some as strange that the mail trains were systematically continued and protected by the strikers themselves. Inspection of the *principle* involved however, shows that it was no marvel whatever. These men owned a certain co-operative share of the contents of the mail train which carried the letters through *government*.

It would have been greatly against their interest to have waged war against the vehicles of the government Post Office. Of all the numerous articles of commercial interchange conveyed by those trains, nothing was theirs in common but the Postal Service of government. This belonged to the Body proper of Society; and was in part, their own. Feeling towards it was harmonious. They felt toward it a protective impulse. To injure it, would have been inconsistent with their possessorship *in* it as fellow citizens, and would have been a violation of an instinct of self defense. So, if the Railroads themselves, the business of which they ordered a suspension, had been likewise, property of government, a similar interest would have articulated between them, and they would have taken far different measures from a strike to redress their grievances. They would have sought the helm of political power.

BROTHERHOOD. It would be disastrous to attempt a sudden change to political action; for while the change were taking place the organization would lose its cohesiveness and perish of discouragement.

RESPONSE. It is not at all advisable to attempt any sudden change. Let them slowly but earnestly introduce a certain plank of political tactics and be satisfied to realize trophy after trophy by it, and your members will all feel an increasing incentive or impulse to organization such as they never before experienced.

BROTHERHOOD. State the character of the plank you

refer to. Persons who have been badly treated, by every political party are not accustomed to venture upon politics.

RESPONSE. That relating to the ownership of Thoroughfares by government. Throughout the Municipal, State and General governments there occur many enormous industries such as the Canals, Public Highways, Telegraphs and so-called Rapid Transit Routes in our cities and towns. This work should come within the power of labor organizations.

BROTHERHOOD. What advantage to us has this labor over any other? It is all of it labor under masters; and men are worse used when so employed than in any other way. There is no advantage in working for government.

REPLY. There is seen an immense advantage in it, when understood; which we want to carefully consider. In the first place GOVERNMENT RAILROADS, TELEGRAPHS and RAPID TRANSIT ROUTES are not individual property. The labor done with them is ordered by the general Community, when they are the property of the public instead of individuals. Votes which created the Heads of all the great public Departments were votes of workingmen. These men are employés of the people. Being yourselves the Community, and these public works in the interest of the Community, they are yours. It is no longer an individual industry for one man or company but a Community of interests. Hence the workingmen have a right to demand to be employed upon them; and it is a right of the engineers to turn the force of their organization toward securing better positions than they now hold. A co-possessorship in a government Railroad would bring back home feelings. This is their first and only incentive to organization; and when they wheel their force into line and combat for this guaranty of labor as a political *principle* they will see opened before them a mightier love of organization than they now realize. It will perhaps, be strong enough to sweep all into organization instead of a part. The procurement of daily food and shelter is the first incentive that actuates all creatures. Lions, tigers, bears, dogs, birds, reptiles fight for it. Men kill each other for it. The means of perpetuating existence is worth thinking, organizing or even fighting for. By the nature of things it is the first incentive for community among men. Had we all we could eat, drink, wear and require for shelter freely furnished us and were not in needof protection, we should not need government. Wanting these, we depend more or less upon a government to furnish them. This is natural; and a government that supplies but a part is defective. Men want something more than protection. Food, clothes, homes, labor are necessary; and governments are learning to supply them as well as protection, which has hitherto been supposed the exclusive function of government and is yet the chief theme of political economists. Government in fact, is a combination for mutual protection and support; and its legitimate duty is to supply citizens a sufficiency of both. All functions of government then, are greater than the functions of trade combinations; because the government is for the mutual protection and support of all citizens. Yet while individuals and companies are wrongfully getting political control of it and working it in their interests, thereby excluding the true workers from its protection and support, these workers are organizing to secure slavery for themselves instead of independence. Were they to work directly for government as they would if at work directly for such Public Highways, they would work for themselves; and would then work for a true Commonwealth. Continuing to work for outside companies and individual managers who have no common interest in them, their labor continues to be what is called wage slavery, and *your organization is only a means of enforcing the privilege of remaining in this bondage.* If they discharge people from their service, it is because their mastery over them is absolute; and they repudiate their claim to enslavement by disowning them. No wonder that more than one half of those who work at the various trades are unable to see a sufficient incentive to combination to keep them organized. All that which in the government, or co-operative industry is paid extra, to make men comfortable, or is abated from their hours to make them manly and independent, in other words, all that which government employment offers them in form of increased wages and short hours, goes to the individual or company in form of profit or dividend. With the toiler is left nothing but reduced wages and social inequality.

BROTHERHOOD. Among other points of interest appears a hint that there are two separate and distinct incentives of citizenship both attributes of a good state of society; that in ordinary citizenship, or where government does not furnish labor as well as protection, only one is used; and that to organize upon these two incentives is to quicken the hopes of humanity.

LABOR PARTY. Our first incentive is the very natural one of self protection, and causes us to be constantly watching for means of obtaining food and shelter. The second incentive is that which we all, as citizens, feel, in favor of good government. Every citizen feels it. Even the individual managers of public industries, however much they may be actuated by personal interest, naturally feel actuated to some extent by this incentive. But it is not powerful enough to combine all. The best part of the people are uncombined. Disgusted with the dishonesty of public rulers and regarding them with a feeling, that to meddle with such corruption is disgrace, they remain away from the polls and thus permit the country's corrupters to carry out their designs unmolested. Some of our good Labor Organizations may be said to rank among these. They have voted to abstain from politics. Doing this is virtually voting not to interfere or in any way stop the career of such demagogues associated to sap the foundations of republicanism and who are leading work-people into captivity,

The second incentive with vague abstractions and theories, has never been strong enough to keep government pure. Exclusively protective governments have resulted in little more than guarding frontier lines, nationalism, jealousies and war. Under its rule, republican governments may seem solid, and may excel abject monarchies in point of enterprise, but there is lacking the first and stronger incentive to pure government. We find lacking the incentive to a citizenship which *provides the peaceful business element of supply*. We find lacking another incentive to combination strong enough to force all chosen Officers of State, to farm productive industries and to distribute their proceeds at cost among the people. There is lacking a determination to kill the commissioning system of executing work; to supplant it with one that works without proxy, from government, direct to people;—the first incentive to citizenship, which will make governments integral, and eternal.

## CHAPTER VIII.

. . . . . . . .

## GENERAL VIEWS, FEELINGS AND EXPRESSIONS OF THE WEALTHY AND HIGH IN POWER, CONCERNING POLITICO-INDUSTRIAL ORGANIZATION.

---

### Colloquy between an Advocate of a Political Party and a Conservative Doctor of Laws.

. . . . . . . . . . . . . . . .

Political Economist. Professional men in law and jurisprudence have been giving attention to the movement of the Working People and observe some very startling points and propositions in certain Circulars issued by those of the Atlantic Seaboard Cities, but nothing remarkably radical or advanced in any of those of the West. What is the cause of this striking difference?

Industrial Party. The radical nature of the Labor propositions is always in proportion with the age of the theatre of congregated Labor. But your discovery is a little late; for the West has already taken up the subject from its depths. The Labor *Principle* —that is to say, the Points at issue of the Labor Movement assume a stronger tone as the Working people study their Question, and as their Organizations grow. The movement is natural to all races and all lands. It belongs alike in the east and in the west; and as it develops, will not confine itself to localities.

QUESTION. What is meant by the term workingmen, or work people?

LABOR PARTY. They are used in a generic sense applying to both sexes and to all grades of useful labor, including teachers and operators of telegraphs, or of musical instruments as well as of hammers, lathes and plows. The term "working classes" or "working people," in labor phrase, sounds awkward; and the term "workingmen" has obtained a recognition as a plain, homely, and expressive word which includes both sexes. Our English language is not as clear in regard to this expression as the German, French or Spanish. We have no simple word that translates *Arbeiter*, or *Ouvrier*, or *Trabajador*. In Latin, the word *Vir*, man, and *Mulier*, woman, and their plurals were rendered in collective expression by *Homo, Homines*. Our language lacks these significant and conciliatory terms. We therefore trust you will not find fault with homely generalities.

POLITICAL ECONOMIST. Why is this movement called essentially the labor problem?

LABOR PARTY. Because established fact, or science comes from mechanics. Voluntary effort, or effort toward the accomplishment of an object, is labor. Theory is unelaborated effort and is not and cannot be science until it is made palpable to our senses. To do this, instruments are required. The moment a wish, ideal, or theory uses an instrument however rudimental with which to build for itself a palpable shape, it borrows from mechanics. Mechanical instrumentalities are, therefore, the means of science. Human hands alone can shape and direct these instruments. Such is Labor; and as the doing of this labor involves the means of existence, it becomes the most important of all questions how labor and its product shall be economized and allotted.

POLITICAL ECONOMIST. The position that science derives from mechanics, needs explanation.

ANSWER. It can be proved, even admitting that all knowledge originates in intuition and genius; though this is by no means the case; for many valuable things are found out by mere fortuity. Discovery of principles which combine and form a sewing machine, a history, or a telegraph, is done by an instrument. The brain is that instrument. It is a species of mechanical instrument. It is a mechanism. It is therefore, not the least point in the Labor Problem to prescribe that the brain be rightly cared for. Bringing these mechanical devices into palpable form and running condition requires a great variety of mechanical skill. Agassiz and Humbolt were scientists; but they were also mechanics. They wrought science; that is, they brought knowledge into the world, and shaped and accommodated it to the perception of others. They could not have done this without the aid of mechanical instruments. Humboldt in measuring the volume of water in river beds and the altitude of mountains, used instruments. Agassiz used instruments in his deep sea soundings. Professor Silliman's Laboratory is a marvel of mechanical art. No scientist could develop a theory without great mechanical skill either in himself or in others. All sciences depend directly upon mechanics.

POLITICAL ECONOMIST. But the greater part of those engaged in this so called Labor movement view the Question in a narrower light.

ANSWER. If they do, ignorance must excuse their error. The truth is, this is not so much a social question as one of Political Economy; and its agitation may be stated as proportionate to the general enlightenment of the human race. A story of the grades of human development makes this fact clear.

POLITICAL ECONOMIST. Working people are jealous of every new invention that capitalists apply to save labor, as well as to lengthen life. It is well known that in many cases where life-saving apparatus have been applied to prevent the cutting out of the lungs as in the case of the steel grinders of Sheffield and in other ways, the men have revolted and combined against it as an intolerable innovation. It is difficult to see any economy in this, political or personal.

LABOR PARTY. There is much meant, which a casual observer does not see. Industries necessarily assume forms and customs. The usages of the workmen are gradually conformed to these; and they have learned, by grim experience to keep on the alert; since oftentimes the least innovation however valuable, is sufficient to change the custom or usage of a particular class of work and displace the workmen. Now, in the case of the Steel grinders, we do not attempt to defend them either from a philosophic, or hygienic point of view; but only excuse their action as the necessary effect of a current circumstance. It is true that the dust of steel when constantly inhaled, is almost certain to produce pulmonary disease. The average length of life of those engaged in this trade is only thirty years; and it must be regarded as something very desirable to invent any attachment, which, without lessening the amount of work performed, would lengthen a lifetime from thirty years, the present average, to sixty years, the average of the farmers who breathe pure air.

But the poorest toiler has neither time nor disposition to consider this question of health. He has a family to support. For his labor he receives barely enough to exist from week to week. Deprive him of a place to which he is accustomed and before he can accustom himself to another his family must starve. Now the simple alteration proposed, may so affect the steel grinder's vocation that it will require a more expert, or even a less ingenious hand to perform the labor, and this may involve his displacement. A dread of these constantly recurring innovations is what actuates him to organized resistance. Workingmen have been called stupid on account of this resistance; but their interest is to handle only such matters as have a practical bearing upon their daily means of support.

POLITICAL ECONOMIST. You say this whole so-called Labor Problem is one of Political Economy exclusively. It sounds vague. All the world is in the habit of treating it as an entirely social affair. Books of all the Socialist Authors make little mention of political elements in it and treat it as an exclusively Social Question.

LABOR PARTY. Our Labor Movement is in its infancy. As it comes out into the broad light of public discussion it takes a political form, and strikes for Economic Emancipation,

LAWGIVER. It looks like a questionable venture, to treat a subject which involves the social happiness of millions of families, under the head of Politico-Economics. Do you not agree that it is the social status of the Working class which the movement is trying to elevate?

RESPONSE. We might question the good taste of writers and thinkers, who give things inappropriate names. It is politico-economic in its true character. Why it is a political problem is because it can only be solved by political means, through the operation of Economical methods. Social conditions indicate society at rest;—the avenues by which we may enjoy, *established.* Economical conditions indicate society in evolution, or agitation. The producing of these means of social enjoyment is, and usually has been the work of gradual legislation. The claim of the Workingmen is that these means are not yet established. The condition of the bondsmen, in chattel slavery, was termed a social one. But that supine condition, apart from degrading, and disfranchising 4,000,000 of the people, and shocking every lover of humanity to revolt, was found by experiment, when taken in full consideration by the great nation, to be *politically*, a failure. It became a subject of national discussion; Then it was political. Despotisms of other countries looked upon its overthrow as the beginning of a political revulsion that would not end until it reached the wage slavery system upon which their own thrones stood. It was, after forty years of investigation by the nation, as a committee of the whole, found to be a vast political evil that entered largely into Legislatures, Municipal Councils, and Congress. Its power made and upheld great numbers of public offices and furnished legislative work for unnumbered law-givers from the constable to the Senator, even to Presidents of the United States. Who then, will contend that the Slave Problem was not a Political one? Was the war of the Rebellion a political or a social affair? Yet what are the general points of difference between chattel slavery and wage slavery? This Labor Question is clearly a political one demanding attention from the nation's political economists. It demands the entire people's active attention. If chattel bondage was an economic failure, this is an economic waste. If chattel slavery exhausted the soil and made the country poor, wage slavery makes the intellect poor. If the nation repudiated chattel slavery as a luxury, so must it repudiate wage slavery. Both conditions demand equally the study and wise executive ability of mankind in order to further true political interests. One thing is certain:—the mere agitations of working people are unproductive of anything realizable except through legislative channels. No proposition comes up that can be solved by mere social talk. It requires intense and assiduous activity or *motion* in a political direction. The social condition proper, is a condition of *rest* —a situation that regards things calmly, as finished. In other words, the true social question belongs to the intimate affairs of private life; and even then, the body politic watches it, for stagnation and decomposition follow rest. Incorrect allotment must then be the natural result. Not a proposition can the workingman make, looking toward his advancement, that does not involve fierce discussion of a political nature, and generally the creation of some statute. A political condition is one of activity. A social condition, one of quiet. The labor question is intensely political for these reasons; and involves for its solution the study and statesmanship of workingmen and women; and though they may look toward a future social condition for the human race, it now belongs to Jurisprudence; since its solution involves the democracy of co-operation. It is no erotic affair, but a strife for law, liberty and bread.

POLITICAL ECONOMIST. Your labor co operations are not generally considered successful. Workingmen are struggling despondently over the practical application of what is called the co-operative principle. The character of American institutions seems to be adverse to it. Conflicting elements manage to break up many efforts at co-operation and there is scarcely a co-operative store, land society, or industry left. Some thief is sure to succeed in getting appointed as custodian of the funds and the poor workingmen are swindled. The fickleness of American people, is something remarkable. The workman of to-day is the proprietor of to-morrow; and this ambition which is both popular and laudable throws life into a constant succession of changes, which involves petty emulations, defeats, and triumphs over each other. We see too much antagonism in American people for co-operation; they are too restless to co-operate; too busy with their own thoughts and hopes; too adventurous. The average American workingman at fifty has had at least one house of his own, been a foreman two or three times, a boss once, been West and settled on a farm, been a property owner, and has had a more chequered life than he will acknowledge; and after all these vicissitudes to which the Trans-Atlantic Workingman is a total stranger, his mind is in no condition to settle down to the paltry idea of co-operating with his neighbor for cheapening the means of life. Now under such circumstances and in the face of the fact that nearly all attempts of workingmen to co-operate for mutual support are failing around us, what hope can you entertain of ever solving the industrial problem in this way?

Answer. Simply by allowing co-operation its natural *political* course.

Political Jurist. We are not clear about the possibility of business enterprise connecting with political action.

ANSWER. Working people alone are forced by grim circumstances to see this clearly; and are beginning to agitate upon a basis of politico-co-operation.

POLITICAL ECONOMIST. Can you cite one instance where your idea has ever been carried out?

RESPONSE. Most certainly. All operations in the United States of which the carrying out is indispensable to community, are the result of the people's co-operation. It is a truism that "the judgment of the masses is purer, surer, and more reliable than the judgment of individuals, when that judgment can be rendered in council." This is as true as the statistical fact, that nine elevenths of all individual enterprises are failures. The great war of the rebellion was a clear case of hearty, popular co-operation through the government. The people had discussed the evils of slavery for many years; and under that school of discussion generations had been born and educated. The majority finally agreed in the opinion that slavery must be put away; and it was done. Their decision was carried out. It was the spirit of co-operation which accomplished it. But the country teems with other specimens. The Steam Fire Departments of our cities are splendid examples and a living proof that the Municipal Government is more capable of performing vast and complicated business than any individual, or company of them. Would the people feel secure if their preservation from the great destroyer, fire, were left to the desultory action of an individual? The Fire Department belongs to the people; is co-operated in, by the people; watched over by the people. Its defects are felt, investigated, censured, corrected, by the people. So far as it goes, it is the community taking charge of the people; and is a co-operative enterprise, whereby each and all have an intense individual interest in the collective management of an *appliance* of protection. Is that not co-operation?

LAWGIVER. It must be admitted; but what has this to do with the labor question? Workingmen are not as intimately interested in the fire department as the owners of property. Indeed from the character of their strikes and the fierceness with which they conduct their evolutions, they seem to have more sympathy with the destroyer than with the preserver. They often boast that the more destroyed, the greater will be the amount of labor in the market for them.

LABOR PARTY. The labor problem as the term implies, is too homely and practical to consort in any grace, with mere theory. The world is now rapidly coming out upon a broader field of practical economies. The fact that nearly nine tenths of our best citizens fail in their efforts to succeed in independent business is the bar over which individualists cannot climb; and it is the corner stone of the new faith in collectivism.

LAWGIVER. Do the masses expect to become a unity? Do they sincerely expect that this collective judgment of all, or of a numerical majority, can wisely dictate the course of industries?

RESPONSE. It is safe thus to reason. First from the success of the postal department in which the general government has almost mastered the company system and nearly caused it to disappear. This bureau is now conducted by the people who, profiting by each year,s experience legislate, improve and extend it yearly. Such is this great National Bureau, wherein community have daily, almost hourly interest. It is an intensely political, as well as co-perative industry. When all officers of this Bureau are elected by the people instead of being appointed, it will make it still more political thus quickening the spirit of co-operation in the people who are to be served or annoyed by the delivery or non-delivery of their goods. In either case, the Bureau for distributing the country's literature is a national co-operative enterprise, working with a marvelous rapidity and precision, extending its almost traceless ramifications throughout the whole nation. It extends to the homes of an immense population whether far or near, and if they wander beyond boundary lines, seeks them out as unerringly, through international articulation, and is thus made universal. Supposing now, all this wonderful net-work were the property of one man. It is doubtful whether any business man exists who has the ability to dispense it. But we will, for the sake of argument, allow that there is an individual possessing great business ability, who, by the monopoly of instrumentalities for moving and distributing the mails might arrive at that result. Would not the Postal Bureau become an intolerable monopoly? What good would legislation do? What redress shall people obtain of abuses in any outside industry? We should be left no appeal. Would it not arrest one of the important business affairs which voters send men to Congress to look after?

Allowing imagination a wider range, suppose that we give other branches of present legislative business to similar monopolies until there remains nothing to send representatives to Congress for; and we find the land a despotism! It is just these few advantages poor people possess, of legislating business affairs, which distinguishes us from arbitrary governments. In the example of the Bureau referred to, if the people are not satisfied they must blame themselves. Let it be explained, that it answers as a prompter to the workingmen to demand that the same form of collective business go farther and supersede present individualist forms in other necessary enterprises which now fail twice out of eleven attempts.

Lawgiver. The assertion that nine industries in eleven are failures would fortify your argument better, if it had foundation in probability. Workingmen are notorious for random averments; and are continually coining guesswork for positive fact. Is it not more probable that no such a percentage actually fails?

Labor Party. Not only do nine elevenths of all individual enterprises fail inside the first seven years, but it is equally true that four fifths of the different Government enterprises are successful if we except those of war, where one or the other of the contestants only, succeeds, and where both lose largely.

Political Economist. What essential difference do you draw between this founder of a great company business and a collective body or Commonwealth that possesses similar faculties?

Labor Party. Supposing this imagined manager of the business in question, after getting his vast industry satisfactorily arranged, dies. As a consequence, the animus of the enterprise which this man has studied and brought to a successful issue, dies with him; because he has failed to instruct others to his own *standard of capability*. This is the inevitable fate of individual enterprises, and is one reason why so large a percentage fails. But in a government enterprise the *régime* is reversed. A government enterprise is collectively controlled from the first. The monopolist referred to who operates this business system through his personal genius, is proud of his secret. Such men generally die without leaving even to their own children, their business secret. Their death is a calamity; because the world needs business ability, though it were selfishly applied. It should be the duty of a people, in a collective sense, to make a study of this business secret of the individual and to carefully teach the collectivity —that is, the body politic,—the same principles of management, for collective use, which the individual has worked out, for individual use. To perpetuate the knowledge of business management wrought by the sagacity and tact of individuals and to inculcate this tact upon the public mind, is to make the spirit of co-operative business through *government*, take the place of individual business through monopoly. Masses cannot afford to lose a great business. These successive losses are a cause of the large percentage of failures. Let people get this business secret and it will *never die*; for although individuals may come and go, and be subject to the vicissitudes of event and change, yet legislative knowledge and tact is ever gradually upward, keeping pace with the progress of human enlightenment, and is absolutely imperishable. It is always improved by practical experience through youth and age as it passes from generation to generation.

Political Economist. No method in business can exist without some basis or theory, and the details of such business are predicated of this theory. Upon what theory do you found this new democracy or ballot co-operation?

Labor Party. Upon the ballot as the only natural share of citizenship. What proves fatal to our small association, is the inequality and changeableness of shares. Fix them upon the *one share, and one priced share basis*, and they are likely to succeed. Otherwise they become a prey to monopoly or are ripped and routed by competitions. Neither one of these evils — competition or monopoly — can enter into Ballot Co-operation. Why? Because the ballot is the exponent, or practical expression of a want, which is felt within the individual. The ballot is a legalized edict. It is indivisible and cannot be multiplied; and if the caster be wise, it is unmonopolizable. Every one feels deep in his nature that if he has a right to exist, he has a right to the means of existence. In the ballot only can this feeling find expression with majorities. In the collective industry each citizen feels this intense personal interest. He has one share in ballot co-operation, and no less;—the ballot share. The government ought to multiply its functions by making them assume many distributive and manufacturing enterprises. It is only in augmenting the number and volume of these public industries that the public can realize the dignity and profit of their inheritance of the citizenship which is expressed in the ballot. What is a share in citizenship? It is nothing unless accompanied by some useful material. The biggest infatuation the public can fall into is to suppose that a commonwealth, every acre of whose land and every manufacturing and distributive industry of which may be taken away from them by the aptest and luckiest of their numbers! The true future value and glory of the citizen's ballot rests in the clue it furnishes him to get these industries and lands into enjoyable fractions, by means of the right or share of citizenship. This can only be realized in *collective ownership:* and if each citizen owns a single untransmissible life share of one such property in common with the rest, it follows that a large number of such properties would be equivalent to a fortune for him. The management of these source-tributaries of their wealth would then make it a Commonwealth indeed.

POLITICAL ECONOMIST. Is not every manifestation of business growth after all, contrary to the very principle involved in this plan of letting government absorb the control of our industries? We see on every hand that the freedom we enjoy only gives license to individuals who possess superior tact or business capacity. The greater number of the people do not possess these talents and fall the prey of a few who do. Mechanics apply themselves in the same manner. Our gifted business man buys a machine which performs the work of a dozen men with their empty nands. It used to require all their time. Now one man, with a machine can do it. What becomes of the eleven? The world is getting full of these business facilities. A little while ago all the small shops in the streets were occupied. Now they are vacant. In place of them, we see some colossal establishment systematically dispensing the needs of the people at a cheaper and more satisfactory rate than has hitherto been done by these numerous, smaller concerns. How many small dry goods stores have been annihilated by the superior method of A. T. Stewart & Co!

LABOR PARTY. This is a most cogent reminder of the progress of science but it is fraught with dangers. It will not do as we are continually arguing, to permit such great establishments which thus supersede and destroy the old and comparatively petty methods of our fathers, to fall exclusively into the hands of individuals. They run into monopolies. The profit incentive of the individual beggars the less lucky masses. Great establishments must thrive for their economical merits. The world needs them, but they must belong to the people as a collective body. Business concerns must be operated by the State. How long must the people be humiliated by a diseased and chronic system of supply? How long must their homes, food, fuel, clothes and other necessaries be doled out to them by mere individuals with special legislation under their control, who operate for special interests? Such persons if unchecked, assume a very arbitrary purveyorship for the defenseless masses, who are, in this way, chained too low to be dangerous; and bind the thongs of poverty and infatuate slavery around them. How long must this last, in the dazzle of such an enlightened age as this, when people have no better excuse for their miseries than apathy and ignorance? A little political organization of the truly useful classes; a little imitation of those magnificent examples already under State control, whose very splendor mocks them; a little wholesome combination of independent work in the direction of Self-Help, would sweep away the shackles from their limbs, the cobwebs from their vision, the lethargy from their nerves, and launch them out upon a field of co-operative economy redundant in manhood and gladness.

## CHAPTER IX.

. . . . . . . . . . . .

### REVIEWING AND SENSING THE POLITICAL PHASES OF THE RISING QUESTION OF LAND AND TIME.

DIALOGUE BETWEEN DWELLERS UPON FARMS AND IN CITIES. FORESHADOWING AN OMINOUS CRISIS.

. . . . . . . . . . . . . . . .

AGRICULTURIST. THE FARMERS WHO ENTERTAIN a lively recognition of the general importance involved in the Labor Movement see much that is worthy of serious contemplation and are preparing to admit even the possibility of a revolution, feel disposed to hold interviews with pioneers of the Labor Party as an expedient, notwithstanding a general belief pervading their organizations, that the theory embraced in the Labor Platform is impracticable.

MEMBER OF THE LABOR PARTY. Then we are honored by an interview with persons in a passive rather than a combative state of mind; and must at once assure them that these are by no means impracticable ideas, but that they are highly practical and apply to immediate home necessities of the whole industrial people, the occupants of the land included.

FARM LABOR. We want to know how they can be so twisted as to apply to that very numerous branch known as Agriculturists. Why should the Farmer take an interest in the question of diminishing the hours of labor?

CITY LABOR. Our Eight Hour Movement sprang out of the increased facilities of machinery for production. Every new mechanical contrivance saves some of the old tugging labor which our forefathers were obliged to perform by the long process of manual toil. Wares of commerce are now produced by machinery fifty percent more rapidly than at the beginning of this century, when people worked from twelve to sixteen hours a day; and twenty percent faster still than in the third, fourth and fifth decade of this century when people worked ten hours a day. The change, therefore, was scientifically correct; the diminution of time being in a mathematical ratio with the increased facilities of production.

FARM LABOR. Your calculations refer exclusively to manufacture. What about Agriculture and distribution?

CITY LABOR. In Agriculture we see a great wrong. Nearly the same increase of the facilities of production exists on the farm that is observable in the factory, machine shop or builder's yards; but while the employés of in-door industries have talked, studied, agitated and partially succeeded in procuring from time to time, a commensurate abatement of hours, Farmers have done little in any direction. They have organized to economize Farm products for the well-to-do proprietors, but have said too little about the drudgery of their help. The same old non-progress humdrum exists. A poor Farmer Boy continues to rise at daylight, do the milking, feed and harness the horses and clean the stables. This is his recreation before going to work.

After this pastime he must plow, drag, harvest or make hay, for twelve long hours, during the warm weather. In winter he is turned out of work entirely; and hunger stares him in the face. All this in a free country where serfdom and slavery are ignored. Compare this Farmer Boy with a young mechanic who enjoys the short day's labor!

FARM LABOR. The comparison is scarcely fair; because the Farm has not yet received as much benefit from labor saving machinery as the mechanical industry.

RESPONSE. This is one of the reasons for making the comparison. The Farm has not developed the boy as has the In-Door Industry. If it had, he would have applied inventions of his own. Farm work still keeps him down. He remains in a state of ignorance; while the mechanic has had a few meagre opportunities. Besides, the mechanic has been subject to a monopoly fastened by speculators, upon his labor saving inventions, which has gluttonously devoured most of his opportunities; while the Farm, by its peculiar character, cannot be subject to the concentrating work of monopoly, to any great extent, except in distribution, or the sale of produce after it is raised. True, there is a monopoly, to some extent in the manufacture and sale of most labor saving implements of Agriculture, such as reapers, mowers, threshing machines, and even the bricks and lumber of which the Farmers build. This, Farmers find, can be abated by *co-operation*, but it cannot be called a monopoly of the instruments in any way conflicting with the wages and hours of the Farmer Boy in question. The study of the age is, how to free the poor and helpless from drudgery that makes them slaves; how to realize *Economical Enfranchisement;* how to best cultivate and apply mechanics as an economic means. In the case of the young mechanic, we already find that the labor-saving instruments produced since the opening of the century have notwithstanding a terrible monopoly of their uses, by individuals and companies, actually liberated him from the old serf drudgery of bygone ages *in proportion as they have shortened his day's work.* The agricultural laborer continues to work from twelve to fourteen hours a day; although an almost incalculable advantage has been realized in agriculture through the introduction of labor-saving instruments. What result do we see? The mechanic, though far less educated than he ought to be, already begins to feel himself a man. He is shuffling off his clogs. His fustian, corduroy, hickory and iron drab are exchanged for the fashion cut. His wan, expressionless eye assumes the keener flame of an unhindered development; and the painful gait, stooping stature, and mournful effort at manliness have so improved that among wage mechanics good appearance need no longer be forced to have effect. Young mechanics are indeed respectable although few are able to find employment more than two thirds of the year. If then, the mechanics have cause for agitating the subject of still greater improvement how much more cause have their suffering neighbors of the Farm to complain of their still unmitigated condition! The comparison must not be understood to refer to the sons of well-to-do farmers who are not obliged to toil but to that great class of hired men and women at this moment doing the hard Farm labor; and who like the mechanics and their wives, sisters and daughters, have no other means but their hands for support.

FARM LABOR. Fault must again be found with this seeming want of fairness. We understand that the great Labor Question touches the whole Farming Community;

employers, as well as our employés. A great political subject like this must not be confined within narrow borders, but should engross all.

CITY LABOR. We are weaving two extremes into an argument which will soon engross us all in the web. The question with all is, with regard to the unscientific use to which the whole machinery of production and distribution is surrendered. Everything in farming as well as in mechanics depends upon the *economic uses of productive facilities.* These subjects we are digesting do not belong either to morality or equity, in the light in which these terms are accepted in society. They are matters of severe science in the adjustment of physical forces to economics. The effect of this adjustment is as computable as an algebraic equation. It is sure to produce more equitable relations in men and things; *is not merely supposable but positively certain.* Science knows no more about conscientious equity or ethics, excepting so far as carrying natural law into effect is concerned, than the inanimate Spinning Jenny. The world must learn to study nature more and accepted usage less. Get hold of solid material and learn to shape its uses so that it will produce and equitably distribute the greatest possible amount of good material with the least possible effort; for in exact proportion as society learns this, will the labor problem come to solution. Within the last hundred years the truly wonderful acceleration of practical, inventive genius has abridged the mechanics' days' work about three hours while it has had no co-equal effect upon the large and useful class of farmers, likewise non-property owners. Can a nation afford this, knowing that the progress of invention is about in proportion with the leisure and consequent disinthrallment of body and mind? Many things have been invented and set successfully at work doing that which formerly was done by hand; but there is much left to be discovered. We have the means of accomplishing with facility, much that formerly cost great pains and patience to produce; but we have yet to invent and apply means by which to correctly distribute these productions. This requires the intelligence of every citizen. What sort of economy is this then, that allows the intelligence of hired men to lie perpetually inactive? Farmers themselves cannot afford it, neither can the nation at large. Do not the sons and daughters of the soil lack many intellectual accomplishments which more leisure and training afford? Comparatively few of our farmers' children feel qualified to go in the company of the young clerks, law, medical or art students or even mechanics of our neighboring towns and villages. It is not because they *cannot* command leisure so much perhaps, as because the whole farming community are in the habit of drudging; and even the grand inroads of economics which the science of mechanics brings forth seem insufficient to turn them from this almost deadly habit of overdoing. The Farmers, most certainly, are thinking people; yet they do not think enough, in proportion as they work too much. A healthy man may work eight hours a day even at hard farm work and think every hour of this time; but if he works longer than this fatigue will arrest his study. If he continues to work twelve hours, bodily fatigue is perpetual; and thought is driven perpetually from his intellect. No wise and really prosperous Farmer can afford more than an average of six hours manual labor per day. With this amount of bodily exercise the easy Farmer attains his greatest average longevity; that of sixty two years! Only the representatives of one class of business men attain this age —the accountants. Many of our most useful tradesmen such as the machinists, glass blowers, steel grinders, brass finishers and of several unskilled occupations die at the average age of thirty two. Gradually an extra lease of average life may, with safety be credited to them, equal in proportion to the amount of time abated from an excessive day's work. So long a life of the thrifty farmer cannot be attributed solely to his advantages of pure air and healthy surroundings; for we find that the average age of the agricultural laborers of Great Britain is only forty eight years. It is not only a great inhumanity to ourselves to exact more than eight hours per day, but it is a bad financial economy leading to disaster. You see by a careful scanning of facts, that there scarcely exists an argument in favor of the long day's work which is not grossly on the side of savagery and human degradation.

Farm Labor. It is desirable also to obtain interchange of opinion with reference to the best manner of distributing farm products. This subject must naturally treat of great Railroad monopolies whose dangerous combinations threaten to intercept and drag down free interchange between the agriculturists of the interior and the consumers of the seaboards. Plainly this evil can never be uprooted until Farmers have the means of conveyance in their own hands. In order to avert this growing difficulty farmers combine with each other; and begin to appreciate the need of an extensive mutual combination with the workers of the cities. Might not a great advantage be thus procured, especially if such railroad lines and water communications necessary for transporting the supplies of both, could be arranged between them entirely independent of the transportation companies? But there are insurmountable difficulties attending co-operation of this kind.

City Labor. People living in cities are acquainted with many of the theories and projects of Farmers, and there are many adherents to them. A favorite idea with the Farmers is to restrict and regulate the freight tariff by legislative enactment and in this way control monopoly.

But this will be slow to succeed. It is true these restrictions will for a time be resorted to as a means of combating the encroachments of great companies. It is the first flank movement upon the enemy. Being the army of resistance Farmers naturally become the army of revolution. Monopoly is the old monarchy revived. A monarch is one who has the power of government concentrated upon himself. It makes little difference whether that power have control over the destinies of men direct, or over the means of their existence. The difficulty to be corrected is brought on by an *accaparement*, and absolute exploiture of the instruments of transportation by individualists actuated by an impulse of exclusive personal gain. All was going well and the building of railroad lines throughout the country in times past was looked upon as a necessary improvement to the country so long as it was in the hands of many companies and there was competition. But gradually the roads are being leased or bought up by such individuals as are shrewdest in control and thus the management of these combinations is turned over to one, instead of many competing companies. The inevitable tendency is toward concentration of our transportation lines, upon *one man*. "Man," typically used, may represent one company or one knot of men vulgarly called a "Ring"

But be sure of one thing, that certain as the law of natural selections, this one company, knot of men, or ring, will always be composed of those who possess the greatest aptitude and grasping ability to manage; for it is by their superiority over other competitors that they get control. This is monarchical in an intense degree; and should be repudiated with the same spirit in which an invading army of a despotic monarch would be repudiated. It is a despotism which may inflame elements of civil war; for it is an onslaught against popular liberty. Should a monarchy undertake to concentrate around a throne the management of the United States and Territories, the people would regard it as an attempt to monopolize their business and a war would be as natural as the uprising of the Farmers against monopoly. A people imbued with the spirit of freedom, arouse and shake off the yoke by force. So they must shake off the yoke of this great transportation monopoly or they will soon find themselves and their industrial interests subordinated to them. But the fathers of all free institutions have always resorted to many a feint and sally before they came to the final grapple with the enemy. So we shall have to resort to all the strategy of legislative restriction, prudential coaxing, and temporary commutations; but the evil remains abroad, and will exist. It is a tumor upon the democracy of the people. We may doctor it but it will grow afresh. It *must be cut out, deracinated.* The railroads must be delivered over to the State and become property of the people.

Farm Labor. But the people have a peculiar dislike of this idea and cite us to the different governments of the world that have adopted the management of railroads, telegraphs and other public works by the monarchical governments, as proof that the system is monarchical and that rather than being diffusive and democratic, it is concentrative in tendency.

City Labor. This is another of many mistakes. The power of central government over public industries of all kinds invariably tends toward popular control; while the power of individual management, invariably leans toward exclusivism. Napoleon Third, one of the severest despots of modern times who was able to perpetuate his reign for twenty years by sheer stifling and fanatacizing the intellect of a great people who rank among the intensest lovers of freedom, found it convenient to keep the railroads out of government control; because the people claimed everything belonging to government, as theirs. Masses never think of claiming that which is owned and managed by individuals. Great railroad companies who were the subservient instruments of monarchy, were thus enabled to monopolize the carrying trade, raise the tariffs to a high rate and enrich themselves by exacting from, and humiliating the people. Close on the borders of France is another monarchy having exclusive control of more than half her railroads. All the world is gazing and calculating upon the results and learning an incalculably important lesson. Little Belgium under the very shadow and frown of her giant neighbor is teaching all people a lesson in this most radical branch of political economy. Her government possesses the railroads and works them in the interest of the people. The whole labor movement is inspired by it into the profoundest hope. Switzerland awakes to find her republican government a monarchy, to the extent that railways telegraphs and canals are avenues of despotism. Italy sees the incompatibility of railway monopoly with her huge progress and is buying up her southern lines. Germany exacts a fourth class government conveyance to accommodate her people. England is cautiously, and successfully applying the same principle to some of her home and colonial lines. Belgium in many respects though a kingdom, is the freest government in the world; and king, people, and representatives are enacting laws and regulations which exclude monopoly from railroad management. The price of railway travel and of freight is astonishingly low as a consequence; because the government has no desire to make a profit out of it. It is conducted on the principle of *serving the people at cost.* Now we have a freer government, theoretically speaking than the people of Belgium; yet our railroads are frowning despotisms and are growing more monarchical and defiant. The only manner in which these threatening innovations upon our liberties can be treated, is to annihilate the monopoly over railroads and substitute our own management in its place. In short, we must follow the example of Belgium.

FARM LABOR. We apprehend it will be long before people are practical enough in their legislation to effect so radical a change. The government has shown itself too stupid, fraudulent and incompetent even to transact its own proper business of making statutes and paper regulations, for the people, without attempting all these intricate evolutions of business management. People are scarcely wise enough to substitute direct for proxy control either in railroads canals or telegraphs. Legislatures and Congress are continually in an entanglement with the people in matters of practical business; and now, you propose that they plunge still deeper into untried adventures, when they are incompetent, even to make regulations for those industries which they already control!

City Labor. The only cure for it lies in co-operation of the people themselves. Government must learn to control them as public works. Government gave away money and land enough to the Crédit Mobilier scheme to build a railroad across the continent, for the people. With this money it might have hired the work done and of the best material, paid its own citizens well for the same and then had this great highway in its own name to run for all time in the mutual interest of the people of both seaboards at cost. To say that government could not conduct an inter-oceanic line in behalf of citizens is equivalent to saying that it cannot work the Postal Department; or that a city government cannot supply itself with a Police Force or with Water, Fire, Sewerage Departments without intermediary managers; yet these are all known to be satisfactory and successful.

Farmer. What is your opinion regarding the management of the Land; or in other words, the control of agriculture by the State or government?

Answer. Mere opinions are of little use in these days of exact knowledge which is sweeping away the creeds and usages of the human race. Some reference to what has been done on Co-operative Farms and Government Parks may not be amiss in affording a subject of conversation.

Farm Labor. Is there evidence enough to warrant this government in undertaking the building of Parks and Farms on an extensive plan? Might not Congress attempt a Farm upon a sublime scale on some of the great government domains of the West?

City Labor. Appropriations of money by Congress will be necessary, for the Yellow Stone National Park. Nearly all the Parks of the country are successful in their objects. They are the breathing places of the great people. But they are all built by contractors, which is a stain upon the principle of collectivism. There are in the world however, a few excellent models which serve to show the perfect capability of the people to work lands without intermediary aid. The Société Beauregard in France has a farm worked exclusively by its members. Many of the great farms of the Shakers are worked by their own members. The Community of Oneida has, until manufacturing called the members away, always done its own farm work, without aid from without. Its success is due to a persistent carrying out of this principle. Of late years, the principle has been necessarily violated; as the domain grew faster than the membership, and outside help was hired. It is, however, the intention to return to the old plan of direct labor, as soon as circumstances will permit.

Farm Labor. What is monopoly in its voted acceptation at the principal Labor Congresses of the world?

City Labor. Monopoly originally signified the one city, or centre of negotiations. Greece had two; Athens and Sparta; and they were rivals and fought. Rome was a Monopoly. The word is consequently applied to any centre of control or power. A modern Monopoly is generally a junto of a few of the shrewdest intellects having financial control over great numbers.

Farm Labor. What is the tendency of the modern Monopoly?

City Labor. It thrives best by obtaining and controlling labor saving appurtenances, which are the harvest of human genius and therefore, common property of civilization; and do not naturally belong to individuals.

Farm Labor. What is the effect of this usurpation?

CITY LABOR. Too frequently it displaces from their positions and forces into the streets, as compulsory beggars, plunderers, and lawbreakers, great numbers who are affected by its introduction. Under the exclusive control of a Monopoly, an invention capable of doing work which formerly required ten persons is made to perform it with one. The power and self interest of this Monopoly are such that the thus economized product is not much lessened in price; but the nine workmen are discharged; and the Monopolist realizes, as his net profit, that which was formerly paid the nine men in wages, less the wear and running expense of the instrument which now performs the ten men's work.

FARM LABOR. Do you want to bridle the invention of machinery?

CITY LABOR. No. We would remedy the evil by making government encourage the inventor, assist him, pay him, and buy his invention if a good one. The State itself must learn to operate the Labor-saving instrument in the impartial interest of the whole people, without profit and at cost; and not allow any exclusivist who is urged only by the profit incentive, to use it as an instrument which can serve the double purpose of making a millionaire of himself and paupers of the people.

FARM LABOR. Do artisans of the city think the introduction of labor-saving implements creates paupers to such an extent as to effect the statistical reports?

CITY LABOR. The growth of pauperism is in proportion to the number displaced by the innovation. It is one cause of so much suffering among mechanics. The tendency is also observable on the Farm.

FARM LABOR. Will State interference, or control of

these implements by the people at large instead of individualists, abate the evil on the Farm and in the Factory alike?

CITY LABOR. *The government must do one of two things:—control the inventions which displace workmen of the land and the workshops, from vocations superseded by their introduction, or shoulder upon itself, that is, the people, the maintenance of the paupers and the cost of arrest, custody and punishment of all criminals, which the consequent idleness, hunger and desperation bring forth.*

FARM LABOR. How can government be made to manage an industry; especially a Farm industry?

REPLY. How can governments manage the care of paupers? Community at large pays their expenses! Communities know how, and make provision for them though they find it poor economy. Are communities ever to remain so stupid that they cannot economize time by putting men at work upon the very machines which drove them into pauperism under the monopolist? This is one great study of this century. Labor-saving machines are innocent and incalculably useful. But their exclusive management by a small minority at the expense of the great majority is an outrage; as our pauper statistics show. Let Government learn this and it will find no trouble in working the land on a vast and scientific scale.

FARM LABOR. What else will be the effect but abolishment of the Patent Office and the substitution therefor of some scheme by government, for incouraging inventors personally so that the community, or people may have the direct use of the invention?

CITY LABOR. We propose no warfare upon the Patent Office. The effect must be to reward the deserving. Competism and monopoly have abused the Patent Office opprobriously; but our object is to discuss the science of land tilling, by the State. Man is so constituted that several aptitudes seldom combine in one person. The true genius often has the least push. The inventor is generally modest, retiring, thoughtful; but what is worse, confiding. As a rule he has not the constitutional characteristics of a manager of inventions. A shrewd manager is usually an employer. He employs, we suppose, among other hands, a man of inventive genius, who almost unsconscious of the good he is doing, invents an improvement in the labor-saving apparatus of the concern. Now the misfortune is, that the manager is too frequently the one to patent this improvement as his own; and often the poor inventor, far from securing the profits to himself, is bought out for a trifle or intercepted and browbeaten or perhaps attacked and discharged at the caprice of the more powerful manager who has money and business tact. So the Patent Office is frequently used in the interests of the shrewd manager rather than of the modest inventor. By the application of money, lawyer's service and circumlocution, this Monopolist gets the honor and emoluments, by patenting the invention as his own. All these difficulties are avoided when the government has control of the industry in which the invention is put to practical use.

What people want in order to be happy, and to live in consonance with the progressive spirit of true liberty and enlightenment, is to adjust their affairs so as to free themselves from business responsibilities, that they may turn their valuable time to the nobler and deeper subjects of social and literary life. Humanity is bowed down with toil. More than half the business, attempted by individuals fails. Wreck, disappointment, social caste, self destruction follow.

Individualism is a scramble for illegitimate profit; and too frequently the undeserving get it. Of this incoherent and incongruous scramble for worldly means, the Agriculturists have their share.

Let them then, join the mighty Party of Politico-Social Industry; unbind the fetters which fasten them to an infatuating habit of selfishness and with the toilers of the cities and the sympathies of science, call upon the people to act collectively in bringing into the world a system of soil cultivation by the State; that industrial responsibility may fall impartially upon great numbers, not unequally upon individuals.

Agriculturist. For the State or Government, to attempt the exploiture of agriculture in all its branches, is a serious undertaking. It is, indeed, a vast adventure. Such an extraordinary leap into the darkness of doubt and inexperience, must and will necessarily be regarded with alarm. What else but wreck and disaster could, by any sane mind, be expected to result from such a stupendous and wholesale departure from the customs and usages of the entire world? Nations vary in their forms of political government. Individuals seem created with great diversity of physical and mental adaptabilities. Even the surface configuration of the land which the farmer tills is intersected with nooks and eddies and boundary lines, seemingly to fit it for individual tillage and to baffle any attempt of a greater administration or domination over the soil, like the government, or the collective individual whose united occupancy of land forms what is called the State.

Response. What is a modern government but an association for protection and mutual well-being? It is evident, not only from statistics, but the open and visible facts, existing on every hand, which accuse farm management of gross incompetence. Individuals undertake, with their meagre opportunities, to control the cultivation of the soil, and fail. We see the precious land under heavy mortgages and often becoming the property of lawyers and others of the highly paid and speculating people of the towns, who do not perform the hard toil of agriculture. Thus the land is gradually drifting into the possession of those who do not earn a living by cultivating it. This is a great wrong. No people should tolerate it. But how can Farmers prevent it, if uncombined? Accumulation of the landed wealth of a people into the hands of individuals and companies, is not only wrong but very dangerous; yet as it is a result of the competitive system, endowed with special laws and powers of immemorial habit and usage, there certainly exists but one sure method of obtaining an equal distribution of this landed domain, and that method is *agitation, as a fundamental principle of a new political economy, supplanting the old competitive system upon which the wrong rests.* The evil, portentous with social and political magnitude, over sweeping the most troubled area of any subject of the dark and difficult problem of Labor, is *failure of land cultivation and tenure, by the individual.* Humanity can devise but one solution resting upon the adamant of impregnable justice and eternal duration:—all individuals must become *one*, by association and agreement;—this to be made a deep, penetrating Principle of the Industrial Agitations. Working people are not slow to see in their own beloved Government or political Empire, an immense and powerful combination of forces competent at their sovereign command, to turn its richest resources of applied sciences, of willing labor, of copious funds to a vast, practical, scientific tillage of the EARTH.

## CHAPTER X.

............

### WORKING PEOPLE THE TAXPAYERS. DUTIES OF POLITICAL ORGANIZATIONS CONTROLLING PUBLIC WORKS.

---

DEBATE BETWEEN MEMBERS OF
OLD POLITICAL PARTIES AND AN ATTORNEY
FOR THE MOVEMENT OF LABOR.

................

POLITICIAN. WE COME DELEGATED BY AN Organized Body, to enjoy an exchange of sentiments with reference to some new opinions you entertain on Political Economy.

ATTORNEY FOR THE PEOPLE. What Body do you represent?

POLITICIAN. A secret society organized and maintained in the interest of many who take upon themselves the manipulation of important details in politics.

RESPONSE. We have never yet been able to separate studied secrecy from deception. We, ourselves, sometimes see the need of privacy in unimportant details; but as for a mere secret club being empowered with the management of so solemn a trust as the people's destiny, human beings must be wise and just indeed, if pure management arises from the hidden depths of their nightly reunions, which the world's sad and sickening picture of poverty and sin, proves to have come from darkness rather than light. The political economy we teach depends for its success upon light; not darkness. It is scientific and provable only in the broadest glare of light. Can it then have sympathy with that which is occult?

Politician. If you are no better posted in details than to begin a political career without the aid of secret political manœuvres you are a failure to begin with.

People's Attorney. Well then, if your organization has any idea of endorsing or of even discussing the merits of truth, whether that discussion be in cells or on the house tops is immaterial, except with the progress to be achieved.

Politician. Our organizations are as desirous as your own of using their power honorably and with discretion. It is a mistake, however perfidious the management of some secret political combinations, to suppose that all politicians are wanting of human kindness.

Attorney. Kindly permit that we address you as one of the aggrieved public; else we may not arrive at an understanding. You are yourself a political officer of some kind. Your bureau is in some City Hall, Police Headquarters, Public Justice's office or Commissioner's department of Public Works. The great public at large had little to do with your appointment to an easy and remunerative office. Your appointment, functions, power, come indirectly. Not through the people with whom you play, but from the Mayor, Governor or President, whose election you instigated the people, through some unseen manœuvre, to sanction. You represent then, the successful side of two antagonists; and this success emanated from the sanction of an occult, perhaps perfectly honorable plan, by a majority of the Public. The Public were admitted into the secret only so far as the general principles at the base of Party Organization required it. All details relating to your appointment, method of administration, salaries, in fact all the details relating to the destinies of the people until the next election, or until the close of said administration are kept private. This is the same as in monarchical countries with this single improvement that *this* monarch and his appointees or assistants, are obliged to abdicate periodically instead of remaining in power for life. You continue to exercise over the people the same supreme control which has marked the career of all monarchies. If the people succeed in holding you in check or in dictating openly what you shall do in secret, it is with the superior mechanical instrumentalities like the steam engine, the telegraph, the press, and other appurtenances of modern practical knowledge. Even this is strongly felt in modern monarchies, working potently in democratizing or diffusing legislation for the welfare of all.

POLITICIAN. Admitting that our system is radically wrong and that the people ought to have the power of electing all subordinate officers and that everything ought to be discussed and arranged in open, instead of secret meetings, it is nevertheless certain that secret political societies exist; and it is this fact which motives our inquiry. We represent a political power that manages details in government. We find that business decays at each great metropolis of the Eastern Sea Board which, if not prevented will cause the industries of those emporiums to be drawn into centres of the West.

People's Attorney. This is natural. Politicians cater to the middle classes and fail to protect industrious elements of society. The government of a city is one-sided, and in the interest of so-called taxpayers. These taxpayers are the owners of property, mostly created within the city. The city has been swindled by political combinations and plunged into debt; and the taxpayers who are obliged to pay the enormous percentage of taxes levied on their property, raise the price of rents and other means of life. This rise in rents is equivalent to a diminution of the salary of every person engaged in the industries of that city. The taxpayer finds it easy to equalize, so far as *he* is concerned, the excess of his tax, by the rise of his rent, and other material in which he deals. He is a *manager of product.* The poor producers believe they have no more effective means of equalizing *their* excess of rent, and means of life, than a corresponding rise of their wages through organization. This naturally leads to strikes, public turmoils, and what is called the disturbance of industry. Immense waste and antagonisms of industry are caused in this way. It makes industries precarious; and few business men can stand both the increased tax and the risk caused by the propensity of their employés whose wages they are obliged to cut down, to strike or otherwise interrupt business. The fatal consequence of this desultory condition of Eastern Seaboard Industries is to gradually eliminate the vital staples of their business prosperity which of course, other industrial centres obtain.

Politician. This brings us to the point. What can political organization do to help the matter?

Attorney. Every thing. It is upon the political action of such that hopes might be placed if integrity could be relied upon. They have power; but instead of using it in the interest of the real taxpayer, the producing majorities, back of whose calamities there is no appeal except in strikes and over whose future there yawns nothing but social caste, they lavish it upon the non-producing middlemen or pseudo-taxpayers who, to bridge over their difficulty, have but to *raise the price of rent and other means of living and cut down the workmen's wages commensurate with the tax-levy and the hazard incurred by this change.* This means war, not peace. One result is to gradually drive industries from the city. Political Organizations show their utter incompetence to legislate for the well being of their great and beautiful city, in persistently refusing to make provision for the safe and honorable employment of the working people who are thus forced to defend themselves, and whose want provokes crime and entails upon the city further wretchedness, shame, bankruptcy. Meantime the Politician does not abate his subservience but obsequiously clings to the middle class, recognizing them as the true taxpayers.

POLITICIAN. What then can be done? Politicians have no following from the laboring people. On the contrary they are generally repudiated by them.

ATTORNEY. Very naturally. These men have the control of whole Departments of Public Works; but instead of attending to this as honest duty and interest instruct, farming the power of this supervision, they lease them out on contract to third parties, to speculate on. The sinking condition of the public treasures and the spasmodic nature of business show that the contract system is defective when the interests of the great public rather than those of public men are considered. Necessary work should always be done for the SAKE OF THE WORK, as well as for the WORK IT-

SELF. The necessity of the work of building a park is the first incentive for that labor, which is felt by the entire community. The number of days work it requires to complete the park and the manner in which it is to be done, is an important matter to those of the general public who would be employed and thereby earn a living. This is the second incentive, which touches the heart and home of the entire working classes. It is also the vital matter these political organizations neglect. The Politician is unable yet to see, that on this incentive he can advance his own and his city's interests.

OPINION. Talk this way to the world and you will be scouted as a communist and an enemy to the leaders of society.

REPLY. Nevertheless the truth shall be spoken. The first incentive to the building of a park is felt by the general public in common as a public necessity. The second is felt by the workmen who are to be employed thereon. A workman feels a double incentive, because in addition to his desire of employment, he, being also a citizen, has a common interest with the general public, in the beauty and health, of the city, town, or country in which he resides. It follows therefore, that the producer of the park takes double the interest in it that any other person *can* take. This doubled incentive is strong enough to promote a political Party. Your organization partakes of precisely the same character so far as it goes. You conduct the details of a government. They execute the details of a park. The general public require a government. The same general community also want a park. This want then, is identical in both cases and is the first incentive. Now the next incentive is the desire of your members to execute the details of this government. They desire it, first because each feels it a necessity in common with the rest of the general public, to have a government; and secondly because they wish to be employed, and earn a living, in the performance of this duty. This is honorable, if there is no dishonest speculation in their motive. If they did not do it somebody else would, and these two combined, form an incentive to organization, which is intensely strong. Arguing then, from a point in principle, no fault is found with your organization. It may be frankly admitted that it is necessary to have rulers, for all citizens's sake and for your own special sakes, when honor lies at the base. What objection then, can you conjure up, to the employment of the people, by the people, *for the sake of the labor* and the consequent means of support, which it affords them?

POLITICIAN. But we do not perform the details of this labor on the parks and public edifices. It is let to contractors.

ATTORNEY. Why then, do you not let the making of laws and ordinances to contractors or middlemen? If you are afraid of one communism why not of another? Why do men no longer sub-let their laws to the despots of individualism? What is the advantage of a democratic government? Why may not a great principle apply to one form as well as to another? To labor as well as law?

POLITICIAN. Do you call the long tried and popular system of contracting the world's necessary work to outside parties a despotism?

PEOPLE'S ATTORNEY. Most decidedly. Any regulation is despotic, whether political or industrial, which does not consult majorities concerned. It is a despotism with which the entire anti-monarchical spirit of civilization is unconsciously at war. It utterly ruins the second and intensest interest of the citizen in an integral government; because the people are not supposed to have either ownership or interest in a private regulation. When the United States Government wants a good, genuine ship it is sure to build that ship itself; but when congress makes an appropriation of money to pay for the building of a ship, and allows a junto of appointed officials to sub-let the work, to contractors, be sure the ship will be next to worthless. The difference between a necessary thing made by ourselves, under our own supervision, and the same thing made in the interest of a contractor, may be considered paramount to that generic difference which exists between selfish interest, and common interest. The only incentive the former feels toward making the thing a good one is fear of popular displeasure, the loss of reputation, and the desire to be honest. The incentive he feels toward slighting the work, is his craving to make money. The world knows this unfortunate craving too often prevails. Wretched patch-work and superficial gloze, pervading a large portion of American manufacture is sufficient proof of this. Now when we do a thing ourselves *for* ourselves, we are, by the force of circumstances, free from all negative motives. We *cannot* make it wrong. We have no incentive for making it wrong, because the pure thing is what we want. For this reason the government gets the best ship when it employs its own supervisors direct, hires and pays its own workmen direct, buys its own timber and other materials direct or independently of intermediary managers, and watches and detects every flaw. Here is seen the reverse of the contract system which excludes this noble second incentive to do right. Our doubled incentive then, is a new urgent of motives in favor of democracy; because it increases the number in the organization. It needs this two-fold incentive to keep the whole general public organized in politics; and every tendency is despotic without it. Industrial equilibriation cannot exist without it. Competism, with its speculative incentive receives no check without it. Human government can never be pure until its details are carried out under the doubled incentive which every citizen must feel, and be, through personal motives actuated by. The fewer the number thus actuated the more closely it verges toward despotism, until it culminates in exclusivism or monarchy itself; as did Rome and all the empires of the past; whereas the larger the number thus actuated, interested, and employed, the more purely democratical and fraternal becomes the government as do the self-help societies of co-operation. If your political government furnishes no second or doubled incentive of organization and labor, except for a mere handful, eliminating and excluding it from the masses, it is monarchical. It may be in a republic. It may produce laudable things. But its character is monarchical. Majorities are excluded and it can only be democratical in proportion to the numbers who feel this doubled incentive of political organization. Its democracy can become general, only in proportion as it multiplies these doubly interested members.

Politician. It is true that we have a Department of Public Works, upon which working people are demanding employment. It is further true that great numbers are in an unorganized state, and those who are associated think of little but Trade Unions.

People's Attorney. It has been explained how this demise of the work they ask for, destroys their strongest incentive to political organization. The sub-agent gets the work; not they. He makes profit out of the contract by exacting an over portion of labor product from them. If you should study their wants as supervisors of the Board of Public Works and employ the men *direct*, to perform this service in which they could take an interest as citizens, hiring them direct and not by proxy, there could be no violation of principle. Its tendency is to elevate the workman instead of degrading him; spurring him to produce genuine streets, parks, city buildings and other public works.

POLITICIAN. You have not made it clear how this sub-agency of labor acts as a tyranny or despotism. Merely the statement has been made but no satisfactory reason and evidence have been adduced.

ATTORNEY. Proof is visible in the degradation of employés. In favor of the direct system of employment the proof is in their elevation. The difference is plain and natural; and being generic, we can attach no particular blame to any person. It is only desirable that men should see that the direct employment of the citizen by a Board of Public Works intensifies and completes the incentive to political organization, watchfulness and purity; while the reverse is the case in the sub-agency system because the strongest incentive of pure, genuine government is destroyed and the inevitable results of political demoralization follow. Instead of the government being watched over and guarded by the majorities, whose labor creates the public improvements, it is left at the mercy of the unscrupulous who, to secure the contracts, would bribe you with the very money they make out of the overwork exacted from these citizen employés whom the direct agency system would enfranchise and elevate rather than degrade, as at present done, by employing them on the principle of increased wages and shorter hours.

POLITICIAN. Would not this increase of wages and diminution of time be a disastrous expense to the city and be regarded by that portion of the general public not thus employed, as an insidious means of buying political organization of the workingmen?

PEOPLE'S ATTORNEY. No; although suspicions might be incited by those interested, or in sympathy with sub-agents who are sometimes powerful both in political influence and in the sway of established public sentiment. A little reflection proves the contrary. In outside industries, the wages as a result of the desultory methods described, are so low that the workman or woman is only able to exist. Comparatively few of the unfavored million can accumulate property. When thrown out of employment they almost immediately begin to suffer. If taken sick, the horrors of a twofold calamity, destitution and pain, befall them. The only mutual aid or burial society they belong to is perhaps their Trade Union or mutual benefit society and four fifths of them do not belong to those. In this helpless state it is easy for the sub-agent of the Municipal Works to exact. There is no resistance. He *can* therefore, true to the instincts of monopoly, he *does* exact. Helpless poor people. become virtually degraded slaves at his feet, because they have no appeal. Beggars for the privilege of remaining servile are truly wretched creatures; yet such are they! A pitiable government then, is this you dispense in secret; and those who tolerate the same, boasting of the management of details in politics to whom are given the destinies of an immense Board of the people's Public Works, are also deplorable slaves both to themselves, and to this sub-agency.

The labor agent after obtaining the contract, hires his men at the lowest compatible wages and even then, constrains them to a constant hazard and fear of losing their occupation. Labor contractors clothed with such power of interest and consequence, can exact a large amount of work from each; and twenty percent more time than the law making eight hours a day's work allows. These employés are of the people who, insofar as means of redress are denied are humiliated. Not satisfied with this, the performer of Municipal Work is by the same propensity for gain, impelled to slight it; and the working people who are the true taxpayers are compelled to pay in exorbitant rents and provisions, for what has not been done. The streets of your city, are proverbially unclean and in summer the stench of carrion and of putrid cesspools and sluices, and the ordures of the open gutters combine their infectious miasma, breeding and fostering choleraic death-rage. Mad dogs rave, spume and snap unhindered; summer fevers burn and destroy while the city surgeons burlesque medical science with autopsies, and learned reports on the phenomena of germ diseases and the discovery of the nerve fatality of hydrophobia. Neglected cities thus make science a satire on the nerve and sinew of their human victims. Evidently it costs the sub-agent money to purify the city; and since emoluments of profit can purchase reputation he has no other incentive to do work well than unprompted virtue. Competitive individualism thus renders employers void of the second incentive of good citizenship; and their workmen by reason of bad treatment are equally void of it.

Politician. Cannot a brighter shading be given to some side of this dark and ghastly picture? Give us an idea from a brighter point of view. The Boards of Public

Work on streets, docks, parks and public buildings are completely under our control or may be made so by a little legislation.

Attorney. Employ the men yourselves and you have the bright side as a consequence. Hire them independently of contractors. Direct and supervise their labor. Hire them at Eight Hours per day if according to law. Give them honorable, living wages. Never turn your good men off to starve. Treat them with respect. Hire men for their intelligence and honesty as well as for their efficiency, as workmen. Encourage them to join and enlarge the political organization, until every person required to conduct Public Works finds permanent employment under your immediate supervision.

Politician. How long before they will get dogmatic and tyrannical and abuse their power? Contrariety and self-destruction seem inborn elements of the laboring class.

Attorney. Because they have never been trained in industrial self-government. But they will never do this. They have no interest in doing it; and if they had, they would be soon self-accused, and detected; for they are too numerous to be secret. They are citizens in actual co-operation with each other for the common good; citizens actuated by the desire to promote the general welfare which forms the first incentive of political organization to which they cannot but belong, and also by the desire to maintain themselves and their families in respectability and comfort, which forms their second and strongest incentive to political organization and honorable citizenship. Do away with this pernicious letting of ferries and other work which begets injustice by opening opportunities for it. Endeavor to institute a direct employment policy and streets will henceforth be kept clean; parks well made public edifices will be genuine; ferries and other steam transit thoroughfares, cheap and comfortable. Employés will be honorably treated and elevated from slavery to manhood; and the cost of doing it will be far less than this indirect patchwork by obsequious sub-agents of the Public Works.

POLITICIAN. Admitting this assumption of control of the ferriage, passenger transit, and other such work, to be charming in theory, it applies only to those improvements over which the Boards of Public Works already hold control. It does nothing in the way of restoring the great ship building and other industries which the country has lost by the ravages of hard times.

PEOPLE'S ATTORNEY. If the country has lost industries, energy will restore them. There is no reason why a city cannot build a ship if it can build a park; nor any reason why it cannot navigate ships if it can conduct intricate industries like Water Boards, Fire Departments and Schools.

POLITICIAN. Do such counsels premise that shipping industries can be assumed by every Seaboard metropolis through political action?

ANSWER. They can be restored by the action of the Boards of Public Works. The shipping industry is a political necessity of the people. It forms an important co-efficient of an integral community. Without it, the strength and symmetry of a Seaboard are shorn away. Commercial plumpness, beauty, prestige and health are lost. It becomes a necessity. Now under individual management the shipping industry has failed and fled from your city; although a public necessity. Being an industry necessary to the prosperity of the public it deserves the consideration of the Board of Public Works. Yet this consideration implies sanction or rejection which cannot be done without resorting to deliberation, and the yaes and nays. In other words the ballot, which is political action.

POLITICIAN. Yes, but what has the Board of Public Works to do with it?

ATTORNEY. Public sentiment cannot find expression, except through the machinery of arrangement and detail. Boards of Public Works represent a political power that manages the details in politics. You seem ignorant of this great politico-industrial necessity: the shipping interest of Seaports. You have never even taken into consideration this important subject.

POLITICIAN. Nor have Boards of Public Works power to authorize such an enterprise without authority from the State Capitol.

RESPONSE. No. But the people have. Public Boards may not have latitude sufficient to cover such an enterprise without some legislative sanction; but organizations have a right to bring it before public consideration, with a view of obtaining this legislative permission. After such preliminary work it belongs to the Boards of Public Works to carry it into effect. It becomes a co-operative enterprise. Work is done by the people after plans and drafts most approved by them. The industry restored to the city is then a democratical or co-operative industry instead of a monarchical one as heretofore. Employés —the managers, draftsmen, carpenters, machinists, blacksmiths and others employed, feel an impulse to organize in clubs politically, and hopefully work for the best interests of the enterprise, because they feel the doubled interest in it:— that of citizenship, and that of duty to themselves.

POLITICIAN. How may that sullen tendency be reconciled, which appears both in political government and that of great monopolies, requiring employés to wear uniforms? People say the uniform designates *caste* and look upon it as an aping at social distinctions. They are told to calm their fears; for it is only a business necessity, very convenient and innocent. But that does not explain. You allow that the Post Office is a proof of the ability of a people to manage great Distributive Industries, more economically than individuals; and point for proof at a growing tendency to distribute and infuse watchfulness among the people, rather than to concentrate upon individuals the great current of control. You even say that the people are mutually impelled to the management of their business concerns by their own intimate, heart-felt and fireside interests; even by the tenderest family and friendly intimacies; that they are compelled as a collective commonalty, each integer of which feels a sovereign impulse to depend upon the mutual combination of *all*, to enforce. This power of popular will, it is argued, is supreme and becomes a true democracy. But how does it look democratic when it shows itself in the very garb of royalty; imitating the hated uniforms of military despotism which has so emphatically spoken in deeds of oppression and of blood? The people will ask for a correction of these discrepancies in logic; because uniforms are forced upon employés of both aristocratic and government industries.

ATTORNEY. The uniform is not offensive to the eye or the taste. It is not only neat, genteel and popular, but also serves the purpose of putting a stop to double dealing. It makes men show their colors. Whims of the dishonest may be shielded under colors of daily life. Uniform dress does not permit occult dealing. A letter carrier or other agent, hired by the State is well dressed, and respected. He is on a par with any person who earns a living. Colors are honorable. The great bank which pays him is the treasury of the people. He is given and must execute an honorable trust. He is more punctually paid and better treated than are the employés of most individual firms and seems by no means dishonored with the uniform of the law. It is a necessity to him, assuring him special protection and a necessity to the people being their means of recognizing their employé and his responsibility. What is said of the letter carrier may also be said of the Policeman. This objection loses force in another point. The Gens d' armes of Europe are uniformed through compulsion. The spy and detective are very careful not to dress in uniform when they have a secret *rôle* to play. It is characteristic of rogues to wear inattractive apparel, and they know each other by wink, grip, blind cypher, *argot*, lingo and other *langue de serpent;* and the shrewdest detective, if he calculate their manœuvres from ordinary lines of action as established in honest, business methods upon which men career, finds it difficult to discover them. The statement however, that all officers should be required to wear their uniform, must refer to society as it is at present; when the number of uniform–wearing officials is as nothing, to the numbers of the *people.* What we may wear when all become responsible, is a distant subject. The uniform *per se,* indicates simply nothing. It is only a matter of convenience. That as a token of military grades it makes some people pedantic is true; but this will, before the criticism of rising public inteligence, be frowned upon and its uses be applied as a mechanical necessity.

POLITICIAN. There appears ogreishly rising before the industrial world, another threatening spectre in form of two or three extraordinary inventions. Within a short period there stalks unbidden into the labor market, an instrument which claims the power of superseding and of entirely supplanting and destroying the great and time-honored art of printing. There are a half million printers making a living by their skill in this art! Shall all these honest tradesmen submit to be driven away from a respectable employment by an inanimate tool with which the tender and comparatively unskilled fingers of a girl, may perform in an hour more work than the printer, with his long earned skill and close practice, is able to accomplish in a day? Allow these sciences and inventions you hold up as elements of a high civilization, to thus undermine the means of existence of this large and useful class, and you make them arbitrary scourges and a curse instead of a blessing. Does it not look like baldest sophistry to maintain that a machine which, in giving employment to one, robs five others of the means of existence and throws them, helpless, into penury, is a benefit?

ATTORNEY. There is nothing within human reach, whereby the wrongs described may be adjusted, so long as a common sharing of the earnings of this printing machine is denied the aggrieved mechanics whose skilled art and whose means of support are destroyed by it. The introduction of inventions no power can stay. Nor should it. We may as well seek to throttle the fount of human genius. We may as well condemn the struggling, aspiring race to intellectual oblivion; for what, more than this unearthing of nature's buried jewels, this analysis and synthesis, this resurrection of her latent virtues, can contribute evidences of mind above brute force? No. Let no man dream of stanching the flow of intellect! It is sacred. The cure of the evil does not lie in an act of barbarity which could produce only retrogression and self-contempt.

But a cure is in your hands, as managers of great Boards of Public Works *whose property they are.* Expect nothing so long as the competitive system rages and the scramblers for the lion's share outwit the working million who struggle and vainly combat to check an emulative career which grasps and appropriates all for selfish ends, giving no quarter to the outwitted victim. No. Hope cannot be looked for in the competitive system. Bitterness, poverty, humiliation, race-degeneracy, and other concomitant crimes against humanity exist filling the world with social ulcers. There is but one method of relief. *The State must become a Coöperation;* and take control of these inventions, as legitimate property or wealth, which enriches a people by enriching such State, Commonwealth, Municipality, in which they live. This delivers the new printing instrument, in full function, to society *by a social compact of citizens; thus intercepting the speculative incentive.* Make this noble gift of the citizens' intellect *common property;* subject to the control of the Boards of Public Work.

Other magnificent inventions like the telephone, which, through a competitive instinct of speculative strife fall prey to, and are swooped up by shrewd individuals and monopolies, with recreant unfeelingness for the fate of masses, must, before a rapidly engulfing problem of Labor's Rights, yield to the altruistic methods of management and become, likewise, the common goods of humanity.

POLITICIAN. Even conceding a possibility that Boards of Public Work under our direction as their Political engineers succeed; that the printing innovation, the telephone, the gasworks and all similar industries now operated by and for individuals on the competitive, or emulative system, become common; what moral or intellectual benefit would masses of the people derive from the change? The same spirit of strife would continue. It would only be forced to course in broader channels. Instead of being personal it would be political. In a few years it would be national. Conflicting with the interests of individuals whose business is differently grounded, it must inevitably tend toward the begetting of strifes rather than the quieting of human passions! Indeed, who shall say that it will not provoke the strifes of blood, by exasperating our emulative impulses?

RESPONSE. Were it a private affair, a conflict between two neighbors, serious results might follow. But this change of management in the applied methods of new inventions, which are as much the common property of civilization as the air we breathe, and as little the prey of individualists as water, or intelligence, or soul, or law of nature, is an affair which affects all humanity. Its province is not circumscribed to petty individual interests. It sweeps over broader areas and covers the interests of humanity. It becomes a problem of Political Economy involving the grandest and profoundest *principle* of mutual self-help and love, such as the world has never known. It becomes a school. There are no elements of strife in a community of interests which its discussions, its reasonings, its moral agitations will not melt, soften, purify, refine, as in the chemist's crucible; for it is the school of schools, the nursery of humanity, the foe to oppression, the messenger of practical wisdom and of reciprocal love.

## CHAPTER XI.

### A MISCELLANEOUS DISCUSSION OF THE FOUR PREVAILING MISCONSTRUCTIONS AND MISTAKES THAT BESET THE AGITATORS OF THE SOCIALISTIC PHILOSOPHY.

A FRIENDLY COMBAT OF OPINIONS WITH SEVERAL PERSONS, ALL INTERESTED IN SOME METHOD OF HUMAN IMPROVEMENT BUT CONDEMNING ALL BUT THEIR OWN. PLAIN TALKS ON GIFT, FARMING AND TEMPERANCE.

OBJECTOR. ACCORDING to almost every sort of feeling that actuates our mind and muscle, the so called Socialistic Philosophy, which requires that Government assume the control of all our economic means of existence, is highly prejudicial to individual liberty. How is it possible for enterprising persons, men, for example, of great managing ability to develop any useful life work, like a manufactory, a farm or an invention, when every free action is curtailed, restricted, and submitted to the impudent censorship of everybody? The idea is distasteful from first to last! It is destructive of individualism and independence. It cannot but have the effect to ruin personal aspirations upon which it is conceded by all writers and thinkers on Political Economy, the superiority of our age over past ages of the race, takes its marked distinction. "What's everybody's business is nobody's business" has long been a maxim which people of experience find to be literally true. Surrender the personal incentives that inspire us to any enterprise, that gird us with that almost marvelous energy which characterizes men of our day, give these longings, cravings, delights and pampered hopes that accompany individual responsibility, over to the many, no matter how well qualified those masses are for the task, and it wlll be speedily seen that the life of all genuine energies has been sapped, perhaps when it is too late to prevent or rectify the disaster.

SOCIALIST. You speak of four kinds of industry. The premises are fair, and very favorable to a fair discussion We will accept them on your own grounds and confine our researches to the three great industrial branches upon which millions are constantly dovoting their genius and practical energies—those of Manufacture, Agriculture and the Invention of labor saving Machinery, much of which is used solely in facilitating the other two pursuits. Let us first look at the subject of Inventive Gift; the most important, being a source, directly or indirectly, of modern development and of much of our shelter, clothing, medicine and other necessaries.

Do you consider that industrial pursuits are, in the main, economically conducted? If the power of individual management is so sacred and unerring as represented, how is it that nine elevenths of the industries in the entire country, fail within a seven years trial? Yet this is lamentably true. When we fairly submit this assumed success of individuals to statistical count, we discover that instead of the boasted triumph of their masterly genius and strength over difficulties, it is, to our astonishment, disastrous bankruptcy nine times in eleven! Now, so far as concerns the exhilarating, delightful or refining sensations and the life duties and responsibilities which make the *incentive* of such duties, we must be honest with ourselves; for instead of actual results leading to this, we find that the disappointment, worry, perplexities of many kinds attendant upon the calamity of so frequent failure, furnish statisticians with a key to that preponderance of suicide among managers, over common, or non-managing people. It is true, that suicide prevails in a degree among working people. This is traceable to almost the same fountain—fears and anxieties—but of quite different kinds. What troubles the journeyman, is uncertainty about holding his situation and the insolent usage he is too often subjected to when he has one. He has no grand "castles in the air". No half developed life-work to be wrecked. No costly hopes long treasured, to be dissipated, and no fears of any ill results of mismanagement except as he ruptures the natural law by violating a rule of the art and mystery of his handicraft. Being always forwarned by ever repeating experience that the punishment for this is immediatly inflicted by nature, he learns care and gradually grows into habits of exactness which produce pleasure instead of pain. Not so, the business adventurer. A large majority of them fail within the first seven years of trial. Many are unwilling to survive the wreck of a life project and as such persons generally spring out of the most enterprising and magnetic class, society in general suffers, in proportion to its loss. The fallacy of your argument that steady self-employment of the people by themselves, will, in any manner, produce hurtful results by cuttting off individual liberty is self-apparent; since a large majority of your independent-spirited citizens are necessarily doomed to failure by the fiat of competitive institutions under which they struggle.

OBJECTIONIST. Still, you fail to meet the great and unanswerable objection to the proposed plan of conducting industries—the objection that it will utterly intercept the *incentives* which now inspirit people to energy, enterprise, and vigor, without which, man would sink into the condition of the naked, purposeless savage. Whence all this delightful, progressive enlightenment with which we are surrounded? Has this been procured by penning up, restricting men's minds, submitting them to the constant inquisition, as well as the glaring censorship of an ignorant populace? Let working people be honest with themselves and they must soon become convinced that their undertaking is one which cannot fail, if carried out, to consign this civilization to decay! The world is not so far advanced that it may not suffer another collapse.

SOCIALIST. To the reasoner who has honestly canvassed this subject for true information, this objection seems not only strange but extraordinary; strange, because it contains no truth in fact; and extraordinary, because it is the first objection raised, hooted at and shaken in his face and the one which is most calculated to bewilder, horrify, prejudice and finally prevent him from studying further. Now, in order to meet this subtle objection plainly, we must begin with the first and worst class of fault-finders—the political office holders themselves. The very persons who most loudly clamor against labor getting a foothold on its own management are those whom Government has been a mother to, or been their almoner. Alexander was born to a throne and consequently to vast means. Did not this circumstance contribute to make him the renowned Alexander the Great? Or did his "Government pay" you deprecate, dull the boy and cut off his incentive and rob him of the means of self development? The fact is, he, like thousands, even millions of less fortunate ones, was born with those life incentives; and the government place and pay he inherited, were just what proved indispensable as means with which to accomplish his purposes. Forgetting the bloody deeds of his brutal age and race, the world owes him a debt of gratitude for the one great act of establishing the Alexandrian School. But if military heroes are objectionable as illustrations, (militarism is condemned by the Industrial Party altogether, not only on the ground of its inhumanity but also because workingmen are its first dupes and victims) we will look at the career of individuals in private life. Let us study biography. Kant, who himself could do nothing till he got a life position in the Royal University of Koenigsberg, openly proclaimed as one of the cardinal points of his philosophy, that *what men ought to do they must do; and consequently, must be supplied with means of doing it.* He taught that it is the duty of man in the aggregate, to help the individual, as an integer. His teachings were intensely democratical. German Political organization of the socialistic School has taken root upon Kant's trenchant theses. Yet this intrepid sage, like millions of the unfavored ones of gift and special genius, might have floundered through the world without writing an essay or delivering a lecture, had he not been provided with means, by an institution with a government pensioned by the State and as permanent as any political institution on the earth. But we can go farther back. Nobody was anybody, without government help in ancient times. Yet this aid was what produced the civilization of

Athens and Alexandria. It is now recognized that the doctrines of the great philosopher, Aristotle, which upheld accumulated investigation of natural law, by means of mechanics, statistics, natural science and comparison, were correct; being exactly the scheme the world is now following in the march of enlightenment. But this celebrated old greek was both a teacher and an engineer under the emperor Alexander and his father, king Phillip, before him. He was, in all repects, a government employé. Did this prove disastrous to this great man's genius or life-hopes? It furnished him means, on the contrary, to popularize and apply his system. What would have been the Alexandrian School without such a founder and such a teacher? Solon was nothing until he got on the government pay rolls. Lycurgus was adrift until he became an employé of the Spartan Government, under the Eurystheneid line. He seems always to have enjoyed the pecuniary blessings of the people's exchequer; but it cannot be said of that eminent Lawgiver, who lived in a comparatively early era of our race, among quarrelsome, ignorant, indeed desperately superstitious barbarians, that his happy advantages had the effect to debauch or demoralize him. How can you assume that government paid service was, in this remarkable case, other than a blessing to our kind? We simply assume, with Kant, that whatever men ought to do they must do; and when it becomes necessary as in the present struggle of the adjustment of Labor product with regard to ownership and enjoyment, the people must look to their government as the natural employer as well as protector. Every man in early days, to bring his inward being out, had to be the protegé of the people under some solid institution. Demosthenes and Cicero were useless lawyers, mere babblers in the field of rhetoric, until they became state's attorneys; until their mighty philippics were heard from the bema and the forum. This does not presuppose that great, even greater souls did not exist. It means simply that those who have nothing can do nothing. In the gaze of modern democracy Spartacus looms up a hero; and his story thrills and gladdens every heart. But even poor Spartacus, a gladiator and a slave was fed, furnished, nurtured in daring deeds and his army with which he carved a page in history was in like manner supplied from the government and this rough host he afterwards led to a remarkable uprising against oppression was equipped with weapons, fed and trained in the arena and prepared for their leader when he came, through the money and the laws of the Roman government; else how could Spartacus have given humanity this wonderful example of revolt against a brutal and humiliating species of slavery—the arena of Roman gladiators. Hardly do we find a man of note in the Middle Ages who was not, in like manner absolved by one of many methods of government guaranty, from the responsibility of property-holding and of private life. Copernicus, the monk of Ermeland, wrought out, brought out and thoroughly demonstrated his inestimable Planetary movements under the quiet bounties of a fixed government institution. Now if servility, or intimidation and fawning obedience are results of such employment, how could a poor mathematician like Copernicus, who got a living by teaching, have succeeded in demonstrating mathematical hypotheses which were not only unpopular in all such institutions, but frowned upon by the governemts of the earth that sustained them, because they were regarded by such governments and institutions as heretical, actually threatening the overthrow of foundation principles upon which those institutions were grounded? Did his steady employment in a solid institution that gave him regular payments for labor, have the effect to demoralize the Monk of Ermeland? Columbus and Magellan who proved by experiment what Eratosthenes and Thales had predicted, were dumb and powerless until governments gave them their commissions, their outfits, their crews and launched them out upon the high waves. For over a hundred years from the great discovery of Columbus the oceans were ploughed in all directions by ships fitted out by different governments of the world, for geographical and other useful researches. Does all this sustain your argument that men of independence and genius become gross, lose their natural spirit and characteristic parts and dwindle into effeteness or worthless political servitude and indolence? On the contrary, Columbus is an example among many others, who have suffered the torments of individualist jealousies because he was successful. Biography proves that inventors who are unprotected by some strong institution like a government, are too often made victims of by grasping, irresponsible individuals. A principle cause of this is attributable to the fact that men of inventive minds are wanting of those aptitudes that characterize men of grasping, selfish minds; and consequently fall an easy prey. Individuals generally succeed in despoiling the researching, inventive, penetrating geniuses who contribute most good to their fellow men, of the honors and emoluments of their gift and their industry. Laws tolerate it. Competition grows out of it. Political and economical affairs are numb to its cruelties in ratio as it fosters greed in individuals and makes them callous to the sufferings of its victims. While the great discoverers and inventors could maintain themselves under the guardian wing of a solid institution, like Government or an endowed seat of Learning which has outgrown individual ownership and management so as to be recognized as common to the world, they could succeed in realizing their aspirations unmolested. But when the insinuating student of narrow egotism and self-interest, who thinks of nothing but moneygetting, fastened upon innocence of this kind, the usual result was to get away from the ingenious man all that was worth anything, of his project, and turn him out to die unhonored and unknown. If the pure truth were acknowledged we should know that the secret of England's glory and success is, that she has always been a wise almoner. What could Newton have accomplished outside the University of Cambridge? But Cambridge is in fact, an institution of the British government; founded by government officers and receiving periodical subventions from it. Newton was the philosopher who could, therefore must and did, give us the facts about gravity. Who shall question that it was the exalted influence of his position, his co-operate help his college prestige and salary that established the man's power and made his success certain? Why, even the quiet of a government prison has educated many a genius for a great work. Bunyan was but an unlettered enthusiast, tantalizing the public ear, vainly screeching at deaf disgust, until his twelve years of discipline in Bedford prison; then he could write the "Pilgrim's Progress". Many a heretic will testify that getting away from absorbing circumstances, even though it be hiding in the clammy dungeon, has the effect to c-ordinate and marshall the tributary requisites of a successful life-work.

John Milton, the great polemic democrat, a government employé under Cromwell, was a gentleman who for many years had received help from government. His genius was strengthened by such help and was perhaps invigorated for the master-pieces that followed. What of splendor that afterwards shone out from this contributor to language and literature, was property born in him; and that wanted only *means* from no matter what source, wherewith to further, encourage and ultimately accomplish his purposes. How, then, did the exalted and ennobling position he long occupied under solid and respectable institutions like the British government, tend to demoralize him or weaken his powers? On the contrary, Milton must forever be recognized as one of the great builders of republican government. Tennyson the Poet Laureate of England has for many years received a large annuity from government. This does not prove his poetical work to be in the least stultified. Would that the ingenious people of every station, who for want of means are lost to the world, might all be equally well provided for! Would not the result be to free inventors and authors from the robbery that is now almost certain to destroy the man or woman of genius, by heartlessly grasping their conceptions away, while in the embryo and vending them as the robbers' own? Fixed or endowed institutions, like a political government, or a university that belong to no persons in particular but are the property of humanity, are generally very honorable in matters of recognition and payment of services. Is it not natural then, for persons of every variety of unprotected genius which has conceived valuable things in the mind, but is unprotected, and surrounded by a thousand greedy sharks of the competitive world who always stand ready to pounce upon anything they are likely to make money out of, is it not perfectly natural and just that all such, including the working masses, worst robbed of ali, should turn toward their staunch, benefficent, magnanimous nation, for safety and for means? "Government" is always common to any people who have the organization and the manhood to assert their claims. Swedenborg owed his ability to produce the "Arcana" and other literary work, to the sinecure he held for many years, under the Swedish government. His salary paid his publishers' bills. The world is indebted, primarily to Swedenborg, secondarily to the Swedish government for whatever the labors of Swedenborg are worth. You will find few in the American Republic who have really succeeded in reaping the honors and emoluments due them from a work of their own genius, who have not had more or less assistance and protection from that great *common* resource, "government". All those perons mentioned, have richly repaid the world for its public favors. A similar story of almost any great man might be squeezed out of the negative reticence that broods over the annals of genius. It is a fact worth knowing, that what sets the British government among the ablest and most successful of Commonwealths, is its munificence in elevating and endowing its geniuses. It is a fact too little known that what made France, during Napoleon, an object of scorn from within and without, was that dynasty's jealousy and exclusivism against literary and originative citizens. It exhibits a steadfast policy of England to lift her genius up, and a fixed determination, prompted by the meanest spirit of jealousy, on the part of Napoleon, to push French genius down. What signalizes the punic nature of most republics is the stinginess of their mediocre politicians and their misplaced, sycophant guardianship of the taxpayers. There prevails a great mistake in the minds of community, as to who and what this "taxpayer" is. The advocate of the competitive system, on which political economists base the dogma of "supply and demand" always imagines that those who have the immediate handling of the money with which taxes are paid must of course, be the taxpayers; whereas, any honest person who reasons, cannot but see that LABOR is the original, the true and only source of all payments on articles taxed. Now, the laboring people are those who perform such labor. Yet managing persons have not only gotten away from the laborer his labor-product itself, but they assume, with the coolest effrontery, that this "gotten" product of the laborers' toil is the *source* of taxation; and consequently, that they themselves are the taxpayers! It is just here, the great Industrial Party takes its source. This kind of thing has been going on long enough. It is an effort in the direction of justice as the hard working, unappreciated, ill paid workers of the country are the owners of it, in justice, having made it what it is. But it will be seen that the labor party does not propose to degrade this citizen's government to the capacity of a mere almoner or almsgiver, the position that governments certainly have assumed in most cases mentioned, toward citizens needing help. The party assumes that the government belongs to humanity and not to any select objects of favor. Governments, like the air we breathe, are *common property* and cannot be construed as the *exclusive property* of any man, or of any set or minority of men whatsoever. As the air man breathes is necessary to bodily existence, so the laws and regulations for national existence called government, are necessary for his moral life; and any effort of a class of men to exclude masses from the free benefit of either, is direct usurpation. We are determined the world shall see a system by which, not ony its geniuses but also that still greater class, the working masses themelves, who go hand in hand with genius, constantly assisting her in all elaborations, applications and toils shall enjoy the strong, steadfast aid of government, in a manly manner. We cannot forget that under the old competing methods, this govornment help has generally been enjoyed under some form of sinecure office. The labor movement regards sinecures in the light of *alms-giving* or beggary; of itself without a shade of manly independence. True, such a benefit as that has generally been regarded as better than proffers from an individual. But a sound labor movement wants only for citizens the honorable labor that government can, and ought to, and must render them, by assuming the management and control of the great people's Industry, altogether independent of managing schemers, who now manage them for themselves. Governments belong to one individual as well as another. Whose right is it to make distinctions in favor of particular persons? Who shall say that a government possessing the ability to work as difficult a matter as an army of conquest, may not also have the ability to operate a cotton mill? Who shall say that if government can, by its well known, successful system of feeding, clothing, equipping its legions of defense, often to a half million men, at rates far more economical than they can furnish them themselves and with better articles, that the same government cannot render anybody and everybody, *every* claim to citiizenship and protection? Who shall say that if a government can conduct a magnificent enterprise like a postal industry, with a great, systematic department, regulated by the people's will at pleasure and run with such cheapness and unerring exactitude for ages, that it is unable to work the telegraphs the railroads and water lines that form a part of it? It is a stupid ignorance of political economy which stimulates them in their denial that government is the only legitimate and natural channel through which the railroads, water lines and telegraphs should be operated; because so long as these instruments of transmission remain property of individuals and joint stock companies, whose interest is advanced rather by exacting from, than promoting the interests of the great mass on whom they thrive by extorting exorbitant rates of freights and fares, just so long will the postal system itself remain incomplete. We hold that the assumption by government of the railroads, water lines and telegraphs, if for no further purpose than merely as auxiliaries to the postal department, would soon cheapen railroading, shipping and telegraphing so as to make these inventions of the laboring people practically usable by them; for as things now are, they are almost totally deprived of their uses. Now, to your question. How is it going to destroy individual incentives? Without economic *means the people are slaves. This is their economic means.* How can a person lose the spirit, glow, animus that nerve him to an invention when he has means with which to carry out the project? On the contrary, these advantages will help people by liberating genius from the shackles of poverty. The almost free postal arrangement of the people makes it possible for a poor man, whether employed in the post office department or not, to write correspondence which used to cost beyond his means before that beneficent service was undertaken by government. He can transmit sums of money in safety; and finds himself facilitated in accomplishing many other things which in the dark incompetence and the gloom of the unlettered ages he could not have done. Does not this explain why inventions are thickening upon us, even with a rapidity which outstrips our corresponding growth of knowledge as to how these inventions should be applied! Had government under the sanction of the people, as in this case of the post office, the control of cotton and woollen manufacture would it not be in furtherance of the people's interest to cultivate inventions? Would government, like the sly, crafty, selfish individual or joint stock company study to cheat an inventor of improvements for facilitating this manufacture? On the contrary, governments, as we have seen, are magnanimous; and in all such cases, it is for their advantage to be so, because the people want to rid themselves of every burden when they do their work in common. The government *must help* the man of genius. How could Cap. Eads have accomplished his work of deepening the channel of the Mississippi, without the help of the United States Government? What a failure would the genius and energies of M. de Lesseps have proved, had not the French Government sanctioned his schemes and rendered him abundant assistance in cutting the Suez Canal and also in his railroad and marine floodings on the Sahara Desert! We find Cap. Ericsson writhing in the slow tortures of the monster of individualism, lashed by its merciless tail, derided by its tongue, shriveled by its breath, until a government took him, in an hour of peril; then his genius taught the nations their greatest lesson in marine armaments of defense and gained for him the imperishable honor and glory of having rescued a fleet and perhaps saved a Republic.

The significant truth is, that if all our industries were the common property of government instead of being as now, the plunder of a system of individualism that thrives best by robbing people of special ingenuity and enterprise and depriving them of both the pleasures and emoluments due by virtue of their originative minds and their labor, if, we repeat, these industries were property of the people, the *Body-Politic*, or general public, they would soon learn to work them collectively and independently of the competitive methods altogether; simply because it would be for their own interests as individuals to do so.

Here we are furnished with a proof that *Collective control of the Economic means of life emancipates, rather than enslaves the mind.* As it is, people make slavery a trade. To delve ten long, dull hours for a person in whom you take no interest, is slavish. But the moment you begin to feel a proprietorship in that industry, you are free. This proprietorship yields *a right* to labor there. If you are abused, you are entitled to redress by virtue of your collective ownership in the business. It is your *right* to labor there that makes you ecoumically free. With freedom you can work out an invention or study the materials for a book or any other life-work, unmolested. What genius, enterprise, happiness want, is FREEDOM from poverty. Eonomic emancipation is the sane, solid, reasonable question before the world. How could prostitution exist if females were furnished good, respectable employment? The disgusting traffic would soon disappear from the earth; because female modesty as a rule can be proved to outweigh both passion and temptation; but the gaunt monster hunger forces her with a cruel grapple to forget modesty and become his slave. Again, as a further proof that the assumption by government, of industries, as in a co-operative society, would be greatly beneficial in encouraging genius, let us look at more *facts.* Whenever it becomes necessary to science that correct observations should be taken on a forthcoming transit of a planet, an eclipse or even meteorological data like those of the weather signal service, we find all the enlightened governments of the earth engaging in a lively co-operative work, fitting out costly scientific expeditions and with a most cordial understanding, forgetting all their petty differences, sending ships and special trains, equipped with the best of instruments and the most thoroughly skilled experts to various points on the earth's surface where the best observations may be effected. Here we find not only one but many governments furnishing the Universities and Colleges of the world with means to do needed work which otherwise would be left undone. We find also that these governments in thus furthering science, are actually employing many working people of many professions and trades who otherwise might have nothing to do. We find governments of various countries, busily assisting each other with plans and equipments for carrying into effect the expeditions of research to the North Pole. The ostensible excuse given for this is, that individuals are not capable nor are they qualified to carry out so prodigious a work. Quite true. Here we agree with them emphatically. Neither are they capable of conducting so immense, so vitally important a business concern as a cotton or woollen mill or a farm, on a scale large enough to be either respectable or successful.

Objectionist. Then you hold that the management of Industries by the State instead of the individual, would have the effect to develop rather than discourage the genius of the people. But what about health? Is it more than fair that we consider the great topic of health in these discussions? Yet you are undermining health—health of society as a mass and health of the individual as a unit of society—undermining health, I say, by driving people into the adoption of great changes sure to produce distempers. Mark history. Wherever bodies of people have been known to enter new enterprizes, involving emigration from home into new tèrritory, we find that generally a large proportion, often half and sometimes nearly all, fall prey to the pestilences that beset the new modes of life. In their eagerness they overlook the deadly malaria that lurks in the damp forests, the wild, unpent blasts of winter, the sultry simoon, whirlwind and tornado of summer, the storms of spring and autumn, interspersed with an occasional free use of the reeking tomahawk, scalping-knife, the desperado's bowieknife, revolver and bludgeon and all this delectably inter-wreathed with failures in the crops, starvation, inability to meet indebtedness, mortgage sales and bankruptcy. Poisonous reptiles, hungry wolves, bears and alligators complete the picture. Exactly so with the greater, mightier and vastly more fundamental changes you propose shall take place in the social and political world. Nothing can prove more disastrous to the social and political health of the people. We know it took thousands of years of growth in human development to grow out of certain forms of socialism, patriarchal and otherwise and get society fixed upon a sound basis of competition. It took many scores of ages to get this splendid enlightenment and now it is dogmatically proposed, by an ignorant rabble, to throw it all away, wheel back into ancient barbarism and violate the decrees of natural growth or progress by swooping humanity into a thousand perplexities that environ a life of new experiences dogmatically forced upon us without even considering their own inability to erect a wiser system and supply it with means and with honest officers and functionaries of experience to take the places of the old. You are plunging the world into an abyss, certain to produce the most terrible moral, social and political ulcers tumors, wens and vital diseases the world has ever known.

SOCIALIST. The answer to this hash of objections is, that *the growth of our knowledge of political economy does not keep pace with the growth of mechanical instrumentalities.* A class of aptitudes for grasping is allowed by this marvelous enlightenment you depict, to hold unlimted, even predatory sway, havoc, rapine and murder over the innocent, peaceful inhabitants, who are endowed with adaptabilities and aptitudes which qualify them only for inventors, producers, workers, builders of this astonishing civilization you glowingly describe. It is a civilization then, based upon rapine and predatory brigandage. Each inhabitant born with the grasping faculty instead of the productive or inventive, becomes a licensed squanderer, practicing a legalized devastavit upon that which ought to be a paternal estate. What a wonderful condition of social, political, individual health must be the inevitable outcome of such a state of affairs! Like the eagle, the lion, the vulture, that are the emblems and symbols of the predatory, hawking competitive system your bloodthirsty military enlightenment stands on, your man of shrewd grasping aptitudes unhindered by either the law, the ruling interest or by public opinion—since all these are moulded, shaped out to best thrive under this system—sallies forth from his home of comforts, pounces upon the defenseless majorities, too busy in the great world's work of production, distribution, invention to defend themselves, and robs, starves and enslaves them on every hand! A most marvelous enlightenment! What other than debased and low and ignorant, may your system's victims be? An enlightenment based upon brute force; advantage getting; ignoble use of power. An enlightenment without magnanimity, bloated in oligarchical rule and living by the beast-monarch instincts of the eagle and the lion, while belying such creatures' true characteristics by aping their predatory life too far, for the animals disdain to feed upon their kin. Such is the enlightenment then, which you call a healthy, as well as a health producing *growth* upon society! Did it not outgrow the competitive system itself, it might be more tolerable. But it builds up overbearing monopolies and destroys the very principle of competism by stealing from the *Socialist his Coöperation and applying it to Joint Stock Companies*, crippling free manufacture, free intelligence, free distribution, reasonable rates of travel and telegraphy, even free circulation of money. This is the enlightenment you live upon and uphold; a civilization based upon the mechanics and mechanical instrumentalities the working people produce, operate, and become the slaves of, through their monopoly by men gifted only with this class of grasping, unchecked aptitudes. The laboring, inventing, creating class, unprotected by class laws, invent the locomotive and weave the railroad system over the country; but are virtually forbidden the enjoyment of these vehicles they themselves construct, supply and keep in motion! Let us look at the effect of this on the health of the laboring classes thus deprived, by exorbitant rates of fare, of the advantages of healthful, cheap travel. The poor, it is well known, are afflicted with many kinds of diseases which only a change of climate can cure. Physicians have geographical charts, delineated from government statistics of the census and health reports, accurately showing the localities where certain diseases prevail and also where those maladies do not and cannot exist. Now let us, to make our argument on this health question clear, suppose that this new democracy or social government were in full play. Of course there would immediately spring into existence workshops and farms, scientifically conducted through every expedient at the people's command, as in a co-operative society. There would, to do all the manufacturing of machinery and other iron work, be perhaps a dozen vast government iron works doing business at different poin.s; one, we will suppose, located in Colorado, another at San Francisco; one in Florida, Maine, Texas, Missouri, the Central States and other localities where resources of health and of iron, coal, timber and other material of success and comfort abound. The railways are also the property of the people and tariffs fixed at actual cost. Now Colorado is, we assume, marked on the map of health as blessed with a climate excellent against consumption. At another quarter no fevers exist. Different maladies fly different countries.

Now, if a man engaged in one of these workshops is taken sick with a scrofulous or consumptive disease any good doctor must advise him to go where he may enjoy a change of air. And he does not have to wait for an occasion; for the workshops are arranged to meet the exigency. A situation is ordered for him by telphone and the sick man is cured by the change, without squander of time or money; for he now rejoices in a true citizen's co-interest in management as well as mere muscular activity in these grand works. Carry out this system and you settle health's darkest mystery.

Objectionist. Do you want the private business of the country to fall into the hands of politicians? This is a plain question, plainly put. Our experience with politicians is, that they are not to be trusted, as a class. There is a sly, impudent, dishonest look upon the very visage of a politician. He always shows a well fed face and does not exhibit the gaunt accomplishment of starvation to be found among your labor agitators but there is seen an undisguisable cunning playing a wanton art upon his lip. He can, no doubt, talk sweet things about giving the starving people employment. He knows how to promise. It is a part of the secret of his false career; and he harvests his successes from it. He is fully prepared to take the poor creatures he deludes, into his most gracious confidence and with reckless promises tell you of his great ability in all the details of business management *if you will but keep him in office!* He wants the Municipal, State and General governments of the country to vote appropriations of large sums of money, ostensibly for building up these government industries which you advocate because he knows that such appropriations are just what is the most easily converted into political plunder which is the only game he is scenting. These coy, shrewd, double-tongued politicians who mostly spring from the unprincipled, if not from the lowlived part of community, are baiting a trap with the soul and body of the working men. They are totally incapable of managing an industry of any kind. All they want is to gratify themselves. Are not we trifling then, with good sense when we pander to rogues?

SOCIALIST. Every Socialist will acknowledge that you are putting the question straight; but your views are all taken from the old competitive standpoint. We have no politicians in the movement.

OBJECTIONIST. That signifies nothing. Politicians are as penetrating as mercury. No matter how much you labor to repudiate them they will always be there; the first to decoy, mislead, demoralize you and the first to assume and shout loyalty to your cause in the light, while stabbing at both you and your principles in the dark.

SOCIALIST. Well, since you hold so bad an estimate of politicians, our only answer to your inquiries can be in straighter terms. We care little or nothing about *who* the workers are. Any man to be elected to a political position in our Party must believe in our *principles.* It stands to reason. When an editor is engaged on your newspaper his sentiments are consulted before his abilities. He must be loyal to the principles of that newspaper. After that matter is settled, the question of qualifications can come in. It is *principles first, qualifications afterwards;* for of what use are his qualifications to that journal, if they are not directed most strenuously and exclusively toward its success? Now, the labor movement must be as practical and business-like. The Progressive move of this age cannot afford to select men who are not well known to it, as efficient exponents of its *principles.* What a foolish thing it would be for an army of conquest, invading a new region, surrounded by all the besetting temptations that usually decoy an invading enemy, to be commanded by a general who were known to sympathize and intrigue with the forces he was sent to overthrow! Yet the cases are parallel ones. If you are unwilling to admit the justice of the cause itself, you must, in candor, recognize the necessity of applying sound business methods in the work of carrying out those principles, whether good or bad. Our Principles are so clearly studied out and so definately put in language, that they become a study; and the most advanced students—those who most ably, honestly, persistently advocate, teach them will naturally be looked to with most confidence, as persons best fitted to become the employed servants of the Party. It is altogether impossible for treachery to exist in this movement for the very reason that *those who are not for the principles are against us.* There is no such thing possible as half way measures in this Labor Question. When the moment for solid, practical effort arrives men must choose and be consistent with their choice; because it is a *principle* to be labored for; not an individual. This is distinctly understood. Now a political party, in point of moral or *ethics*, resembles the newspaper or the military scheme referred to. Each has its curriculum, its peculiar ethics or moral ideas of right and wrong, without which no newspaper, invading army, college of learning or Political Party ever has thrived or perhaps ever will succeed. It matters little then, what the likes and dislikes, the whims and petty caprices, notions or tricks may be, of the exponents of *principles*, who are elected to work out those business objects, assigned to each through the fiat of creed. We care little whether our agents be inanimate instruments or living men. Be he saint or devil, humane or selfish, the man's merit, or usefulness does not consist in this. It consists in his showing his constituents who elected him to office, that he conforms to the oath of fidelity to his Party's Principles.

OBJECTIONIST. What are the principles of your organization expressed in short terms? The reason why the movements of Labor in different parts of the world are so vague and unappreciated is because nobody knows what the agitatators want. They get themselves flurried over some real or imaginary wrong and without even knowing or reckoning upon the exact or probable results, send out wild and fierce men incompetent to state even a proposed plan of relief.

SOCIALIST. The exact wording of the principles of the Labor Party would be a difficult thing to give, because at nearly every congress or large conference, where the working people meet, the words of the so called "platform of principles" are changed to suit some trivial necessity of the moment without altering the general sense; but we can give you the most important ground-work or *theses*, in a few words:

Platform of Principles for the Socialistic Labor Party.

Labor being the creator of all wealth, through and by it alone is civilization possible. It rightfully follows that those who labor and create all wealth are the most necessary part of society; and hence should enjoy the full results of their toil.

An equitable distribution of the products of labor is utterly impossible under the present system of society. This fact is abundantly illustrated by the deplorable condition of the working classes, who are in a state of destitution and degrading dependence, in the midst of their own productions. While the hardest, most disagreeable work brings to the worker only the bare necessaries of life, others who do not labor at all, riot in labor's products, having everything which wealth can purchase.

The present industrial system of *competition* causes the intensity of this inequality; concentrating into the hands of a few, all the means of production, distribution and the products of labor, thus creating gigantic monopolies, dangerous to the people's liberties.

Monster monopolies and extremes of rich and poor are a natural outgrowth from the competitive system of conducting industries which are supported by class legislation. They are subversive of all democracy, injurious to the national interests and destructive of the practice of truth and morals.

The resources of life, that is, *the means of production, transportation and interchange must become* as fast as practicable, the social property of the people under the administration of government so as to institute direct popular Legislation and enable the people to propose or reject any law at their will, thus securing self-government in the interest of each.

DEMANDS.

First. Revision of the Constitution, or Frame-work.

Second. The right of suffrage shall in no wise be restricted.

Third. Political Equality before the law, to all citizens.

Fourth. The establishment of a National Ministry of Labor.

Fifth. All Conspiracy laws operating against the rights of the working people, must be repealed.

Sixth. Congress (and Parliaments) shall provide for an immediate creation of National Bureaus of Labor Statistics.

Seventh. The rigid enforcement of the eight hour law in all national and public works. We also demand an amendment to the Constitution of the United States, legalizing eight hours as a day of work in all industrial employments.

Eighth. All uncultivated lands shall be taxed equally with cultivated lands in the same locality.

Ninth. Government alone, shall issue all money; and such right shall not be delegated to any banking or private corporation.

The Socialistic Labor Party struggles to carry out the following measures in states where they are not now the law:

First. State Bureaus of Labor Statistics.

Second. Eight Hours as a legal working day and strict punishment of all violators.

Third. Abolishment of the system of hiring out by contract the labor of convicts in prisons and reformatory institutions.

Fourth. Strict laws, making employers liable for all accidents resulting from their negligence, to the injury of their employés. Mechanics and laborers are thrown upon the mercy of greedy management, unless protected by rigid Life and Limb Laws through which justice may be obtained.

Fifth. Entire legal restriction of the labor of Children under fourteen years of age.

Sixth. Universal Compulsory Education; all school materials to be furnished at public expense.

Seventh. Factory, mine and workshop inspection; and sanitary supervision of all food and dwellings.

Eighth. All wages shall be paid in the legal tender of the country; and violations of this law shall be punished.

Ninth. All ballots to be printed by town and city govenmants. Ballots containing the names of all candidates for public office to be sent to all voters two days before each election, and all election days to be legal holidays.

Tenth. All property whatsoever, without regard to the purposes for which it is used, shall be impartially taxed, so as to bear its just proportion of this burden.

All so-called tramp laws punishing unemployed workingmen as tramps are unconstititutional and inhuman, as poverty is thereby made a crime. The immediate repeal of such brutal class laws is demanded.

By a deep laid scheme against the people, carried through by means of class, or lobby legislation, over 125,000,000 of acres, good government land, comprising an area of territory larger than ten states—sufficient to furnish farms of fifty acres to over 5,000,000 of our citizens—have been given to sharp, arrogant corporations whilst great masses of the citizens are cringing with but a scanty existence, too destitute to enjoy either home or competence; and at the moment these wrongs exist the great, reigning parties which manage the nation's destinies are joining hands, South and North.

PLATFORM OF PRINCIPLES ADOPTED BY THE "NEW DEMOCRACY", NEW YORK, 1858.

The following Platform may be instructive, being in substance and very nearly in words the same as recommended at that time for the people's consideration:

1. As all legitimate property is the product of Industry it rightly belongs to the producer.

Eight hours of labor should be the extent of a legal day's time, being as much as the health, happiness and progressive improvement of society will permit.

3. As the earth is the common parent of all mankind, from whose bosom each individual inherits the inalienable right to live and draw subsistence, therefore any and every interruption of the enjoyment of this right by the monopoly of traffic in the soil is a violation of the sacred principle of justice and must ever be attended in the future, as in the past, with direful consequences. Land then, being a common element (not property), should be supervised by society for the benefit of the people, upon the basis of equality.

4. To secure the greatest advantages of economy from the improvements of the age, and to guard against the cupidity of contractors and organized monopolists, the system of contracting public work should be abolished, and all public improvements, such as railroads, gas-works, canals, mining, post offices, expresses, telegraphs, &c, should be public property, conducted by government employés, at cost, for the benefit of society.

5 As ignorance is a fruitful source of crime, therefore every facility for the acquisition of useful knowledge should be equally guaranteed to all and schools, colleges and scientific institutions must be supported by the government, free. That the people may be enabled to convene frequently, to

consider subjects of public welfare and revise the acts and propositions of their public servants, the school-houses of the land should be open at least two evenings in each week for the use of the people.

6. To develop the resources of the country and afford just protection to the useful classes against the avarice of capitalists and the derangements of trade, an Industrial Bureau should be established by government, upon equitable principles of time and compensation, thereby preventing the necessity of strikes by furnishing employment to those who might otherwise suffer the pangs of hunger or be tempted to crime.

7. For the protection of the people in cities against exorbitant rents, the unimproved property belonging to the cities should have economical residences erected thereon by the city authorities, and rented to the people at cost, in the same manner as they are now supplied with water.

8 To prevent the further practice of fraud by municipal authorities, the people must have new charters for cities, containing clauses to the effect that all tax levies, and other important measures must be submitted to the people for approval and rejection; and further, that the head of each department must make and publish monthly returns of the business done and all the particulars of receipts and disbursements.

9. To protect the poor against the impositions practiced by soulless speculators, the authorities should purchase, in proper season, a sufficient quantity of coal for the domestic consumption of the people, at cost of mining and transportation.

10. As the declaration of Independence affirms that "all just governments derive their power from the consent of the

governed" themselves, therefore, the right of suffrage should be secured to every citizen of mature age regardless of sex, color, or condition.

11. To remedy one of the most corrupting customs of the present system, we demand that all fee offices shall be abolished, and all lucrative salaries be reduced to comport with the wages paid to mechanics and persons of other useful callings; and we further demand that whatever labor society requires a person to perform, said person shall be remunerated therefor upon the principle of *Equal Compensations.*

12. The Currency of a nation should be issued by its government only; be a legal tender and bear no interest.

13 The sad experience of all peoples exhibits the fact, that wherever irresponsible authority is conferred it is liable to abuse; whether it be exercized by monarch, lord or delegate; therefore, in *political* institutions, the inhabitants should retain the sovereign function of ratifying or rejecting all acts of their authorized servants.

14 The demands of the Labor Movement are extreme of necessity; that all individuals desiring reform must, on the merit of the principles they strive for, place themselves on this Platform; while those not favoring reform will naturally rally on the other side.

The above Platform is remarkable if only on account of its age. There is no better arrangement and wording of these great, fundamental truths to be found. Ever since the war of the revolution boasted of as having given *liberty* to the inhabitants of the United States, there has been much dissatisfaction manifested, and frequent grievances, to the effect that this liberty was a sham. These democratizing amendments have been agitated many years, as a relief.

The following is taken from a code of principles adopted by the Social Democrats, formulated at the different European congresses of the labor movement and often quoted as reference by the Industrial agitators in America:

PLATFORM.

A. The Social Democratic Workingmen's Party seeks to establish a free State founded upon Labor.

B. Each member of the Party promises to uphold, to the best of his ability the following Principles:

1. Abolishment of the present unjust political and social conditions.

2. Discontinuance of all class rule and class privileges.

3. Abolishment of the working people's dependence upon the capitalist by the introduction of co-operative labor in the place of the wages system, so that every laborer will get the full value of his work.

4. Obtaining possession of political power as the prerequisite to the solution of the labor question.

5. United struggle, united organization of all workingmen and women and strict subordination of the individual, under the laws framed for the general welfare.

6. Sympathy with the working people of all countries, who strive to attain the same object.

C. We further demand:

1. *a*) All public officers shall be elected by a direct vote of the people.

*b*) Every inhabitant over twenty years of age shall be entitled to suffrage.

*c*) Introduction of the one-house-representative system.

*d*) All enactments shall be laid before the people for ratification or rejection.

2. Improvement of the present judicial system; and in-

troduction of free administration of justice, *without favoritism.*

3. Abolishment of conspiracy laws in all the states.

4. Abolishment of all indirect taxes and introduction of a single progressive income and property tax.

5. Abolishment of all monopolies; manufacturing to be carried on by free co-operative labor societies under the guarantee of the people, with government credit.

6. Adoption of obligatory school-laws for all children between their seventh and fourteenth years; free use of all necessary books and other public eductional appurtenances. Prohibition of the labor of children in industrial concerns.

7. Introduction of the eight hour system for all.

8. Regulation of female labor in occupations injurious to health or morality. Equalization of women's wages with those of men.

9. Prohibition of work in prisons being done in the interest of private persons. The prisoners' time to be managed by the state and *only for public purposes.*

10. As the contract system tends invariabiy to corruption, bribery and felony, we demand its abolishment by the State; and that every kind of work done under the auspices of either the general, the state or the city governments, be done by days' wage work, according to the Eight Hour System as designed by the statute.

11. Sanitary inspection and authorized care, over the workingmens' and workingwomens' habitations and work shops.

12. State and National bureaus for Labor Statistics to be established.

13. Banking and insurance to be conducted by the State.

## CHAPTER XII.

## THE GREAT LAND QUESTION.

---

### FINAL AND BOLD WORDS ON THE NATIONALIZATION OF LAND. QUACKS, STANDARD PHILOSOPHERS, BUZZARDS AND FILIBUSTERS WHO HANG ON THE OUTSKIRTS OF A GREAT SCIENCE.

---

CONVERSATION BETWEEN A SENATOR AND A SOCIALIST.

STATESMAN. There appears in many parts of the country a strong desire to understand exactly what organized labor is going to do as a finality with the Land Question. What is the action resolved upon, or what is going to be resolved upon, by your Organization if it succeeds in ultimately reaching a majority?

SOCIALIST. The ultimate Land Question, unlike many other and more familiar forms of the great Problem, is necessarily kept in abeyance. When the proper time arrives and the movement is in readiness all along the line, with a reliable force of speakers educated to the idea; in short when all preliminary arrangements have been completed, minor demands realized, the party out of infancy and in dignified attitude, it will do to sound loudly the clarion of Land for the People.

STATESMAN. You claim to be the Party of science; to be the only and original among many which you accuse of selfishness and insincerity. Now, fairness and sincerity demand that you frankly impart to all who are anxious to know what in your theory is to be done with the Land. We want no half way language but the simple conception entertained by you as to what is to be done with Land when labor comes into political power and control. What will you do when in power, to realize your Land theory?

ANSWER. The question is fair. One thing in answer is that no inhumanities would ever be tolerated by the Party of Labor. Neither honor, science, justice nor humanity can afford to do a cruel deed. This movement cannot prosper except on principles of strictest equity. No arbitrary assumption of titles, no dispossessment of inheritances, forcible evictions or cruel confiscations can ever be countenanced by it. As in the formation of society or social conditions among men, long ages of time have been consumed, so now in its completion, no man should impatiently hope for nature to hasten beyond her usual pace. The Land question be it ever so radical or formidable need frighten no man; for correctly considered its nationalization on a large scale cannot take place until the people are first in possession of the scientific mechanical instruments with which to cultivate land and make it fruitful.

STATESMAN. We understand that this nationalizing the machinery of labor—that is, the improved facilities used in modern production and distribution—means with you, their social ownership, management and impartial yield. This is quite plain and comprehensible; but it is very far away from the Land question. How are the land and its products to become social property?

ANSWER. By nationalizing Land is meant both the word and the deed to their full extent.

Question. Land among the earlier nations largely belonged to the state. Having the failure of many states that once held it in common, as examples of stupendous follies of the dismal past before us, how can we indulge anew the hugging of that ancient phantom, which never realized a proposition for humanity and has only nourished individualism and the most ghastly forms of slavery and other cruelties which have always widened the gap between rich and poor?

ANSWER. Land it is true, was in some ancient countries, as Rome, nationalized by the barbarous ordeal of force; but it was never social property. Your question must be answered by the political economist. Government should not only possess but should also cultivate the landed domain. In doing this it must bring into activity all its immense powers of capital, genius, science and prerogative. Being the natural organization of the people it should be their basis, bolster, employer and insurance fund. People are gradually but constantly becoming wiser and surer in their legislation; are growing out of their old warring habits and getting so practical as to dare undertake through their government or popular organization, large business enterprises. These they have found to be much more economical and safe, less partial more democratical and true to the masses, than the old competitive ones still existing about them. People are learning that there is nothing so great, so intricate, so difficult that this great common organization, the collective unity cannot better and more satisfactorily do, than the old snarling, short-lived, competitive concerns which have hitherto undertaken business for purposes of profit. In short, people are discovering that this sort of business management is just what causes the poverty, ignorance and misery which surround them. Looking then, at the past, its nationalized land and celebrated landless agricultural laborers with their enormous and bloody agrarian convulsions, it is fair to reason that while men were ignorant of collectivism, they could do no better than to accept individualism. Collectivism was too scientific for that time. Individualism was fierce, selfish, competitive and warlike. But it was the best system known. Now, men are more advanced and better qualified to comprehend the three great improvements inherent in collective ownership and control of the land, namely: brotherhood that does away with warfare and cruelty; understanding that makes clear the methods and possibilities; and lastly, the opening up of a new set of incentives of good citizenship.

Now, this collectivity is the people's co-operation for a better management of the land. Men are daily taking fresh lessons in government and thus gradually opening their eyes to the practicability of engaging in business upon a vast rather than a petty scale. You cannot any more reasonably doubt the ability of government to cultivate a farm, hiring men at good pay and exercizing modern inventions, modern short hours, modern humanity and kindness, modern public watchfulness over state, general and municipal transactions than you can doubt its ability to conduct the postal system, the Erie Canal, the schools or the railroads and telegraphs. It is absolutely preposterous to argue against the ability of government, the natural organization of every people, the collective mind or state, to assume with the utmost confidence and certainty the control of any enterprise whatever. Most especially do these words apply to scientific cultivation. But they apply anywhere. Man as an integer without the mutual co-operation of his fellows, when out in the cold, competitive world is a failure. This fact is seen in the mortgages on his land wherever we go. True, large numbers succeed; but if a majority fail the proposition holds. Individualism has had a fair chance for thousands of years and failed; and it is high time for co-operation to be tried.

Statesman. You speak of this proposed assumption of land ownership and cultivation by the state, in other words, state farming, as if you were discussing a society for mutual co-operation! Can any stretch of imagination picture the slightest analogy?

Answer. Yes, in the outward appearance, but not in the outworkings. As individualism is precarious in its isolated forms, taking advantage, like the hawk, the tiger, the huntsman, of superior gifts of cunning, of strength or vested rights and opportunities to destroy its competitors, so in the proportion of the numbers, the whole system of co-operation as known in modern days is little better than the creature of prey, even attacking distant efforts of its own sort, when not affiliated in some clique of the craft. The socialist is too poor, too meagerly supplied with the leisure that begets competitive wit; too hard-worked to attempt the half-way policy of petty co-operation which has proved itself so hawkish, that in Germany and wherever it has existed as long as a quarter of a century the favoritism natural to its loop-holes, openings and chances, was found always to fall to smart people who bought more shares, exercized more wit, bullied more cunningly, and were soon seen strutting about with plenty, while sweating toilers got little except leers. In fact, co-operation is oligarchy from the start, dwindling down into monopoly—oligarchy while its joint stock features last and are more numerous, monopoly when the wit has succeeded in outwitting, displacing the many. This however, he is sure to do. Thus the dribblets of the many become the capital that starts the thief in business. Co-operation then, is monopoly in embryo while the joint-stock concern numbers many; for the hateful germs are there. Its tendencies, like those of the joint-stock company, are to gradually push out the many after using them in establishing a business, to assume individual control, enrich a paltry few and end in an individual concern at last. Especially is this petty co-operation worthless in America where the nature of institutions is political, with a hypocritical gloze of freedom and an actual monopoly of wit and its concomitants of victimized poor. Wit has it all here. The poor on ten to sixteen hours hard labor have little wit, however bright and brainy they may have been born. And wit and its oily offspring modern monopoly, are many times bound to thank some petty co-operation for their start in the world. Search for the root of poverty and evil and you shall find it so. How are poor men and women going to apply co-operation to land-tillage? What can petty co-operation do, even if it possess honest wit, in a scheme to own and cultivate land? How long would it be before a cunning wit of superior business abilities would spring some poisonous wrangle on the unsophisticated membership which would terminate in hoisting him up as the manager? Of course the rest soon become subordinates, then mere agricultural laborers, afterwards serfs. So wit sets up as getter; all others are outcasts; and the thing winds up in one man becoming owner, boss, landlord, congressman, monopolist; and the rest, common people of no account, with their ordinary quota in the poor-house and their darlings in unmemorized graves. Why friend, unless you allow your moiety of statesmanship in this gravest of social problems, you are admitting absolutely no proposition for ameliorating the growing horrors of monopoly! While you object to our scheme of state co-operation because it involves so vast a measure, you yet do not object to the insidious and constant growth of land monopolies almost equally vast. This individualism is enlarging with prodigious strides. Its attendant roll of poverty-doomed names is equally alarming. Great grievances must be met with radical rights. Labor is blest with the unique quality of harboring no ancient, rooted prejudices; it hugs no traditional fancies of history or of family. It has resolved that since the isolated individual is a failure, the business capacities of the *collective* individual must be tried. The individual cannot farm the land; else why a majority of farmers or agricultural workers in poverty? why a small minority in affluence? why bankruptcy, mortgages, squalor? why thistles and choking tares, weevil and rot? Could not capital, well paid energy with the well known scrutiny of government, make a farm blossom as well as a park; protect us from starvation as well as from fire; control public farming as well as public schooling; bring us our food as well as our letters; fertilize and work the acres of the country as well as the gardens of the cities; employ the wanderers and tramps as well as political partisans? Do you for a moment imagine that any argument to the contrary can hold against evidence so sensible and self-convincing? Away with prejudice and tradition fostered in wiles of individualism which have led men astray! What the workers want is statesmanship founded in the sciences whereof their own skill and toil have created in these modern days the mechanical tools. The state can farm the land, if the makers of the tools, the majority of voting citizens will it; for possessed of such mechanical means, it can put capital, with which its treasury is burdened, into it as a public enterprise and veritably "make two blades grow where one grew before." A change thus determined upon and thoroughly discussed by labor as an organized political party, nothing can satisfy us until it is in force; until the sources of fertility are thoroughly tapped; until practical skill in chemistry or ground-constituents, and in machinery shall be the prerequisite of a first class appointment thereon. Then our youth will have some attraction to labor, to knowledge and lofty attainments; whereas the craft of thievery is now too often the attraction because it offers higher rewards. Cannot government see to land as well as mind-tillage? Yet we see it busy everywhere cultivating mind—a new function not yet a hundred years on trial but already a vast success and being copied by all governments claiming title to the rank of civilization. Before this prodigious undertaking was begun ignorance infested men's households keeping pace with war, social corruption, kingcraft, standing armies, toadyism and their natural associate poverty. How foolish to cling to the old traditions based on a system of rank individualism which has forever kept men upon the land as serfs or slaves and is little better to-day! Already the sane and entirely scientific proposition has gone abroad that war is useless, brutal, always selects its victims from the laboring masses, does not belong to a truly enlightened age or country. This idea born of the labor movement, receives most of its aliment and impulse from the educating power of the public school system of the world. Had this great state undertaking not existed, workingmen would not for ages have discovered the uselessness of war and it may be regarded as certain that the nobility and wealthy who reap the emoluments of war would not have introduced any such life-saving measures. It is the work of this tillage of the mind of great masses by the state. So this proposition to cultivate the land in mass in the manner that states are cultivating mind in mass, though it startle some nervous folks, is really the one to bring wars to their final termination; because agricultural prosperity belongs to peace and cannot go hand in hand with brutality and suffering.

All this however, does not allege that the hard-worked men and women engaged in the tedious field of labor, with all their opportunities of the public schools, do not lose much of that wit and independence which are necessary to the watchful care required in the management of a small co-operative concern. It is just here that statesmanship based on so-called *platforms of principles* is, in this progressive form of government management of land and implements of tillage, secure from all danger of being wrecked by business sharpers such as have cursed all our efforts at co-operative stores, building societies, farms and manufactories. It is easy for the workman ever so sadly dulled by his enfeebling work, to catch on to a *principle* determined by his political party. The poor thus wrongly characterized as witless unfortunates, are not fitted for co-operation, because not prepared to cope with the competitive system, but are certainly in a good frame of mind to urge the same idea by means of the ballot. This bears a portent and power of inspiration which works upon his pride. The idea of compulsory fraternization for neighborly help conveyed in schemes of petty co-operation, is always extremely offensive to the average American voter no matter how lowly his social condition may be. This feeling seems inwrought into him by American institutions and makes him a natural politician and a bad co-operator. Thus when once set and determined on state co-operation, he will, with a rough, uneducated, less sensitive mind-condition into which hard fare has brought him, be in exactly the right mood to use his vote towards the indiscriminate dismissal of all public servants who would turn the arts of trading against his jealously nourished hopes of realizing the principle of his political platform. The poor man, in fact no matter how benumbed his sensibilities, is, in any country better qualified to guard against political knavery than he is to watch and detect the financial knaves who hover about the co-operative enterprises.

STATESMAN. Then this system of land ownsrship and tillage clearly means that your party hope to reduce the ownership and cultivation of land, from its present tenure by individuals, to one of common or popular ownership through government tenure and tillage. May it be asked, if once this theory be practically inaugurated, where will the matter end?

What will become of the world? How soon will the revolution be at hand and your overthrow of institutions collapse society? When is the first blood of our desperate resistance to be spilled? We are anxious to know because, being ourselves the owners of the land, having the means to institute a formidable resistance by employing the too willing talents of your own purchasable members and by a wholesome creation of repressive laws for the occasion, we promise to be faithful to our duty in maintaining good government.

SOCIALIST. Now, let us reason well and exhaustively first We are opposed to this impatient, not to say inflamatory method of argumentation. It leads to neither Christian-like nor rational deductions.. We would ask for nothing which the calm reason and fiat of an honest majority does not recommond after great discussion, deliberation and comparison with the history of the past. You recoil before what you imagine to be a revolution. Not a whit more momentous is this turn of things than one just gone through with in the great mechanical world—the cotton manufacturing industry. The relative difference in the comparison is, however, very great; since in this case it was the poor and helpless who were deprived, even of the use of the skilled art at which they earned a humble living. This mighty revolution was the result of the invention of machinery. It turned thousands of worthy people out of house and home, caused starvation, great suffering and death all over the civilized world. It caused rioting and organized resistance of the victims and was fraught with deeds of blood. Your class sanctioned this revolution, quelled the riots, used your prisons, enacted your favorite laws, hoisted up your alleged inventors who had stolen the honors as well as emoluments from labor—your Arkwrights and others—and knighted, glorified, feasted them, crushing and humiliating the deserving. Yet we do not complain, because it was the natural outcome of a science. Nothing can resist its inroads. Neither can anything resist the scientific, onward tread of the movement before us to-day But now comes the answer to inquiry as to when this change shall come. It is not *now* even asked for. Outside parties may seize on to the land question and attempt to project its issues in advance of their time but nothing could be more dangerous. The history of the past to which you justly allude, is a most memorable warning to all men, to beware of the mere nationalization of land. Why, it was that which under Roman control, plunged millions of free men into slavery! All through Greece, Sicily, Italy, and Asia Minor land, before the Roman conquest, was worked by small farmers, who, although as we have shown, were liable to failure like all others in the competitive conflicts of business, were comparatively prosperous and contented, working their bits of land as individual tenants on the same system of small holdings as that prevailing at this day. Un ions of trades existed all around them; for the ancient laws tolerated labor societies. The farmers themselves sometimes had their grange organizations. They were respected and probably were as well off, all things considered, as many of our farmers to-day. As Rome spread her conquests of arms these lands fell into her clutches and became nationalized. They became *ager publicus*, or public lands, incorporated with the Roman domain. Beautifnl farms, village homes in Asia, Greece, everywhere, fell by seizure and cruel confiscation into her rapacious hands. Rome assumed ownership of it all and the working people lost their homes. And what was Rome? Nothing but the lords, blooded grandees, millionaire politicians, braggarts of boasted family and their toadies and speculating fortune-hunters all maintained by the military, the armed force and repressive laws of which you so grandly speak. These were the statesmen. They constituted all that was recognized of Rome except her enormous wealth robbed and plundered from labor. Such statesmen made laws to suppress the labor and other social organizations everywhere, taking advantage of a monstrous military power to seize those happy farmers, degrade them to slavery, trade and interchange them as goods with one another and thus establish on this nationalized land the foulest, most gigantic system of human slavery ever known. This is what would become of nationalizing land prematurely, as advocated by many foolish agitators to-day, and right here. Should land again become militarized, as it surely would without an immense, counter-checking organization of laborers, whose teachers are educated and alert on these momentous, would-be-repeated tragedies of history, our newly inspired hopes would be dashed to atoms upon the despotic flints which line your ambuscades. No, no! We shall profit by the lesson taught by that old republic; and beware the premature nationalization of land; we shall thoroughly watch the land sharks who, even now, are eagle-eyed, regarding from afar the hopeful turn the land license question is expected to take, which may, in due time result in opening the American public acreage, in that loose, unwatched, desultory way that our domain will be as it was in the days of the Roman conquests—nationalized, without pre-arrangement or order. We can see these tactics already begun—the same old squatter tactics of the arrogant *gens* families of Rome. Cæsar had his elegant estates, as squatter on the public lands. Lawyer Cicero whose most eloquent bursts rang against the working people whom he twitted of being without an immortal soul, because too poor and lowly to possess a family name, drove to his squatter country seat, on the high road to Capua regaling the ladies who shared his chariot, on views of the six thousand revolted mechanics, enslaved farmers and gladiators, whose crucified bodies for long months dangled on ghastly gibbets because they dared to strike against their bondage. And Crassus, Pompey and Lucullus who thus murdered them are lauded by Rome's flunkies of the quill, because, like our modern railroad statesmen, they won their power through this pernicious old system of legalizing the occupancy of land that always belonged to nobody when it belonged to the state. We are a more watchful and guarded people, it is true, than were the ancients; but this system of land grabbing, even here may yet plunge us into war. Ireland has been almost literally swallowed up by rapacious land gluttons. Trace this mischief to its true source and you find all the trouble in the desultory, unscientific nationalization of land. In early times the land was worked by farmers on the aged and still prevailing competitive system of small holdings. The kings came and arrogantly made presents of large tracts of it to their favorite lords and ladies; for the very fact of kingly possession bears on its face this nationalization through cruel confiscation. England has plodded into the same egregious error, titling her grandees, one by one, until little remains for the impoverished toilers. War and violent revolution—which we always deplore—must inevitably follow, so soon as labor organization shall have awakened the aggrieved, landless poor to a full sense of the enormity of their grievance. How long will it be ere the squatters upon our recently nationalized geyser-park will turn up as the undisputed owners and lords of their leases and have to be driven off at last, by the enraged community for the same unwarrantable, insidious encroachments upon the public domain? Had government in either case, kept the nationalized lands; had the people tilled them without using the contract system at all; worked them scientifically employing unsparing capital; made a noble study of this great and difficult business art; banished from it by degrees, the competitive system entirely and always employed men and women as much for the sake of the labor as for its profits; and finally had all this been done at the sanction, and under watchful direction of such people employed and fed, be assured that there would exist no land question to-day. But alas, these are conditions of that great democracy, at whose millennial camps, swords shall be turned into pruning-hooks, the lion shall lie down with the lamb! The story of the terrible revolts, or strikes of those downtrodden slaves, freedmen and small farmers everywhere on the national lands, has been mostly suppressed; because, threatened by the bayonets of the ruling despotisms and coaxed by honeyed cajolements of patrons in power, historians have failed to do their duty; but enough has come to us to illuminate the path of this our second progressive movement of labor, setting its teachers on their guard against all agitation for land nationalization, until the implements of its productive management are all practically and thoroughly in the hands of the workers; the nation itself in their hands; the standing armies—if any be needed—in their hands; a progressive party of labor in their hands; for nationalization of whatever sort, being in the past, an instrument of all that is fierce, selfish and cruel, is susceptible only under the highest enlightenment, of becoming the basis of that new form of co-operation destined to ensure all against failure and injustice. For the present, then, we argue, "let the land question alone". Matters are bad enough now, without further aggravation. Our old, warlike, competitive system has, so far as the welfare of working and useful people is concerned, proved itself an utter failure; since our blood was shed in those conquests that wrested the lands from their original owners.

STATESMAN. If this be the correct method, socialists' views are far more conservative than violent; at least on the land question. We shall be constrained to acknowledge their measures on land reformation to look less violent and less disposed to rupture the existing laws, than certain other contemporaneous propositions offered by gentlemen claiming to be of your class. What are your notions on the idea of a progressive income tax, a tax on the values of land and other panaceas, such as are being pushed with considerable vigor from time to time?

ANSWER. We have never advocated any panacea. In fact, we simply recognize scientific management of every industry upon an equitable co-operative basis; the governments, of which we are the citizens, owners and directors, sanctioning, lending moneys for, and assisting to control them. This, on the whole, ought not to disturb the good sense of any one. A real and honest labor movement will want this, because its members are the millions of humanity who cannot cope with the inimical competitive system. Men have tried it. Sharp idlers have always got away their last garden patch and they are landless to-day. Is it not time that a radical system were tried? And is a tax upon land values, be it ever so violent, a radical measure? Would it not leave us still where we are now, scrambling, seething, failing, in this same old competitive cauldron? Suffer your standard philosophers to tax land even to dire confiscation and thus force its nationalization; what would it all come to if you fail to exhibit that great and crowning stroke of statesmanship that shall arrange for the governments to which such lands might fall, to immediately assume its cultivation on behalf of their citizens, using all necessary instrumentalities known to mechanics, chemistry and industry? Such hobbies are destitute of any power to effect what we only desire:—a final escape from the horrors of the competitive system. Imagine a tax on land instead of incomes, machinery, fine yachts, or vaulted gold, silver, interest-bearing bonds, or man-grinding mills, or coming inventions of a perhaps near era enabling men to live upon the air and defy the sweating denizens below; or big monopoly-run conveyance-hulks! Why, half the taxable values of our orb would be made to float air and sea! All this and land the only source of revenues wherewith to defray expenses of good governments! Ingenious doctrinaires' heaven of monopolies! Land owners, celebrated in the records of all times and countries, as the class of humanity most liable to failure, must, we are told in these days of glittering sciences whose progress is built upon other branches of industry, pay all costs, on pain of confiscation! And all this cruelty is demanded by gentlemen who claim to loathe the preparatory and truly humane proposition of labor, to science down this great land problem to a basis of practical co-operation in order to finally root out these features of competition and bring land cultivation into an attractive, desirable and prosperous pursuit.

A still further and more complete answer to questions

of this kind must contain two distinct paragraphs. In the first place, a truly scientific, progressive labor party must be based upon that excellent aphorism: "judgment of masses is always surer, purer and more reliable than judgment of individuals when those masses can agree in council"; and this we must treat first. Land-tax ideas, and others of which you speak, belong to one man; that is, they are generally the outcome of a single brain, or a single conception; whilst this peaceful, equitable solution of the problem by means of co-operation and government aid, of which we speak, is the outcome of ages. It was the too advanced study of the forefathers. America's Jefferson hobnobbed with Saint Simon, then a soldier boy under Washington, wounded in the revolutionary war, years before he started his school in Paris for its propagation and became the teacher of great men. Some of the finest talent of the great German philosophers has also contributed to this principle while the Jews who are homeless, are rejoiced to find it a dead letter in the good old law of Moses; and their wonderful forces of intellectual insight are now being resurrected and reapplied. Finally, it is this sort of co-operation that is always agreed to in all important world's congresses and conferences of working people themselves, whenever they have met for deliberation and at which this country, as well as those of other continents have been represented. No man can say that the question is undignified by being the foamy creation of a single brain. It is veritably the deliberate and unimpassioned judgment of many.

In the second place, the realization of the co-operative idea as applied to land cannot at present, nor perhaps yet for ages be even asked for. The nationalization of mines, railroads, telegraphs, telephones, lumber mills, factories, everything requiring the use of mechanical implements; in short, the tools of manufacture and distribution, which means, the natural common property—they having been invented and applied by the common hand of labor—must come first. All these natural tools of the great laboratories of civilization are products of human toil andh ave never been paid for. Their nationalization means simply their restoration from the hand of profit-getters, to their original makers and owners. But man's labor did not invent and create the land.

Such is the modernized form of co-operation. Governments that have ever stood over and watched and upheld the minority, are hereafter to protect the true owners, the makers, the majority. Is not this democracy? Why, correctly viewed, ours is the genuine democratic party, asking for nothing but what we create. When the people own this, when the mechanical tools of labor hitherto used by exploiters of profits wherewith to deprive men of comforts become the people's own, when they shall thereby find themselves out of danger of their immediate oppressors, then, this more distant and dangerous question of land nationalization may be carefully and humanely approached. Or, it may commence sooner, by piecemeal, as in cases of persons leaning to socialization of lands, through common, or state management, or tillage for the people; but no threat to wrest homesteads from the honest farmers, mechanics or others by exorbitant taxation or any other cruel device can for a moment be tolerated.

Now a word as to the peaceful achievement of great measures sooner, by avoiding violence. Correct ideas of political economy are henceforth to be based on evolution or steady and natural development. A plan of land taxation sufficient to exact a revenue for defraying the vast expenditures of governments, unavoidably leads us to anarchy if not to violence and bloodshed. Land owners, an enormous class, would be driven to rebellion. Better to suffer the old system, bad as it is, to plod along until men see their way clear to introduce the more humane and democratic finality which, when they have studied, and gradually become convinced that it is better, they will of themselves develop into the acceptance of, and allow it to sweep out the old obnoxious competitive system root and branch. But an unobtrusive and law-abiding piecemeal system may, without the least danger of rupture, be allowed to take its course.

Show up the evils of a thing to an intelligent public, and if there are no obstacles in the way, such as the old vested rights of kings, the intelligence of such people will of itself, decide against it and it must go. Monarchy was driven away from the American borders by a bloody revolution and its train of vested rights have gone with it. And this introduces us to the piecemeal or fragmentary system—the gradual substitution, little by little, or slice by slice, of the old by the new. We find instances of this elsewhere, where true and correct methods gradually and harmlessly supervene upon old and clumsy ones. There is the spelling reform for the English language. We have methods of eradicating from it this nuisance of bad spelling. But while earnest doctors are busy tinkering it with their half-way system at the schools, never deigning to acknowledge anything but the worshipful old alphabet of Cadmus, a modern literary economist invents a new and marvelous lightning system to supersede Cadmus himself.

So our genuine labor party should be such as will never need to be radically altered and only revised from time to time, at the suggestion of experience. Each experiment must be a germ which will generate a permanent institution. Now, applying the illustration, we find the orthography of the language an acknowledged abomination. Phonography, with the unscrupulous characteristics of all inventions, sweeps out all these rediculous incongruities by its new method of spelling by sounds. Boys learn it in the schools; and as they have to learn the other also, the absurdities of the old are brought into comparison with the beauties and economies of the new and often disgust them. By and by, when the "rising generation" come to have their way, the letters of Cadmus, like the bones of the dodo, will have to be sought among the fossils of things extinct. Any method of doctoring up the old system is not only useless but a waste of time.

Now, let us more lucidly apply this illustration to the argument in favor of an agricultural system to supplant that of competition under which the masses have failed. Like the old Cadmian letters, competition is of mythic origin and comes of kings. Applied to agriculture it has been a wretched failure. It however answers the purpose. Through it we get enough from the soil to feed us; and if it come to us perfumed by the poison of the huckster's adulterations, it is not the honest farmer's fault. Although a large amount of the cultivated land is in the clutches of lawyers holding mortgages against farmers who perish with overwork and broken hearts, yet their thankless toil is enough rewarded to support the human race with the viands of life. The mountain of wrong in the old competitive system is too prodigious to be spaded down. Its evils must be supplanted by the new and better one. But this co-operation must eventually take control of lands and till them with the scientific implements of man's invention, the most perfected application of chemistry, irrigation, machinery and labor-saving art, and thus finally solve the problem in the unbiased interests of all; that all may direct, all partake and enjoy and all grow into the true understanding of the word *Democracy*. We are not, therefore, in the incipiency of the practical application of the great finality, so wanting in good sense or so undiplomatical as to require a wholesale adoption of this boon or even to admit it as a plank in our platform.

Now the acceptance of land nationalization slice by slice, so to speak, may be compared with this spelling reform whose new measures are so radical and novel that even the prejudices besetting roundabout reform methods of the earnest doctors are forgotten; because boys learn phonography as a business qualification. In like manner, no prejudice or evil can result from any person bequeathing parcels of land to society or the state or government, if such person desires to have an experiment tried. But in both cases it is admitted that these experiments are founded upon the correct and final methods. The principal difficulty in either case is first to ascertain, when a new experiment is to be tried, how to make it a success. In the new system of phonography, its very practicability and demand have rushed it forward. To acquire it was to be qualified with a neat and genteel accomplishment, often an indispensable one wherewith to secure a position under government. So likewise this new proposition to radically change the method of land cultivation will create great numbers of neat and most highly respectable positions.

But the evil tendency against which we work is this determination of industrial capitalists to get rid of paying taxes. The richest men are too shrewd to covet land. Out of mere land there is no comparative profit. An instance of a great monopolizble industry such as better suits their purpose, is seen in the telegraph and telephone that can reap enormous profits, scarcely using a foot of land. It can be made to occupy neither soil nor surface. It soars and sings high in the air, an aeolian harp that harmlessly thrums among the aerial haunts of wild birds, squirrels and bats. If land is too precious for its owner to set its poles of the size of a bucket's bottom, at intervals in the hedge, or bog, or wayside waste, it has an anchoretical faculty of insulating and isolating itself from the world's gaze by plunging under ground, there shyly performing duty to the enrichment of mortals above. A cellar-way is good enough for its offices and thus its taxable land values are reduced to nil. It works best at the unknown bottom of rivers, lakes, gulfs and oceans, or wherever the hope of taxing land is most absurd and impracticable. Yet the telegraphs and telephones become not only gigantic industries but are classed among the most defiant monopolies of the earth; overcoming by bribes and other resistance all efforts of the taxgatherer, while millions of profits flow into the vaults of a few men who own and control them.

Even the railroads are leaving the taxable land; and their proclivity for worthless fens, hollows and rivers is familiar to all. In the cities they soar above the heads of animals and men without molesting or endangering them or their cares and toils below. They run through tunnels deep under ground where earth and granite are valueless and cannot be taxed; for no sane person can think of land values in connection with their subterranean tracks. In London the great railroads are sources of enormous profits and likewise making millionaires. To avoid taxation is a study of their owners. They all plunge underground, below the surface limits of the tax-gatherer.

In the same manner other industries successfully avoid the payment of taxes wherever they can escape the legalizable claims of real estate. And should the ideas of our land-tax theorists be realized, they would inevitably resort to the subterfuges of wit and opportunity to dodge the normal occupancy of land, rather than submit to paying their quota of revenues assessed upon the land.

Money, another great vehicle of human activities, also possesses the same invisible, subterraneous characteristics; and can to a still greater extent, exist and career without occupying taxable space. Who would think of levying a tax upon an underground vault, commensurate with the vast and uncertain because constantly moving values which huddle and sequester themselves upon its bottom?

A broad range of criticism thus uncovers to view the utter absurdity of any attempt to shirk upon real or hypothecated land-values the burdens of revenue supply. At every glance of reason fresh loopholes discover themselves wherein are secreted these venomous creatures of subterfuge. To avoid paying taxes is the well known and too successful determination of wealth owners; and these land-tax theorists though undoubtedly at heart the kindest of men, will be looked at by farmers as plotters of a plan to assist them in securing its avoidance.

Land can be socialized slice by slice, so to speak or little by little. The progressive industrial party may plausibly demand that government, either municipal, state or general, adopt it upon a scale of a few acres, a few hundred, or even if there be enough faith among the people, a thousand acres at a time. States are continually trying hazardous experiments; let them try this one and get their hand in. They may be called upon to help us on a larger scale by and by. We are constantly to bear in mind that socialism is the reverse of anarchy; it may be called the world's law and order society. As with the spelling reform system, boy after boy and girl after girl learn the new and outgrow the old method the youngster becomes the adult and from the private it gets into the public school and soon becomes property of the state, so this system of land tenure and cultivation may commence with the individual, converted and leaning to its ownership by co-operation of many, and as the small experiments succeed grow into universal adoption by the governments of the world. But no half-way substitutes are wanted, that will tend to decoy the people into antagonism against the final end. Nothing will do which enlightened intelligence and lessons of experience by trial from year to year, shall not cause to be enacted by law. Any whims to patch up the old competitive system by taxation of land values, by new-fangled schemes of rent or confiscating land and selling it again to the highest bidder, must be regarded as dangerous and misleading.

QUESTION. We have labored under the perhaps wrong impression that this social democracy was an organization of malcontents who, with firebrand in hand and vengeance in spirit were contemplating no peace nor harmony but violent and indiscriminate overthrow of present institutions. If, however, your measures, be they ever so extreme in the ultimate, are both humane and peaceable, even though contemplating the abolishment of the present system of business which men are forced to compete against rather than co-operate with, that is, selfishly array themselves in warfare against, instead of coming into Christian brotherhood mutually with and for one another, heaven grant that it be done, and our echo shall be Amen! And if it apply as a finality to the great and vexed land question so much the better. But how, we would ask, can men know just at what moment to strike for these things, each in its turn when ripe and ready? How are we going to rightly judge the auspicious moment?

ANSWER. By letting it assume the political form. We always know by the signs of the times just the right moment to bring to the front and push a political issue. It is one of the redeeming virtues of politics. It may be said of these days of innovation and change that another important discovery has been made, namely: that there are two classes of industries, or of industrial management in the world at the present time, vigorously competing with each other for existence—the ascendant and the moribund. We may assume all necessary operations requiring human activity and devotion to be industries; the hall of legislation, the court of adjudicature, the workshop and the farm—all these are industries, indispensable to human government, safety, comfort and nourish ment. The judges as well as carpenters or farmers are paid; the court is therefore, technically considered, an industry. To work as a member of congress is often arduous and there are many who cannot stand the strain. But these are industries of the genuine communistical class. The great and growing postal industry is now one of the largest and most flourishing in the world—pure communism in germ, and rapidly developing into perfection. Every industry that is co-perative rather than competitive, is communistic at root and all such are of the ascendant class of industrial activities. A co-operative farm or a piece of land, as a park, garden, botanical or zoological grounds or experimental lands for food fishes or seed raising, where governments conduct the operations, are of the ascendant class of activities in the category of economies for human support. At present this co-operative method is especially in the ascendant, urged on by almost every species of labor organization in all parts of the world where labor has taken a stand.

On the other hand, industries which are operated on the profit or competitive system where the welfare of the community supplied, stands as a secondary consideration, may be denominated the moribund class. They compete with one another, are the instigators of an emulous, often unfriendly spirit akin to warfare and are the cause of strikes and misery among those who, for want of more of the co-operative, or ascendant industries in which to find self-interested employment for their heads and hands, are obliged to barter them to bosses on terms that under a hackneyed law of the competitive system on which all moribund industries are based, forces them to suffer and is a cause of their organizations of resistance against capital. These are two mighty forms of managing our means of producing and distributing the necessities of life. They are at war to-day, because the ascendant, communal system upon which all governments and courts of justice are founded—the most ancient, most just and imperishable of all known forms of management has, through the agitations of this labor problem, been discovered to be also most harmoniously applicable to the management of industries and everything else. If common or state co-operation can martial great armies and cause men to brutally murder and destroy, the same principle under wise and humane statesmanship, can be made to operate a manufactory or cultivate the land. All that is wanted is collective will, intelligence and statesmanship. But labor, feeble, ignorant and unorganized, never took political issues upon this mighty discovery before. Old industries were run on the competitive system then as now; corrupting, tangling and usurping; constantly drawing like leeches, from the co-operative system to gratify private ends. Thus, although the mutual system was the best, the usurpation by egotistical individuals has prevented its application to business functions, other than such as best subserved the selfish purposes of kings and bosses.

The fact is, the true interests of labor have not kept pace with her amazing products of every other kind. She now awakens to find herself cheated. No statesmen ever did, or ever will represent her and work for her interests. Labor must go into the political field and henceforth assume the management of her own affairs of statesmanship and legislation. She has built the splendid things on which human welfare rests; it is high time for her to take a stand politically and most energetically in their defense.

Now, so long as competition could maintain itself in this way, it could exist; but when it began to turn the communistic or co-operative principle towards furthering and maintaining monopolies by which the great inventions of labor were robbed, even of the little advantage that resides in cold competition, a veritable rebellion followed, which has already outlined an attack upon both competition and monopoly, by means of a counter organization in politics. The natural offspring of competition is monopoly; and its whole great line of tactics having proved a failure, may be regarded under the pressure of its bad record and in the light of the nobler system of co-operation, as in a dying condition. All around we see examples of our sweeter mutual method rising into power. Nations have taken hold of it. Cities build beautiful and useful things upon it. Great non-competitive establishments like public schools which develop our intelligence flourish upon it like the green bay tree. Immense labor organizations and social parties look forward to it as an only basis of hope. It is coming;—the grand old socialism taught by our Master, having put its slanderers to shame; and at its approach the selfish, rotten old competitive system is doomed to take its final leave.

Now, as this true co-operative system comes slowly, piece by piece, into the world it is preparing itself to grasp the land problem and sweep all other industry with it. Co-operation then, applied to land, is the distant and difficult work of statesmen, chemists, mechanics—all science, art and energy combined;—for it is here upon the vital and perhaps final question of land that the greatest duties, responsibilities and dangers of its experiment must culminate.

Finally, a word cannot be amiss regarding the very important matter of health. Of all the many enemies of human sanity the competitive system is the most appalling. The vocation once learned, whether that of farming, carpentering, mining, stitching or any other, the poor wage slave under this baleful profit system is bound to delve a life-time without hope of accumulating enough to pay the costs of travel and other changes prescribed by either physician or the common sense rules of health. The employer generally goes and comes at will; often necessarily, on account of the requirements of business. but in obedience to the rules of physical health just the same; thus escaping those dangerous, often deadly chronic maladies which come of constant exposure to the malaria-breeding sameness of drudgery. This fearful sameness of habits is the origin perhaps, of more chronic diseases than all else known to the dispensary It heaps on its melancholy burdens of helplessness as it fiendishly forces its victims to gulp the same poor nourishment and breathe in the same fumes of virus from year to year. Add to all this the still worse poisons of despondency and hopelessness and their ghastly companions, recklessness and the bowl, and you have a too correct picture of the competitive system as now applied.

But the cure comes in a vast swoop, with this nationalization of land, also the implements of labor, mines electric contrivances, the railroads, manufactories and expressage. The world is large and its surface configuration is full of charming, inviting and health-restoring varieties. There are climates where no consumption is known. Others where catarrh is a stranger; and again others whose bracing air heals those infected with malaria as if by magic. Obstinate diseases are frequently cured by their contact. Physicians often know this but are powerless to prescribe except for the rich. Nations have prepared charts of these excellent and beautiful lands and we know where they are. Yet those suffering, who have no means to go there must remain and tug and rot. A co-operative or government farm as described, located in a non-consumptive region would, with the transfer system and the nationalized railroads, naturally invite such people to its anti-consumptive or anti-catarrhal, or anti-malarial home not only to continue their regular and useful vocation, but also to be permanently cured. The mere beginning of such a salutary system of transfers would tell upon the longevity of the working classes. Owning their means of travel, their farms, shops, mines, and being themselves the authors and directors of the legislation by which these industries were maintained, they would not stop with the cultivation of land by co-operation but would erect workshops in those healthful places, offering workers of many callings an equal opportunity to work for themselves and breathe the air of heaven. But alas, the good question, nobly coming into being is yet too blind and too sadly chained to the old obstinate stumps of ignorance!

No. Nothing portends more gloomily an evil future frowning both suspiciously and ominously near than this new and unexpected slogan, the single land-tax theory. Especially is this a darkling foreboding to the farmers. Mr. Mulhall, in a sound work on "The Progress of the Nation within 40 years," shows in a diagram the relative advance of different industries in England. The lines start from nil; the comparison of actual growth beginning at 10. Commerce which is susceptible of the greatest range of profits and makes the most millionaire speculators, runs up to 550 on the scale, while manufactures, the next greatest resource of the monarchs of wealth, rise to 450. Several other great industries which make rich men are shown to have similarly risen. But where stands agriculture? Instead of rising it has actually fallen and stands only at 8! And yet it is this most unproductive, most unfortunate of our industrial resources, the land, which is to be made to pay all of the enormous expenses of government! This proposition for an exclusive land tax relieving these speculators of commerce, manufacture, distribution and jobbery from all burdens of assessment, however plausible it may be made to appear, looks most ominously suspicious. It is well known that the great millionaires of monopoly are constantly on the alert to avoid payment of taxes. They would combine and pool enormous sums of money to secure such indemnity from paying their quota of taxation. And through scheming advocates of so-called single land-tax throwing the entire burdens of taxation off the heads of these colossal and might-wielding millionaires of the speculative, money-winning businesses, the silly people, like flies in the spider's deadly decoy, plunge into an inevitable doom that yawns behind the insidious veil of fascination and enchantment! Land, and toil, old twins of poverty must as usual, continue to delve, supply all wants, pay taxes, and get nothing!

You may crowd the art of agriculture to the highest point but you cannot under any conditions get from it more than a given product, acre for acre the world over; although science and capital may combine to increase it above what it now is. But the labor monopolist well knows that he can crowd workmen upon a given piece of land and by owning their patents and exploiting their toil, force from a small piece of land an ever increasing product—aye, make them stand at their forges, anvils, workbenches and looms so thickly together that even the free air is vitiated by sheer monopoly of it through his exploiture of labor. One may here see that while an acre of land-muscle, so to speak, can but produce wealth in arithmetrical ratio, an acre of human muscle, crowded almost from the earth, or even out upon the waters, is made to produce in a geometrical ratio;—exactly what many industrial managers desire. This shows why our millionaires are so determined to rid themselves of the payment of taxes on products.

Confiscation of land is well known to have ever been the source or foundation of the great and arrogant families of England. This mischief has been done at times when nobody thought of the state farming them for the people on equal footing for all men. The ancient Demesnes of the time of Edward the Confessor, were crown lands. All Demesnes acquired by escheat, forfeiture and feudal delinquency were crown lands;—all nationalized lands—just as the proposed land-tax theories admittedly would reduce lands here, should not the implements of its cultivation be also transferred to the state or people. The seizure by Henry VIII. of the vast Monastery estates made them all crown lands. Indeed, Great Britain, now the true battle-ground of the land problem, is the country of nationalized lands. What became of them? Why, they were alienated to court favorites through the tricks of politicians and used to found the great overbearing families; as a study of the reliable blue-books reveals. Against the tyrannies of these usurpers of the people's birthright—the soil—there now arises a prodigious conflict! Beware then, this careless meddling with land! Let the agricultural question grow with other questions of social ownership;—ownership of the tools by which labor is performed and product created and dispensed. Statesmanship and benevolence must socialize themselves and get out of the competitive rut. Savagism which is still building its landmarks on this our boasted age must be outgrown. When people possess full knowledge of the correct methods of conducting industries, there will be no danger. What men are commanded to do is to love one another; help one another; take care of one another; and they must narrow down their isolated, precarious and predatory individualisms until they can nationalize and mutually employ as by co-opration, all instruments of land cultivation as well as of manufacture and of distribution, upon an altruistic, Christian-like principle. This is to begin the work of reconstructing society for the sake of human happiness.

STATESMAN. But what can be the harm, even if these land theories be tried? Would not the general tendency of such an agitation be in the direction of the finality toward which you aim?

## CHAPTER XIII.

### GOVERNMENTALIZED WEALTH WORTH MORE, DOLLAR FOR DOLLAR TO THE INDIVIDUAL, THAN PRIVATE WEALTH. SYSTEM OF GENERAL AVERAGES.

CONVERSATION BETWEEN A BANKRUPT AND HIS MORTGAGEE.

BANKRUPT. I HAVE grown old in honest manual toil to accumulate for myself and my family a fortune which would not only act as a capital whereon to be emancipated from want or care, but which my stock or race and inheritance bearing our name, might perpetuate a true family in honor. In the ups and downs of this exciting career, often sorely tempting my honesty and beckoning me many times to become a knave—temptations which I have struggled against—I find myself in bankruptcy with nothing but my gray hairs and a sullen future before me. I have made up my mind, since I am at least of average ability to make a living and yet having failed, that the mass of the human race fail; and I believe they wlll continue to fail unless the conditions are changed. In other words, I have been driven to believe in the doctrine that if the property which all so easily create but which so few can keep their share of, could be held in trust for them by their government, then each and all might own an ample competency and prevent bankruptcy and the pinch of poverty altogether.

MORTGAGEE. Well, you are reiterating a doctrine which, as I discover going the rounds of my business and collecting my dues—often a heart-rending duty I must cordially confess—a good number are becoming converted to. But what, in such a case as you instance, is to become of us who *are* successful? We do not want any change of conditions. The world offers a free chance in the competition. If I succeed and you fail this does not justify you in advocating institutions which would make my business impossible; for this would invert the matter by making me the failure and you the success.

BANKRUPT. I am too much withered and solemnized by age, toil and adversity, and too near the grave to discuss with you in a spirit of unkindness; but a zealous, truthful argument may take place without a vestige of bitterness, and only in this feeling would I speak.

MORTGAGEE. Speak, but allow that I have the same liberty.

BANKRUPT. Of course. You have made each of your enterprises pay its own expenses, and the plan that I propose shall be based upon the same principle, with the addition that a system of *general averages* is to be admitted, by which the people may pay, out of a common fund, such deficits as may occur, until the methods of any one branch of business newly taken in, can have time to adjust themselves so as to attain a paying basis.

Mortgagee. I would like to hear an explanation.

Bankrupt. I am the head of a family of ten; a nation is a family of millions and as all wants are common, supplies should be common. My family are a community by themselves. Had I escaped bankruptcy and succeeded in business as I once hoped, I should have been able to found an estate or a property of $50,000. This would have been a matter of $5,000 for each. But we are a loving, well-regulated family; and mutual sympathies and interests so fairly cohere that should one of our little enterprises fail, all the others would fly to its rescue; that is, if one branch should fail to pay its own expenses while all the others succeeded, then, the prosperous part of our community would, by a mutual understanding, straighten out the unfortunate one; and with this valuable experience it would result in its success the next year. This is the system of general averages on the inter-mutual or co-operative plan of assistance and common security—the idea being to secure a comfortable living for all, from generation to generation of our stock. I must now however, acknowledge that it is a pernicious one; since the inevitable outcome of it would have been to plant another family or nucleus of power whose gradual growth into the world, would, like all the families of history, continue to browbeat the unfortunate. On looking it over I have arrived at the conclusion that a system of general averages might be applied by a still more powerful institution than the family—even by the family of man, the political governments of masses—and I am convinced that such management, being naturally like a father or head of a family, would furnish labor and the necessaries of life to all of the children with strict impartiality.

MORTGAGEE. That might answer very well for a mere family affair; but the question is, how are you going to apply it to your state?

BANKRUPT. It must be left to the people, to discussion, to a political party, to public common sense. What is the real difference between a state, which is the head of its family of citizens and a father who is the head of a family of children? I take it, however, that the state has the advantage by far, over the father; for statistics tell us that while individuals who engage in enterprises of business, fail on an average nine out of eleven times, the state is proved to have failed only once in five times, or twenty in a hundred. The reasons for this are that the state, having capital, talent and experience, and being, so to speak, immortal or undying, can be more positive, stern and sure-footed than any short-lived, erring, stumbling individual; especially when the former is above competitive strife while the latter is tormented by competitors at every step and stage of his existence. That the state, then, has a large advantage over the individual in matters of industrial enterprise of every kind, is seen in the fact that whenever it undertakes any enterprise it is almost sure to succeed, while the individual proves himself to have failed as many as nine times out of eleven, from century to century, which leads me to the bold opinion that the individual is a failure. These remarkable figures convince me that a large and powerful institution, like a nation or country—which is in fact, a species of collective individual—may and ought to undertake business enterprises on my family principle. I am one of those who have failed. My steady and arduous labors have, in the course of many years of hopeful youth and middle life, built up this fortune which you now possess, through one of the wicked kinks of the dangerous competitive system. You may not have committed the least guilt as the law reads; for the heartless law was the robber that ruined me in foreclosing the mortgage and its insidious grippers have at last crushed me to the grave. You are but the instrument of the law which throughout the country is foreclosing mortgages and ruining homes, and everywhere blighting the hearts of honest men. I would see a radical change. I would see the nation's government of which I am a citizen, assume the mutual care of its family just as I desired to do with my own children; and in view of my own failure because isolated and uninstructed, I am constrained to believe that no government will ever be perfect and long-lived until it is really what it pretends to be—a protective power over its citizens like the father over his family

Mortgagee. There is in your mind a certain improvement on the leap from sublime to ridiculous; your portly assurance adds to it a sprinkling of the charms and splendors of Utopia. I apprehend that you are going to have each industry managed by the government and fix things so that each one will pay its own expenses. What then becomes of the systems of rent and taxation? And will not the thing tumble like all other top-heavy contrivances of which bad temper is often the inventor?

Bankrupt. Eventual free trade would result from such a system, because each industry produces for itself, employs its own numbers and pays its own expenses. In your competitive world taxation must always be necessary; but that does not make the taxation, which is compulsory tribute, interest, customs duties, rent, any less a robbery. The inter-mutual state which I desire to see, possesses no inherent attributes of these in its nature. It would not fight with bloody weapons against the present method which destroys citizens, but it would supplant the whole evil by a better system through which citizens could be furnished means to live. By this means every industry is self-supporting in the end; each being aided by the averaging process during its incipiency or youth, until it can stand alone like a child. This is but nature. Already we have instances. When the government post-office was undertaken, it was so infantile and inexperienced that it could not stand alone. It had to be supported by deficit appropriations, as the parent supports the child. In fact, it never will be able to pay its own way and do its duty without such support until perfected. Then it will not only go alone but will be able, by a surplus over its own expenditures, to in turn, help some sister industry to a share of deficit money. To become perfect, it must have all the railroads, steam lines and electric transmissions incorporated as parts of itself. If the state or collective body assume all industries as it has the post-office, it would soon get them all on a paying basis, after which there would be no more taxation because everything would pay for itself. Incomes more than sufficient to pay the expenses of each department would flow in from the business, and the system of taxation would cease, giving way to unlimited free trade the world over. Now while I would go softly I would push these matters with energy. I would seize nothing, but would work with the still more powerful and convincing weapons of persuasion, experiment, experience. When one of your old murderous industries of the competitive system is found to be regarded with dissatisfaction by its own victims, the work people employed in it and the masses deriving their supplies from it, then the government should assume it by purchase. As soon as one of them shows signs of a general dissatisfaction, be assured that it is in a decaying or dying state. I call it moribund. We will illustrate by this moribund industry, answering your questions by it. The reason why the government assumed the mail service was simply that the joint stock company could not do it. Company and individual business proved a failure and they died—a very profitable demise for every nation; as by their death the true owner takes possession, and that owner is the people. But the system is still faulty as we know and the reason why is that it does not possess its plant. The very wheels by which mail and other express packages are carried, still belong to individuals who control other inventions of the people. The people or community invented and constructed engines, railroads and all the make-up of this vast business. Somebody who possesses no genius to invent but simply a genius to make money, got away the machines from the people; and while citizens own the government post-office in common, this individual owns the machines; thus crippling government by placing himself as a managing monopolist over the whole. Now, as this glaring wrong is studied by the people, they begin to demand that the machinery be restored to them, in order that their postal system may be completed and that they may get letters, packages and wire messages transmitted to them at cost.

As this question comes up and is discussed and carefully studied, the old system becomes tasteless and stale and finally gives way to it; because it cannot offer any plausible argument in its own defense. It is in a moribund state. It has been attacked. The same is to be said and done with other business, even with cotton mills and flouring mills—all machinery both of manufacture and distribution. The people need only to be awakened to perceive the wrong that lurks in this individual ownership of their machines. Why, it is little less than the old legalized brigandage. These things belong to the people, the children of the nation. We invented them and many of us have starved in carrying out such labors. A shrewd individual has worked so well his tactics that the true owner is left but the miserable inheritance of bankruptcy. A mere family like mine is too weak to grapple with the wrong. The great family of man must grapple with it, and the implements of labor must become their own and be operated and held in trust for them by their natural business and protective association, which is their government. No tenable argument exists to support the opposition to these burning truths. Every sort of industry, be it distributive as a store, or constructive as a cotton mill, should belong to the nation and not to the individual. So long as it is run by the individual as personal property it will partake more or less of the spirit and practice of robbery. When it is endorsed and absorbed by the nation it will quickly learn to work in the unbiased interests of all, and gradually become, with the growth of public wisdom, the employer as well as the source of supply for all of us who claim to be members of itself and of the human family. The plan of government industries will not only simplify all methods of business, cause them to grow honest by making their value common and distributing their blessings equally, but it will enrich the citizen through a permanent possessorship of actual property so that he or she will be wealthier, freer, more dignified and self-supporting than by the plan of the single family, such as I failed in attempting to create; besides it eliminates an element of hypocrisy which I am willing to confess, undeniably exists in my family arrangement.

MORTGAGEE. How can it enrich each? Distribute the property of the country ever so equally among the citizens and they would not be worth twenty-five dollars apiece.

BANKRUPT. We shall come to this phase of the inquiry soon. On the contrary, it will be proved that each citizen, as a co-possessor of the property of his or her country, becomes possessor of a sum in sterling money, if you like, so considerable, that with a small amount of well-directed labor each day, there will be plenty; and there need be felt no fear. Even as it is now, with all the enormous, incomputable waste which flows from the systematic jargon of competitive business, there happens always to be enough. Want is not known except where distribution is defective. If one side of the earth suffers loss from war or drouth, the other side contains an overplus. If one family starves, the near neighbor wallows upon a surfeit which he cannot devour. There is always plenty. What the hungry want is the possession of it. This is of itself sufficient proof that if the present wealth-values were in the hands of the people as they ought to be, there would never occur another case of starvation.

MORTGAGEE. There is such a thing as making, at least, an approximate count of both the actual value of all property now belonging to companies and individuals in any given country or nation and the amount of the population of each. Your idea becomes interesting if for nothing more than the prodigious dimensions of its scope. Have you ever drawn upon figures for a conclusion as to the amount of property, under your theory, that would, as you say, be owned in a bond of equal citizenship, if all the property, say in the United States of North America, should become nationalized by government and worked under your system, or upon a method by which no one person could rule or profit on a larger quantity than another? If there were such a thing possible, it might be worth more than a fleeting consideration; for I admit that things are not always as they should be—a lottery in which I have gained and you have lost a fortune. But first it would be very necessary to make a thorough computation as to how it is going to turn out, even upon its most sublimely enormous scale; and as I am, on my own acknowledgment, a victim of one extreme, while you are the victim of the other, both feeling our consciences to be involved, I am ready to say that if the figures warrant, so also the law of equity warrants, that you try it.

BANKRUPT. Very well then. Nothing is easier than to get at a fair approximation of the actually paying property that would become, under this system, the *bona fide* state of every citizen alike. And the freshest gem of hope that each man or woman's property possesses, is that the property employs every human being of right condition, holding claim thereto, and this not by any speculation of the mean competitive system, but by virtue of the birthright of humanity; and under a management which is their own. It will be a management that gives a certificate to labor as the first right—a right which by the simple law of equity, cannot, under any conditions, shut out from them the offer of free labor or deprive citizens of its enjoyment or of the full product, penny for penny, of that which their labor creates.

Parceling out, item by item, the vast property on which these 70,000,000 people live, we shall find that there are two bases of calculation: the real and the hypothetical values, the latter being often merely asserted without any proper estimate and with an object to speculate. It goes by the name of "watered stock." Between the two, we may—although they are constantly varying—get a rough estimate which will be sufficient for our purpose, since a fair approximate is what we want. In order to do this we shall draw from the Interstate Commerce Commission for railroads, and from books and lectures for estimates of other property.

The entire amount in linear miles, of railroads in the United States reaches above 150,000. These railroads cost on an average, a trifle less than $60,000 per mile. In other words the railroads are worth $9,000,000,000 in round numbers. This gives for each man, woman and child, a sum of $129 nearly. But as each head of family has the care of four persons at the lowest average, and of six persons at the highest, the property in charge or control, under his trusteeship for the children, that is, goods citizenized, so to speak, in joint ownership and enjoyment of each head of a family of four, would be about $514 for the small number, or $774 for the larger number. Thus in the matter of railroads alone, he is in control of no inconsiderable sum. All good things accruing from this, are equally participated. The average workingman of our times does not probably possess so much of the goods of this earth; or if he does, they are not as profitable and steadfast a property as is the said amount invested in these great public works.

Then turning to the telegraphs, telephones and land, which several authors, arguing against nationalization, in books and lectures on economic philosophy, estimate at a value of $25,000,000,000, and at this low price we shall find, if it were possessed alike by all, that each inhabitant would become by this natural title to existence which I advocate, owner of a snug little sum of $350 or more. This is for each and all, including children of tender age. But as the head of the family or somebody must attend to their wants, we shall have under his supervision of the family of four, a sum of $1,428, or of the family of 6, $2,140.

But we have said nothing as yet, of the vast values of mechanical property upon which the working people are best entitled to ownership because they are its inventors, its manufacturers, its repairers and its operators. This property exists in shape of tools, factories, mills and water powers. We have said nothing of the enormous wealth in form of steamships, steamboats, ferrying and coast-lines. Nor have we spoken of the immense stored wealth of navies with their armaments of protection; of the war department with its munitions of defense. We have not considered the still greater value of stored wealth in the coal, iron, silver, gold, copper and other mines which can not be estimated until our labor has been applied. This, of all other property, should be owned by the people. Then there are to be added the vast values of the oil wells and natural gas as well as the pearls, the mineral waters and other resources of incomes and of health and comforts. None of them should be monopolized by owners, as in the present manner, or held in trust as some people imagine is done by individual possessors who thus in their legal fashion carry out and perpetuate the ancient system of brigandage or something that is little better—seizure and appropriation by the one, enslavement and degradation for the other—but these things should be common, as a birthright to humanity and enjoyed by humanity by means of state, or government management, which is the new and final political economy, since all other forms have failed.

Now, if we rate all this immense and growing property at no more than the railroads, electric appliances and land, we shall, even at this low valuation, have a round sum of $34,000,000,000 which would give to each one of a population of $70,000,000, about $485, say $500, in valuable productive property, such as becomes more and more respectable and dignifying as the ages and the enlightenment of humanity proceed. These $500 belonging to each person, as in the previous cases we have given, cannot be managed or participated in by all, because some are children, some idiots, some insane or othewise disabled. Continuing the enumeration on the same basis of the family of four under the paternal head, as in the family with the father at its head, we will reckon from this figure as the minimum and from six the maximum number, we shall have for this guardian's trust, $2,000 for the smallest estimate and $3,000 for the highest. In our calculation on the land and the machinery of distribution we obtained nearly as much more. Adding the two sums which engross all property of the country, into one estate belonging to the family of man, or that branch of it residing within the limits of the territory mentioned, we have for each individual without distinction of age, sex or condition, living under the birthright of humanity, a sum of about $1,000; and we have provided for its proper management by entrusting it to guardians, like the heads of the family, each of whom holds four to six thousand dollars. Hopefully, some method may be introduced by coming statesmen whereby this patriarchal idea may be superseded by a better one; we simply use this form to illustrate by, because it contains within itself somewhat of my family plan and will therefore be found more intelligible to beginners.

MORTGAGEE. But you wanted $ 50,000 for your family or $5,000 for each, and thought that amount necessary in order to make yourselves decent. But here, on computing the whole value of the country's wealth, and dividing it b. the population, you only have a pitiful thousand. You wanted $ 50,000 for the paternal control, or the trust as head of the family; and all you can make out of your estimate for the socialized wealth, is from four to six thousands. I fail to see how this plan, at that rate, can ever avail towards producing an independent fortune, or even raising them out of the the slums and mire of poverty.

BANKRUPT. This is met by two arguments: First, as I have shown, whatever store we may set upon values the fact remains that there is enough. There is no such thing as estimating values amidst ease and plentitude There is always enough—enough for everybody at all times—if it could only be had by the people. And mine is merely a method by which they are enabled to get it. It brings this property which already produces enough for all, within their reach, by involving only a change of its management from the present individual and competitive one, with its enormous waste and embittering strife, into a co-operative management through statesmanship that leads to the elimination of both waste and war.

The superior advantage of the system is in the power that large, rich and powerful concerns possess over small and weak ones. This power resides in all governments and is greater than that of individuals and companies. Being conducted for the people by the people, and not for merely speculative purposes, but for an object of producing for and supplying all alike, it can perform many times more work in a year and produce many times larger results. It can therefore, make a dollar worth many times more than the individual can; since he is obliged to struggle with competitors, breaking down and rising up from the ashes of ruin and such other tormenting vicissitudes as characterize the wretched management of individuals when depending only upon their shrewdness, or failing under the lack of it. A nation that has its force of inventors, of designers, of mechanics, of laborers, in a collective body, knows nothing of death. It is a stranger to bankruptcy. It knows no such word as fail. Its citizens die but they reproduce themselves, and the nation lives on forever. It can improve but cannot deteriorate and retrograde. It can plant an industry which may stumble for a generation but this only acts to lend experience making of it an undying success. It is the only kind of management that possesses within itself all the requisites of power, wealth, popular love, self-employment, scientific resource and long life, necessary to rise without any fear above competition. It is the only species of industrial direction that has inherent to itself, the germ of growth into absolute perfection; for the greatest companies are dependent on the ability of individuals who die without transmitting to posterity their capabilities to outlive the strain of competition. Consequently it is the only kind of management destined to live forever. With all these advantages the state, when it assumes the control of business affairs, one by one, for the people its citizens, is morally sure to succeed, and can make a given or stated sum invested in a concern, worth much more to the owners than the same sum can be worth, if in the hands of an individual or company; because it can produce all that is required, by a calculation so exact that there is neither waste through overproduction nor prodigality in consumption. The individual or company cares little or nothing for this central and sole consideration prompting true co-operative industrial energy. It only cares to sell its wares at a rate above cost, being based upon the speculative idea—exactly the opposite of the incentive which actuates and energizes the inter-mutual state. If the employé of the individual concern is sick, loses his work or perishes in the misery-bound slavery of the system, the individual manager cares nothing; whereas to succor such and provide for them, is the principal motive that inspires the inter-mutual state; for this is its harvest of citizenship.

Thus a thousand dollars invested in this magnificent co-operation, is practically worth more than twenty times that sum invested in a more precarious business under a joint-stock company or individual management; for its first incentive is to furnish permanent employment to him so that on his stored capital thus invested through the birthright of humanity, he is afforded a place to exercise his natural capital which is his labor of brain and muscle. This is what men are organizing for to-day—a place to work, where all and not a part of what they produce will return to them; for in this, their *natural capital*, or power to labor, lies the true fortune and independence of humanity. This, the individual or competitive concern will not do. You now have the full reasons why I so clearly perceive that the individual in the competitive world is a failure. Moreover, under this form of co-operative control, the tendency will be to multiply inventions and produce labor-saving machines; which is again, the reverse of the wish of organized tradesmen engaged in the terrible scuffle with them because they have proved their enemies. The machine is not nationalized. It is not their own. It belongs to individuals and companies who use it for their destruction. Give to the workers their implements of production and distribution and let them be operated under their own eye and management, through government guarantee, so that they shall all receive employment and the agonies and turmoils arising from such cruel misallotments will be forever at an end.

MORTGAGEE. But it seems to me that you are going to sap and undermine the whole great, living principle of patriotism. What becomes of protection? Where is the patriotic force which stands at the helm of nations; the vigilance inspiring a military prowess on which all true statehood rests? What, when you take away their property, remains with citizens, to give them the love of country which makes men fight with self-sacrifice and intrepidity, such as protects and perpetuates a state?

BANKRUPT. Ah! You have now tapped a subject that covers new ground and opens new fields to the science of statesmanship! When the Franco-Prussian war struck Europe it found among the brave Franks a discouraged

www.ingramcontent.com/pod-product-compliance
Lightning Source LLC
LaVergne TN
LVHW020223110826
845151LV00003B/810

* 9 7 8 1 4 2 5 5 3 1 7 3 7 *